Debate Aborted
1789–91

Debate Aborted
1789–91

Priestley, Paine, Burke
and the Revolution in France

P. O'Brien

The Pentland Press
Edinburgh – Cambridge – Durham – USA

First published in 1996 by
The Pentland Press Ltd
1 Hutton Close,
South Church
Bishop Auckland
Durham

ISBN 1-85821-366-5

Typeset by Carnegie Publishing, 18 Maynard St, Preston
Printed and bound by Antony Rowe Ltd, Chippenham

In memory of an inspired, inspiring and much loved teacher of history and literature – Matthew Bodkin, S J, to whom I owe so much.

Contents

Illustrations

Illustrations – Sources

Portrait of E Burke   National Gallery of Ireland

Portrait of J Priestley   National Museum of Science and Industry

Portrait of T Paine   (Norfolk County Library) A J Ayers book

Paine Cartoon   American Philosophical Society,
                                 Philedelphia

Burke Cartoon   British Museum

Priestley Cartoon   Birmingham City Council

Priestley Home Wrecked   Birmingham City Council

Priestley Statue   Mike Boden, chief photographer for the
                                 Warrington Guardian, and Priestley
                                 College, Warrington

Paine Statue   (Norfolk County Library) A J Ayers book

Burke's Reflections (Title   British Library
                    page)

Burke's Appeal (Title page   British Library (*Factotum*)
              and 2 pages)

Acknowledgements

I AM INDEBTED TO THE FOLLOWING LIBRARIES:

Warrington Local History Library, its chief librarian, David Rogers, and his staff, especially Peter and Bob; Newcastle Lit. and Phil. Society and Miss Norwell; British Library ESTC section and Laurence Wood, editor of *Factotum*; Dr. Williams' Library, London, and John Creasey; The Leeds Library and Geoffrey Forster, Manchester College, Oxford; Norfolk County Library; Thomas Paine Society.

ALSO TO THE FOLLOWING:

Jen Darling for the typesetting and her husband Chris for his technological advice; Peter Andrews for indexing and corrections to the text; Prof. William P McCarthy, of Iowa, for advice on presentation and content; my editor Jill Cole and publishing manager Daniel Russell, for encouragement, courtesy and patience with an incorrigible client; Profs. F X Martin and K B Nowlan, of the History Department of University College, Dublin, for advice on Irish aspects and, in Kevin's case, for steering me away from fiction (although it might have been much more rewarding), and finally, **to Sheila, my patient, long suffering, forbearing wife**, and Mary Denton.

RÉFLÉCTIONS

ON THE

REVOLUTION IN FRANCE,

AND ON THE

PROCEEDINGS IN CERTAIN SOCIETIES
IN LONDON

RELATIVE TO THAT EVENT.

IN A

L E T T E R

INTENDED TO HAVE BEEN SENT TO A GENTLEMAN
IN PARIS.

BY THE RIGHT HONOURABLE

E D M U N D   B U R K E.

L O N D O N:
PRINTED FOR J. DODSLEY, IN PALL-MALL.
M.DCC,XC.

RIGHTS OF MAN:

BEING AN

ANSWER TO MR. BURKE's ATTACK

ON THE

FRENCH REVOLUTION.

BY

THOMAS PAINE,

SECRETARY FOR FOREIGN AFFAIRS TO CONGRESS IN THE
AMERICAN WAR, AND
AUTHOR OF THE WORK INTITLED COMMON SENSE,

L O N D O N:
PRINTED FOR J. JOHNSON, ST. PAUL's CHURCH-YARD.
MDCCXCI.

LETTERS

TO

THE RIGHT HONOURABLE

E D M U N D   B U R K E,

OCCASIONED BY HIS

R E F L E C T I O N S

ON THE

REVOLUTION in FRANCE, &c.

THE THIRD EDITION, CORRECTED.

By JOSEPH PRIESTLEY, L.L.D. F.R.S.

AC. IMP. PETROP. R. PARIS. HOLM. TAURIN. ITAL. HARLEM. AUREL. MED.
PARIS. CANTAB. AMERIC. ET PHILAD. SGC.

Eloquence may exist without a proportionable degree of wisdom.
Mr. Burke's Reflections, p. 245.
Steady independent minds, when they have an object of so serious a
concern to mankind, as GOVERNMENT, under their contemplation,
will disdain to assume the part of satyrists and declaimers.
Ibid. p. 187.

BIRMINGHAM,
PRINTED BY THOMAS PEARSON,
AND SOLD BY J. JOHNSON, ST. PAUL's CHURCH-YARD, LONDON,
MDCCXCI.
(PRICE TWO SHILLINGS AND SIXPENCE.)

A

V I N D I C A T I O N

OF THE

R I G H T S   O F   M E N,

IN A

L E T T E R

TO THE RIGHT HONOURABLE

E D M U N D   B U R K E;

OCCASIONED BY

HIS REFLECTIONS

ON THE

REVOLUTION IN FRANCE.

By MARY WOLLSTONECRAFT.

THE SECOND EDITION.

L O N D O N:
PRINTED FOR J. JOHNSON,
NO. 72, ST. PAUL's CHURCH-YARD.
M. DCC. XC.

Original title pages from the principal texts

Introduction

OUR NATION IS FACING MANY CHANGES IN THE YEARS AHEAD and many possibilities will be explored in the run up to the next General Election, with politicians proposing a variety of solutions to the problems presenting.

What of our health and comunity services? It seems unlikely that they will remain in their present form. What changes are desirable and what will be acceptable? Whither public ownership? What of the monarchy? What is its relevance any longer? Should the monarchy disappear, will aristocracy remain unchanged? and what of the House of Lords with its large, residual, hereditary element? Does the Commons need reform? Should this nation have a written constitution? What of the United Nations? And of our place in Europe? Is an Established Church acceptable in a community where its practising members are but a dwindling minority?

These were questions which were being vigorously debated during the early stages of the French Revolution by Priestley, Paine, Burke and others, but Edmund Burke, who initiated the debate, broke off abruptly in 1791. Many believe that this was because he found himself unable to handle the arguments. Tom Paine in the Preface to Part II of his *Rights of Man* says: *'I am enough acquainted with Mr Burke to know that he would if he could'*.

The major works here considered are Burke's *Reflections on the Revolution in France*, Paine's *Rights of Man* and Priestley's *Letters to Edmund Burke*. The first of these had almost attained the status of holy writ in Britain up to the mid 20th century. *Rights of Man* had a considerable vogue, at least up until the Reform Act of 1832, but Priestley's *Letters* were soon ignored after he was forced into exile in 1794. Burke was an accomplished and leading politician whose literary style was brilliant and overpowering but not always logical; Tom Paine was a homespun, largely self-educated philosopher with a gift for logical analysis uncluttered by party prejudice; Dr. Priestley was a non-conformist minister, a philosopher, an academic, a polymath, with a sound education, who was absorbed in the struggle that Dissenters were having to recover basic human rights denied to them after the Restoration.

Paine was preoccupied with issues of Constitution, Government, Monarchy, Aristocracy and, above all, Human Rights, with far sighted recommendations for reform, including a vision of badly needed Social Services way ahead of his time. Priestley's major concerns were with church establishment and its abuse, with restrictions suffered by Dissenters, particularly in Education, but in other areas as well. In his *Letters to Burke* he not only highlighted these issues, but also addressed himself to Paine's major concerns. Burke's *Reflections* touch on all of these issues, but his approach is quite different: he is uneasy about any suggestion or proposal that may threaten the status quo; approaching the end of his life he had become more conservative, even, than many Tories.

Readers may be surprised at the topicality of so much of this material for problems facing us today. Finally, for scholars of that period the book provides a compendium of major works by these leaders of opinion from the late 18th century; in the case of Priestley it ressurects long neglected writings of one of the great philosophers of that era, who never merited suppression, and deserves a belated revival. We must learn from our history and pursue it without prejudice.

In November 1789, four months on from the fall of the Bastille, Dr Richard Price, a colleague and friend of Priestley, delivered a Discourse *On the Love of our Country*, to the Society for Commemorating the Revolution (of 1688–90) in Great Britain. He had the temerity to applaud what was afoot in France and, in his *Nunc Dimittis*, rejoiced that, '*after sharing the benefits of one Revolution, I have been spared to be a witness to two other Revolutions, both glorious*'.

Edmund Burke was so incensed that he devoted the next year to writing, repeatedly revising, and eventually publishing his *Reflections on the Revolution in France*. This, in turn, was so provocative that it drew critical replies within a few months from Priestley in his *Letters to Edmund Burke* and Paine's classic, *The Rights of Man (Part 1)*. These were powerful critiques by two well known and distinguished authors, both of whom were acquainted with, and even asserted former friendship with, Burke. Mary Wollstonecraft also contributed her *Vindication of the Rights of Men*, in fact she was first.

James Mackintosh (1791) characterised Burke's tour de force as a '*most undisciplined rabble of arguments*', entering in triumph, and with an ability to '*put to flight a host of syllogisms with a sneer*'. Paine lacked Burke's higher education and parlimentary experience, so his style is less polished, but his logic is sound. Priestley was, by then, a very experienced author, who eschewed Burke's flowery rhetoric, and whose logic was on a par with Paine's. This is not to suggest that Burke could not also deploy well organised and logical argument, because he had shown such ability consistently over many years in parliament, as evidenced in his *Thoughts on the Present Discontents 1770*, in the debates on the American revolt and in the ongoing Impeachment of Warren Hastings, to mention but a few highlights from his outstanding achievements. However, come the 1790s, nearing the end of his life, a new spirit of hysteria seems to have seized him when contemplating the events in France.

It is a notable fact that, having started the debate, he never directly replied to either of his two most prominent adversaries, but on further consideration this has to be qualified, and we are left in grave doubt as to Burke's motives. For a start, it must be stressed that most of the current literature, considered here, is no later than 1791, well before the French Revolution degenerated to its Reign of Terror ('92 to '94). Previous works of the protagonists have been drawn on to a lesser extent, together with works of other commentators, since that time, where they are particularly relevant. For example, Winston Churchill on the Hanoverian succession and on the early Whigs, is utilised to sharpen focus and broaden the perspective.

The year 1791 was critical in British politics, as these related to the Revolution in France, and were largely conditioned by Burke's *Reflections*, which had appeared towards the end of 1790. Priestley's *Letters* and Paine's *Rights of Man* spearheaded the debate, which was fiercely pursued in Parliament in the succeeding months, and then ostensibly brought to a conclusion by Burke in his *Appeal from the New to the Old Whigs*. It will be argued here that this was no more than a ruse to abort the debate with his more serious and thoughtful critics, who were of no political party.

He was acting very strangely indeed at this time in his life, and has left some questions to be answered, which seem not even to have been posed in his lifetime, because he so dominated this whole field in British politics, and carried Pitt's government with him. In his *Appeal . . . to the Old Whigs* he employs some very shady tactics which are explored and analysed in the final chapter of this book.

This work sets out to provide an anthology of the varying ideas and views of the protagonists, and to reconstruct the debate, as far as it went. Each author has followed his own sequence, and none is the same as any other. So, the logical solution has been to bring together relevant passages from each in a thematic arrangement. Many quotations are quite lengthy, although much pruning has taken place as the work proceeded; to reduce overmuch would spoil the balance of crucial passages. Inevitably, there is some overlap but every effort has been made to reduce this to a minimum. It may also be objected that a quotation under one heading contains material relating to a different section; this again has been accepted to preserve balance in those instances. The authors themselves have been repetitious and often long winded; an overall aim has been to give them rein so that the reader may have the full flavour of the original works, and of the debate proceeding.

Above all, this work sets out to explore the charge that Burke's attitudes and, in many instances his conclusions, had changed from the days of the American revolt or, as he himself expressed what he believed himself to be accused of, '*that by one book he has disgraced the whole tenor of his life*'. Not surprisingly, this author has reached his own conclusions after long exposure to this voluminous and detailed literature; his bias will be clear enough, but every effort has been made to keep a balance, so as to allow each reader to make an individual judgement. I did not set out to denigrate Burke, for whom I have a considerable regard, but unanticipated facts were to emerge in the course of research which could not be set aside.

Some friends have commented, as this work was in progress, that there were a few chapters which seemed to have little direct bearing on the debate; they do, however, throw light on important aspects of the backdrop, and thus provide a clearer focus overall.

CHAPTER I

The Nature of Revolution

Not to know what was done in former times is to be always
a child, if no use is made of the toil and trouble of past ages,
the world must remain forever in the infancy of knowledge.

Cicero

R EVOLUTION IS A COMPLEX PHENOMENON, that comes in many different
guises. It may take the form of a swift fundamental transition, with a
minimum of immediate trauma. At the other extreme it may incubate slowly
and, when it comes to a head, evolve gradually with or without bloodshed.
All this depends upon the circumstances generating reaction, and the milieu in
which it occurs.

There have been many commentators at the time of the French Revolution,
and since, who have seen it as deriving from, or being akin to, the 17th-century
English Revolution, or even the more recent American revolt. On the day the
Bastille was taken, Dr. Edward Rigby of Norwich (a former pupil of Dr. Joseph
Priestley at Warrington Academy) happened to be in Paris with friends on
vacation. Writing home to his family from the safety of Geneva, a month later,
he gave a graphic account of that momentous day in Paris, which included
getting caught up in the mob as it was celebrating its remarkable triumph. He
reports: "We were recognised as Englishmen; we were embraced as freemen,
'for Frenchmen' (said they), 'are now free as well as yourselves; henceforward
no longer enemies, we are brothers, and war shall no more divide us." (Rigby's
Letters pp.62–3) Prophetic words, but alas somewhat wide of the mark.

It is such sentiments that create confusion, because conditions in France in
1789 were very different from England in the mid 17th century, and conditions
in the New World across the Atlantic were nothing like those in the old nations
of Europe.

England, breaking loose from its medieval roots, and disturbed by an
evolving Reformation, had a three-stage revolution: first, the Cromwellian,
then the Williamite and the Hanoverian. In the reign of Charles I it was a
newly enriched Tudor aristocracy with Puritan squires and businessmen, han-
kering after a fully fledged continental style Protestantism (Lutheran and
Calvinist), which was revolting against the reactionary Anglicanism of Archbishop Laud, and kings with Divine Right. Was this, "an attempt to reconstruct
an entire system of government upon a theory?" as Burke would have it. If it
was then it was a quite different attempt and any theoretical basis was far from
being novel. There was a populist undercurrent, as seen with the Levellers and

the Fifth Monarchists, but these were tightly controlled, contained, and soon sidelined by the super-efficient discipline of Cromwell's Model Army. The new aristocracy prevailed, the king, a would-be Machiavellian, but not Machiavelli's Prince, was a victim of his own inept and foolish machinations, so Parliament triumphed, and he lost his head.

At the Restoration a reactionary Anglican Parliament was quick to stem the tide of nonconformity and of a royalist trend to restore Catholicism, at least in part. With the accession to the throne of James II this latter threat seemed to increase, and the king, who might in other circumstances have been quite a benign and indifferent monarch, seeing out his time in peace, was soon translated into an ogre. This was due much more to the fact that he was seen to be the client of Louis XIV of France, than to any formidable qualities of his own. The result was the second stage of the English revolution, designed to copper fasten a Protestant Church and King establishment, through the Act of Settlement of 1701: no popular uprising, merely the actions of a scheming and very determined gentry.

It might even be allowed to describe the Hanoverian accession of 1714 as a third and final stage of this English Revolution, designed, on the face of it, to ensure the same protestant succession, but in truth it was much more a golden opportunity to introduce a truly inept and foreign puppet, not even English speaking, which would ensure the absolute dominance of Parliament. France never handled its problems in such a subtle way and, for this reason if none other, the English and French Revolutions were entirely different.

In the 18th century, England experienced yet another revolution of an entirely different sort.; this was the great religious revival brought about by John Wesley, George Whitfield and their disciples. The country was still experiencing a residual feudalism, more paternalistic than the French, and which lasted up until the First World War. The residual shadow was a smouldering resentment at the continuing enclosure of common lands. There was a great moral renewal with Wesley's revival, which brought in its train a new level of literacy; men and women, enlightened by scripture, wanted to be able to read their Bible, and this led to a thirst for knowledge in secular affairs also; thus arose the *articulate artisan*.

The printing industry, released from its earlier confinement to London and Oxbridge, was growing apace and spreading throughout the land, and so, even before the French Revolution, tracts which were critical of government were now reaching a wide audience.

The writings of John Wilkes, in his *North Briton*, were snapped up avidly. William Cobbett had started his literary career, but his populist phase did not emerge until the next century. However, with the onset of the Revolution in France it was Tom Paine's *Rights of Man* which swept through the land. Those who could not read it themselves gathered together to have it read to them and then discussed it tirelessly. The Wesleyan revival in its initial form damped down any enthusiasm for bloody revolution, but seeds were sown which blossomed into more positive and largely peaceful action in the period leading up to the 1832 Reform Act.

In the interim, some notable Human Rights abuses were alleviated, but not without pain. In 1797 the Naval Mutinies at Spithead and the Nore nearly brought down William Pitt's government; mutiny brought about by the appallingly harsh, inhuman discipline in a service where life at best was by nature harsh. John Howard was uncovering unspeakable brutality in prisons, not only throughout these islands, but also across the European continent as well. His efforts led to timely reform, which badly needs updating again today, and Britain's involvement in the slave trade was coming under slow but relentless attack, by Wilberforce and others.

The American revolt of 1776 was of a different character again. A well established Anglophile and mercantile establishment on the New England seaboard was pushed into revolution by an overweaning British parliament and monarch, believing they could effectively govern and extract taxes from an ever compliant race of settlers. But they found a nation which was leaving puberty behind and, like all late adolescents, might be led but would not be pushed. An umbilical cord stretching across the Atlantic Ocean eventually snapped.

France joined wholeheartedly in this American adventure against its old enemy, and thereby hastened its own day of destiny. Its large national debt, already rocketing out of control, was further exacerbated by naval and military activities upon, and across, the Atlantic. The economy of Great Britain suffered likewise.

In spite of Tom Paine's significant input in the early stages of the American War, the rebels, although they were convinced republicans, were not truly democrats on the French model; they were no disciples of Rousseau. Paine's short tract, entitled *Common Sense*, was an early draft with basic ideas and ideals which he later expanded into *The Rights of Man*. This tract was supplemented by the succeeding *Crisis Papers*, and these were a great morale booster when Washington's army had its back to the wall, especially during the first disastrous winter at Valley Forge.

The democratic deficit, highlighted by the continuance of slavery in the southern states, not to mention total indifference to the fate of indigenous American Indians, reaped a bitter destiny in the Civil War of the succeeding century. These features of American politics are still reflected in the fact that, to our own day, the Republican Party is the conservative element, whilst the Democrats are, on the whole, more liberal.

France, in the years leading up to its Revolution, was in a state which was closer in nature to Russia a century and more later. The glorious years of The Sun King (Louis XIV) and his immediate successor, were years of vast expenditure without an adequately compensating growth in income to sustain it. The royal family and the nobility lived away beyond the nation's means, while poorer people were in a state of virtual serfdom. The nobility included the swollen ranks of the higher clergy, many of whom were besotted with power and hedonism bred in agnosticism. Their philosophers, lacking any strong moral leadership and guidance, but having such a poor example, were in the main agnostic.

Priestley, visiting France with Lord Shelburne in 1774, found that,

". . . all the philosophical persons to whom I was introduced at Paris (were) unbelievers in Christianity, and even professed Atheists. As I chose on all occasions to appear as a Christian, I was told by some of them, that I was the only person they had ever met with, of whose understanding they had any opinion, who professed to believe Christianity. But on interrogating them on the subject, I soon found that they had given no proper attention to it, and did not really know what Christianity was."

                                                    Autobiography p.111

Once when he was dining with Turgot, another guest remarked that, "the two gentlemen opposite me were the Bishop of Aix and the Archbishop of Toulouse. 'But', said he, 'they are no more believers than you or I'. I assured him that I was a believer; but he would not believe me, and le Roi, the philosopher, told me that I was the only man of sense he knew that was a Christian." *(intro. p.22)* Priestley notes that the French are "debarred from the discussion of politics by an arbitrary and consequently a jealous government." *(p.110)* He is not impressed by their manners.

The Barbaulds, friends of Priestley, were somewhat taken aback when in France in 1785, "their curiosity led them to visit the *Chanoines de St. Victor*, an aristocratic monastic order, each member of which had to prove that his claim to nobility dated back no less than 150 years". Mrs Barbauld was surprised at their tolerant, almost cynical, attitude. "They are polite and hospitable and far enough from bigots; for we were surprised how freely to us they censured auricular confession, the celibacy of the clergy, and laughed at some of their legendary miracles." *(Georgian Chronicle p.95)* These same visitors were impressed by the clean and well equipped hospital kept by the nuns at Besançon, but distressed by the condition of the galley slaves working in the arsenal at Toulon.

The poverty-stricken state of many of the poorer classes was frequently commented upon by visitors. Tobias Smollett was shocked by the sight of many French peasants who appeared more like "ravenous scarecrows" than human beings. Arthur Young, the contemporary landlord, traveller, observer, and agricultural philosopher, saw in France examples of the most abject poverty: ploughmen and women without any footwear; hungry children "terribly ragged, if possible worse clad than if with no cloaths at all. . . . They did not beg and when I gave them anything seemed more surprised than obliged." The worst feature of all was that it was the poor who bore the heaviest burden of taxation, whilst the nobility got off quite lightly. The Salt Tax was one outstanding example.

The Encyclopaedists and French philosophers, in the period leading up to the Revolution, are frequently condemned as the evil geniuses responsible for the whole vile movement; but a whole nation will not be led by mere thinkers and writers, into the sort of excessive action which characterised this revolution in the end, without mundane causes. Rousseau and his *Contrat Social* is distinguished as the chief of these pernicious leaders-astray.

Admittedly, it is easy to portray him as the great ogre; his personal life was far from exemplary, but this does not excuse us from taking a cool and objective look at his ideas and ideals, especially as expressed in the *Contrat Social*.

Hilaire Belloc, of mixed French and English stock (and, incidentally, a descendant of Dr. Joseph Priestley), in his short work on the French Revolution, has an interesting assessment. He says of Rousseau that, "his character was of an exalted, nervous and diseased sort", but of his critics that, "few who express themselves in the English tongue have cared to understand (his power) and in the academies, provincial men have been content to deal with this great writer as though he were in some way inferior to themselves". Many of the critics have either not read, "or having read it did so with an imperfect knowledge of the meaning of French words. . . . For there is not in this book *(Contrat Social)* an apology (defence) for democracy as a method of government, but a statement of why and how democracy is right." He sees in Rousseau's analysis: "reservoirs from whence modern democracy has flowed; what are now proved to be the errors of democracy are errors against which the *Contrat Social* warned men."

(The French Revolution pp.16–21)

Belloc, who was one of the leading Catholic apologists of his time, tells us how he considers that the church in France, at the time of the Revolution, was its own worst enemy. He believes:

> "that the Revolution would, in France at least, have achieved its object and created a homogeneous, centralised democracy, had not this great quarrel between the Republic and the Church arisen." And this because there was no "necessary and fundamental quarrel between the doctrines of the Revolution and those of the Catholic church. . . . The Republican cannot by his theory persecute the Church; the Church by her theory cannot excommunicate the Republican."
>
> "France . . . in this period of settlement, (post Reformation) became an absolute monarchy whose chief possessed tremendous and immediate powers, and a monarchy which incorporated within itself all the great elements of the national tradition, **including the Church.**" But, "the very fact that the Church had thus become in France an unshakable national institution, chilled the vital source of Catholicism. Not only did the hierarchy stand in a perpetual suspicion of the Roman See, and toy with the conception of national independence, *(Henry VIII's model)* but they and all the official organisation of French Catholicism, put the security of the national establishment and its intimate attachment to the general political structure of the State, far beyond the sanctity of Catholic dogma or the practice of Catholic morals."

(pp.169–178)

There is a strong echo here of England's Church and State Establishment, so strongly defended by Burke and abhorred by Priestley. "Overt acts of disrespect to ecclesiastical authority were punished with rigour", and no-one could gainsay *Lettres de Cachets.*

"The bishops found nothing remarkable in seeing a large proportion of their body to be loose livers, or in some of them openly presenting their friends to their mistresses as might be done by any great lay noble round them. . . . Unquestioned also by the bishops were the poverty, the neglect, and the uninstruction of the parish clergy . . . (with) the abandonment of religion by all but a very few of the French millions . . . the state wore Catholic clothes, . . . public occasions of pomp were full of religious ceremony. . . . Great sums of money . . . were at the disposal of the Church; and the great ecclesiastics were men from whom solid favours could be got."

Belloc concludes:

"You could not have had the revolutionary fury against the Catholic Church in France if the preceding generation had been actively Catholic, even in a considerable proportion."

Later he comments on a more general line:

"The immediate peril of the state was financial," observing that, "There was no immediate and easily available fund of wealth upon which the Executive could lay hands save the wealth of the clergy. . . . The Charge for debt alone was one half of the total receipts of the state, the deficit was, in proportion to the revenue, overwhelming."

The French Revolution ch.VI

The Church had a great income from feudal property and in addition, from tithes; temptation for the state was irresistible, and thus in 1790 came the Civil Constitution of the Clergy. Apathy, and a somnolent, pettifogging indifference to the threat which faced it, brought the Church to a condition which was well nigh irreversible.

By contrast, and as an example of what might have been, there is a story recounted by Mrs Barbauld, one of Priestley's friends, who, as mentioned earlier, had toured France before the Revolution. This is entitled, *A Curé of the Banks of the Rhone* (1791); it is included in an edition of her works published by her niece in 1825 (Vol.II, pp.260–7), but the original source is not given. It is a tale of an older parish priest in a small village at an early stage in the Revolution, who is in sympathy with what is happening and· what has been achieved up to then. He is much aware of the nation's great need for capital, and having discussed the matter with his parishioners they decide that their church can function quite well without its gold and silver plate, jewelled ornaments and other valuables; the church itself they will give for use as a hospital. A small deputation is chosen to go to Paris with these treasures. They have a rapturous reception from the National Assembly, where it is not unnaturally assumed that these are a typical group of agnostics.

But, the priest disabuses the assembly, explaining that in fact they are faithful and devout Catholics who have decided in the present time of crisis that they can well function, just like the earliest Christians, stripped of all finery. All the normal ceremonies can take place, and the sacraments can still be administered; the priest can teach and lead his flock without anything essential being lost. He concludes by telling the deputies that they should "let everyone choose the religion that pleases him; I and my parishioners are content with ours, – it teaches us to bear the evils your childish or sanguinary decrees have helped to bring upon the country". The Assembly and its audience are somewhat taken aback, but still grateful for the generous gesture. Had this been the nature of the church throughout France the Revolution itself would have had a totally different character, but the common pattern was as Belloc tells it and so the church had much to answer for; it was largely the author of its own misfortunes.

When Lafayette proposed to King Louis that he should summon the Estates General, a consultative body of clergy, nobles and representatives of the Commons, or Third Estate, which had not met since 1614 in the reign of Louis XIII: "The foundations of authority were completely sapped. . . . A great famine occurring at a time of great political excitement strengthened the elements of disorder. The edifice of government tottered and fell, and all Europe resounded with its fall." France was ripe for revolution. It had a king, very different from his immediate predecessors, a kindly man well disposed towards his depressed subjects, but not a natural leader. Although he was no academic, there is little doubt that he had a clear idea of the way in which events were moving, and that he was not disposed to resist; not because he was weak, but because he saw that radical change was necessary. He had little sympathy with autocratic, arrogant and oppressive nobles who surrounded him at court. Had he been a stronger character the revolution might have been a happy event, and had he enjoyed the gift of diplomacy he could have had powerful allies, not least across the channel to the north.

It is important to stress that this work is concerned almost exclusively with the Revolution in France and its repercussion in England *only to August 1791*. It is from the perspective of Priestley writing to Burke early in that year and referring to "the late revolution in the French government", as if it were already a *fait accompli* – a superb and glorious chapter in the history of mankind. The last of these *Letters to Burke* is so wildly utopian that, in retrospect, it can bring us close to tears or else provoke sardonic laughter. (It will be dealt with in chapter 15.)

Tom Paine had similar, though somewhat more moderately expressed, views of Utopia. In his *Rights of Man*, at the end of Part I he states:

"Time and change of circumstances and opinions, have the same progressive effect in rendering modes of government obsolete as they have upon customs and manners. . . . As it is not difficult to perceive, from the enlightened state of mankind, that hereditary governments are verging to their decline, and the Revolutions on the broad basis of national sovereignty, and government by representation, are making their way in

Europe, it would be an act of wisdom to anticipate their approach, and produce revolutions by reason and accommodation, rather than commit them to the issue of convulsions.

From what we now see, nothing of reform in the political world ought to be held improbable. It is an age of Revolutions, in which everything may be looked for. The intrigue of Courts, by which the system of war is kept up, may provoke a Confederation of Nations to abolish it: and an European Congress, to patronise the progress of free government; and promote the civilisation of nations with each other, is an event nearer in probability, than once were the Revolutions and Alliance of France and America."

Rights pp.168–9

It would have surprised Paine to know how long it has taken to achieve a European Union, which is still incomplete and clouded by residual British chauvinism. Like Priestley he would be amazed to discover that wars still flourish and that, as the power of monarchy and hereditary aristocracy has diminished, their role has been assumed by a new breed of entrepreneurs, especially those heading multinational and supranational corporations.

The Industrial Revolution

This was yet another movement, more peaceful, gradual and progressive, which nevertheless had profound effects at all levels of society. It has particular relevance here because of the close involvement of one of the main protagonists in this chapter of history; in fact J E Hobsbawm, in his *Age of Revolution*, devotes a whole chapter to this particular revolution. The Lunar Society of Birmingham was the great *think-tank* of the Industrial Revolution and Joseph Priestley was one of its most brilliant philosopher scientists.

It is a remarkable fact that this outstanding Society has been so little explored in its own native land; the major encyclopediae have no monograph between them, although its existence is acknowledged in monographs on the leading members, and related topics. Were it not for one American academic, Robert E Schofield, there would be no book on the topic (although it must be stated that his publisher in England was the Oxford University Press). Winston Churchill, in his *Age of Revolution*, has a few passing references to the Industrial Revolution but shows no appreciation of its philosophical heartbeat.

Hobsbawm has numerous references to the Lunar Society and some to Priestley also, but he under-rates Britain's contribution to science, stating categorically that: "Chemistry, like physics, was preeminently a French science", going on to hand the major prize to Lavoisier. This outstanding scientist deserves great credit and also our sympathy as a victim of the French Revolution during the Reign of Terror. He was a gifted amateur, like contemporaries in other countries, who frequently collaborated with one another. It is true that he was the first to give oxygen its name, but he was not its discoverer; this was Priestley, who reported the event to Lavoisier, in Paris, in 1774.

Hobsbawm, like so many others seems to know Priestley only as a chemist, although he was primarily a physicist and an advanced thinker in that field. He also had outstanding achievements in literature, history, constitutional law, and finally in politics, as we shall see from his letters to William Pitt and to Edmund Burke. The notable private laboratories of Cavendish and Joule, Humphrey Davy and Michael Faraday, are mentioned, but what of Isaac Newton and Joseph Priestley, who had perhaps the greatest and most comprehensive laboratory of them all, which was recorded in detail by loss assessors after the Birmingham Riots in 1791.

Hobsbawm mentions the outstanding role of Manchester's Literary and Philosophical Society alongside the Lunar Society, but has nothing to say, apart from a passing reference *(p.46)* of the Nonconformist Academies, which had been contributing so much to the cultural and academic life of the nation for more than a century, which educated and provided opportunities for men like Priestley, and left Oxbridge in the shade at that time.

CHAPTER II

The Protagonists

You've got to be taught, before it's too late,
Before you are six, or seven, or eight;
To hate all the people your relatives hate,
You've got to be carefully taught.

South Pacific – (Rodgers) and Hammerstein

THE PROTAGONISTS, in this review of England's reaction to events in France, were led by Edmund Burke, Tom Paine and Dr. Joseph Priestley; traditionally Burke takes precedence, because it was his views and his lead which prevailed. There were many others as well, including the Prime Minister, William Pitt; the Leader of the Opposition, Charles J Fox; the monarch, George III; and Mary Wollstonecraft. But for a start we must focus on Dr. Richard Price, who kicked off. Taking them in sequence of events, the order is as follows:

Richard Price, DD, LLD, FRS (1723–91)

It was his *Discourse on the Love of our Country* (4 November 1789), at the Meeting House in the *Old Jewry* to *The Society for Commemorating the Revolution in Great Britain* (1688–89), which started significant debate in Britain within months of the fall of the Bastille. This has been characterised as the "red rag that drew Burke into the arena" and provoked his *Reflections on the Revolution in France*. Dr. Johnson grouped Price with Priestley, Wilkes and Horn Tooke as troublesome agitators.

Price was born in Wales, of bigoted Calvinist stock, but so bigoted was his father that Richard, in reaction, developed liberal opinions and a benevolent disposition, to become a leading Unitarian in his later years. His friends included Benjamin Franklin, Lord Shelburne, Priestley and Hume. He was a writer on Morals, Politics, Economics, and such advanced themes as Life Expectancy and calculating Population Growth. The university of Glasgow awarded him a DD in 1769. In the following year he addressed the Royal Society on calculating values on contingent reversions, and is recognised as one who laid a sound theoretical basis for mutual insurance. He was a student of natural philosophy (science), especially mathematics.

In 1771 he published an *Appeal to the Public on the subject of the National Debt*, which is said to have influenced Pitt in 1786, who re-established the sinking fund for the extinction of the national debt. In 1776, having been opposed from the start to war with the American colonies, he published a pamphlet, *Observation on Civil Liberty and the Justice and Policy of the War with America*. Several thousand copies were sold within days, but it was not universally popular. His critics included John Wesley and Edmund Burke, even though Burke himself was opposed to the war. In 1782, when his friend, Lord Shelburne, became Prime Minister for a short time, making peace with the Americans, Price was offered the post as his private secretary, and wrote a contribution to the king's speech in Parliament. In 1783, Yale University acknowledged the support America had from Price, conferring upon him an LLD, at the same time as they honoured George Washington. He also became a Fellow of the Philosophical Societies at Philadelphia and Boston.

Like Priestley and others who shared his views, Price was lampooned by the cartoonists. Perhaps the best known effort of this kind portrays Price standing in a tub inscribed *Political Gunpowder*, which rests on a book inscribed *Calculations;* below this is a caption: *Tale of a Tub,* and below that, *Every Man has his Price.*

The famous *Discourse* of 1789 is our particular concern here. Reading this today it can hardly be described, by any stretch of the imagination, as an inflammatory or revolutionary tract. It is a thoughtful and well balanced review of the problems facing every civilised nation, at that crucial point in human evolution, and significantly, it predicts a universal form of citizenship. There are points on which many might disagree, but nothing that might not be debated and settled in a civilised manner.

To start with, Price stresses community before territory, and that loving our country "does not imply any conviction of the superior value of it to other countries". (cf. C S Lewis, *The Four Loves*) He decried, "forming men into combinations and factions against their common rights and liberties", foreshadowing "The Church and King Mob" which was, so soon after, to wreak havoc in Birmingham. He criticises the ancient aspiration of the Jewish people to become "lords and conquerors of the earth, under the triumphant reign of the Messiah", and contrasts the "recommendation to Universal Benevolence (by) Our Lord and His Apostles". Our "narrower interest ought always to give way to a more extensive interest (and) . . . we ought to consider ourselves as citizens of the World". (United Nations)

"The chief blessings of human nature" he declares to be "Truth, Virtue and Liberty", very close to the ideas of Priestley and Paine. He decries oppression of the many by the few, keeping them in darkness by suppressing knowledge, and refers to the *Declaration of Rights* by the French National Assembly. He bemoans the perversion of religion, by its too close association with civil government. He extols Liberty in an enlightened and virtuous community: "Civil Government is an institution of human prudence for guarding our persons, our property and our good name. . . . Civil laws are regulations agreed upon by the community" and which should save that community from "falling into a state of anarchy that will destroy those rights and subvert that liberty, which government is instituted to protect". He abhors adulation and servility, especially as it exists under monarchical rule. He believes, "The potentates of this world are sufficiently apt to consider themselves possessed of an inherent superiority, which gives them a right to govern and makes mankind **their own**", which he states is "fostered in them by the creeping sycophants about them".

"Civil governors are properly the servants of the public; and a King is no more than the first servant of the public. . . . His sacredness is the sacredness of the community. . . . His majesty is but the majesty of the people." For this reason alone, "he is entitled to reverence and obedience. The words Most Excellent Majesty are rightly applied to him; and there is a respect which it would be criminal to withhold from him". (Is this regicide sentiment? – as critics would have us believe of the Discourse as a whole.) Price believes the British king to be "almost the only lawful king in the world, because he is the only one who owes his crown to the choice of his people"; a view not universally shared, even by his friends. Introducing the divine element, Price quotes St. Paul, saying: "Rulers are ministers of God, and revengers for executing wrath on all that do evil". Next he warns of creeping despotism in government if "people are not vigilant . . . and determined to resist abuses as soon as they begin". Earlier English writers also had quite an influence on French thinking, for example Locke, who stated: "There remains in the people a supreme power to remove or alter the legislature".

Price now goes on to extol the benefits of the English Revolution a century earlier, as he sees them. He sets out the basic principles: "1) The right to liberty of conscience; 2) The right to resist power when abused; and 3) The right to chuse our own governors; to cashier them for misconduct; and to frame a government for ourselves." Getting away from "the odious doctrines of passive obedience, non-resistance and the divine right of kings". He admits that "the toleration then obtained was imperfect" and cites the Test Laws still in force as evidence. His next target is "Inequality of Representation . . . When representation is only partial, a kingdom possesses liberty only partially", which can lead to "government by corruption". But he warns against intemperate reaction which may "disgrace the cause of patriotism, by licentious, or immoral conduct. . . . I cannot reconcile myself to the idea of an immoral patriot," he says.

In conclusion, Price returns to Scripture and the example of our blessed Saviour who "possessed a particular affection for his country, though a very wicked country", when he wept over Jerusalem, which brings the preacher to mourn over his own country in which "increasing luxury has multiplied abuses (with) a monstrous weight of debt crippling it". (And that was two centuries ago!) So, to his *Nunc Dimittis*, rejoicing that, having shared in "the benefits of one Revolution I have been spared to be a witness to two other Revolutions, both glorious!" This, in brief outline, is the *red rag* which agitated Edmund Burke and other establishment figures.

From Old Jewry the Revolution Society repaired to the London Tavern for an anniversary meeting chaired by Earl Stanhope, at which Dr. Price moved a Congratulatory Address to the National Assembly of France, which was carried unanimously. In correspondence between various bodies in France with the Revolution Society it is obvious that the French at this early stage in their revolution had high hopes of British support.

Edmund Burke, BA, LL.D (1728–97)

He was born in Dublin, the son of an attorney who had converted from Catholicism to the Church of Ireland (Anglican) to facilitate his career, but his mother remained Catholic, and the wife he himself married was also Catholic. But according to T P Power, "Conversions in 18th century Ireland were largely induced by legal requirements and hence were nominal in nature". So we cannot be sure as to Burke's father; he was certainly not biased against his fonmer church; he was described by Daniel O'Connell as "a fashionable lawyer acting in the Catholic interest". *(The Great Melody p.3)* The mother, Mary Nagle, was of a prominent Catholic family in Cork's Blackwater Valley, of a species described as sub-gentry and, like many others in that part of the country, descended from Norman stock. At the age of six young Edmund was sent to live with his maternal uncle, Patrick Nagle, so that he gained a basic Catholic education in rural County Cork, a strong influence that was to remain with him for the rest of his life, explaining some features in his later career which are otherwise difficult to grasp. (pp.19–23)

At the age of 12, Burke was moved to a boarding school, kept by a Quaker named Shackleton in County Kildare, near to Dublin. The milieu here was that of protestant dissent, something akin to the Dissenter Academies of England and Wales. Here he formed a lifelong friendship with Shackleton's son, Richard, who went up with him to university at Trinity College, Dublin. He had a good and stimulating education there, better than he would have had at one of the English universities. * *The Fellows of the College were said to be careful and diligent in their lectures, and the academic requirements more exacting than at Oxford or Cambridge. (J L McCracken in A New History of Ireland* vol. IV, p.51). In fact there was quite a parallel between his education and that of his one-time friend and later adversary, Joseph Priestley, in that freer, broader, and less inhibited discussion was a feature which both had enjoyed, but which they would not have had in an English university. (This will be enlarged upon in a later chapter.) Burke graduated BA in 1748; his doctorate, from TCD, was conferred shortly after the publication of *Reflections . . . in 1790.*

At 18, Burke moved to London to begin his studies in the Middle Temple, which made him a man well fitted for a career in Parliament. He was never called to the bar, to the chagrin of his father, who withdrew his allowance. He spent some years travelling about, making some significant friendships, frequenting theatres and debating societies, and earning something from his writing. He lodged over a bookseller's shop in London. *(Great Melody pp.23–37)*

In 1757 Burke married Jane Nugent, the daughter of a Catholic physician. There is no record of the marriage which, it is thought, may well have been in France, in a Catholic church. Some reports state that after their marriage

---

* Trinity College, Dublin, has reciprocity with Oxbridge but had not sunk so low at that time.

Portrait of Edmund Burke. By James Barry

Jane conformed to her husband's religion, but others insist that she did not. There are also suggestions that Edmund himself *regressed* to become a covert Catholic, but that again is doubtful. What we do know is that throughout his political career his sympathies were always with the Catholic cause, and whenever the opportunity presented itself he took any action he could in its favour. However, he also realised that for a British politician there were real risks in espousing such an unpopular cause. But, although he was discreet in this matter, he was never deterred. Goldsmith regretted his accession to party politics in place of literature, saying that "to party he gave what was meant for mankind". *(O. G. – Retaliation)* But few others agreed, although his opponents might have preferred the other choice. For many years the frontage of Trinity College, Dublin, has been dominated by fine statues of these two graduates – Burke and Goldsmith.

Burke first entered Parliament in 1766, for the pocket-borough of Wendover, to join the Rockingham Whigs. He had a talent for attracting wealthy patrons, who had such gifts to dispense, but he could still make it clear that he was not one to sell himself, and would return an early pension, at a time when he could ill afford the gesture. It was a weakness in his constitutional armour that only from 1774 to 1780 did he hold a seat at Bristol which he had to contest. Before and after that he owed his long parliamentary career to patronage and the corrupt system of pocket-boroughs. Perhaps this is why, "He always looked on any meddling with the constitution as a dangerous matter, and this reverence for the established order sometimes led him to speak and write as though its preservation were of greater moment than the liberty which was the very reason of its existence". He did, however, take a clear liberal stance on several crucial constitutional issues. *(DNB vol. vii, p.351)*

In his later years, and especially during the French Revolution, he was disdainful of philosophers, sophisters, agitators and lawyers engaged in politics. But, was it not through his legal training that he himself was fitted to enter the arena, even if he did not soil his hands with the craft, like those French practitioners of whom he was so dismissive? And was he even being consistent? Were not many of the American politicians, whom he had supported, lawyers also? As to philosophers, he was no mean specimen himself, even if his knowledge did not have the breadth of some that he haughtily puts down. He had great capacity for assembling a complex web of fact and analysing the outcome, which is surely a notable philosophical accomplishment, but he is wedded to existing time-honoured systems and shuns the speculative.

Burke's parliamentary career concentrated on four major themes, as set out by W B Yates and analysed in great detail by Conor Cruise O'Brien in *The Great Melody.* *("American colonies, Ireland, France and India Harried, and Burke's great melody against it." from WB Yates, The Seven Sages)* With them all there is a common underlying theme which is abuse of power. *(Yates' it)* Burke's effort was tireless in these causes and, though never a party leader, he led his party and its leaders over many years by the sheer persuasiveness of his arguments, drawn from detailed research and careful analysis.

His great causes were:

1) gross abuse of power in **India** when the imperial authority was in effect
   the East India Company. This culminated in the impeachment of Warren
   Hastings, who was the most powerful figure in the company, as well as
   being Governor General of Bengal. Even though the House of Lords
   exonerated Hastings at the end of a long drawn out and tedious process,
   the moral victory was Burke's, who led for the prosecution.

2) the **American revolt** in which he supported the colonists against both king
   and parliament. He strove hard to prevent the breach between Britain and
   the colonies; he did his best to avert war, but when it came to this and
   Britain was defeated, he favoured independence.

3) **Ireland**, which was a major concern, but not always brought to the fore
   in debate or in published works, as he constantly feared unfair and bigoted
   rebuff. He always felt he could be undermined when he showed any
   sympathy for Catholics in their struggle against oppressive penal legislation, which has to be the reason that the first Catholic Relief Act in 1778
   was steered through Parliament by Sir George Saville, even though Burke
   was its real author. This Act was carried, not because Burke or Saville
   converted Parliament, but because the king had been persuaded of a tactical
   advantage in having a very modest Act passed which would enable him to
   recruit Catholics into the army, which was in dire need, and facing defeat
   across the Atlantic. Burke was a notable target in the subsequent Gordon
   Riots of 1780, but when his erstwhile friend, Priestley, was victim of the
   equally vicious Birmingham Riots in 1791, Burke seems to have forgotten
   the lesson of his own earlier experience. *(E E Reynolds in The Tablet, 3
   June 1978 p.531)*

4) the **Revolution in France**, which was the last of Burke's great causes and
   the one where his critics say that he was inconsistent in adopting a stance
   so much at variance with his former principles. His contemporaries, who
   were former friends and supporters, such as his party leader, Charles J
   Fox, whom he abandoned and undermined, and others like Priestley and
   Paine, certainly held this view, which will be explored in considerable detail
   in this dissertation. As we have noted Burke reacted strongly against the
   Dissertation by Price. Then in January 1790 his erstwhile friend Thomas
   Paine had written enthusiastically from Paris, detailing the course of the
   Revolution and predicting its spread beyond the borders of France. Al-
   though Burke seems not to have replied, his reactions to the Revolution
   hardened upon receiving this letter.

(Keane, pp.286–7)

Among his supporters, O'Brien in *The Great Melody* has an interesting thesis
which throws new light on Burke's motivation, making it credible, even if it
is still not exactly watertight. His belief is that Burke saw in the French
Revolution, with its agnostic tendencies, a great threat to all that he had striven
for towards Catholic emancipation in general and in particular the relief of
Irish Catholics. A chauvinistic nationalist view of events in Ireland during that
period, which has been handed down through generations, and prevailed at

least up to the middle of this century, bemoans the fact that a successful French invasion did not release Ireland from British domination. This gave rise to the popular slogan: "England's difficulty is Ireland's opportunity".

Burke was almost certainly right in this aspect of his concern for Ireland. English domination was a factor that his native land was at least accustomed to, and with his guidance he believed that a British government could be persuaded, in its own interest, to make significant concessions to Catholic Ireland, to wean young gentlemen away from continental seminaries where they might be contaminated with the French fever. This is borne out in the foundation of a national seminary at Maynooth in 1795, funded with British capital, and where Irish bishops were given effective control. Had the French invasions of 1796 or '98 been successful the story would certainly have been different, and, in view of the Revolution's record, unlikely to have favoured the Church, thus undermining so much that Burke had striven for throughout his career. Ireland might have become part of Napoleon's Empire, with extremely doubtful consequences.

A J Ayer in his book on Tom Paine concludes:

"I have been convinced by Conor Cruise O'Brien . . . that Burke was chiefly moved by what he saw as the similarity between the situation of the American colonists and that of Irish Catholics. He had no such motive for sympathising with French Republicans".

(p.57)

His monograph in the *Dictionary of National Biography*, by Rev. William Hunt *(p.359)*, provides an interesting view of Burke's position within British politics in his later years. Saddened by the death of his only son whom he had expected to inherit his mantle, and embittered by the widening breach with his party leader, he retreated within himself and, as this writer says, "Burke now held a unique position," then going on to quote Sir G Elliott of Minto, who wrote, **"He is a sort of power in Europe, though totally without any of those means, or the smallest share in them, which give or maintain power in other men"**. A perceptive analysis.

The circumstances, outlined above, were those which determined his *Reflections on the Revolution in France,* and later writings which placed him so much at odds with old friends and allies. Among those who did approve of his attitude to France was the king. Eleven editions of *Reflections* were printed within the first year with the endorsement of George III: "A good book," he said, "a very good book; every gentleman ought to read it". *(DNB p.358)* This was a considerable accolade when we consider that Burke had been a thorn in the royal side over many years. The considered view of Hunt, however, is rather less effusive; he writes: "The book contains the pleadings of an advocate rather than the reflections of a philosopher. It exhibits ignorance of the character of the French constitution before the Revolution; it fails to recognise the social causes of the movement, and dwelling on the sufferings of the few it ignores the deliverance of the many". Oxford snubbed him then just as it did Margaret Thatcher in recent times, by voting

Portrait of Joseph Priestley. By William Artaud

against granting him a doctorate; when it was offered in 1793 he declined in pique. (*DNB*)

Joseph Priestley, LLD, FRS (1733–1804)

He was born of humble parentage in Yorkshire's Spen Valley, with a background rather similar to his friend Dr. Price: a restricting Calvinistic congregation from which he made an early break, going off to one of the more liberal nonconformist academies at Daventry. He was a precocious student, mastering the classics at an early age, and acquiring Hebrew during school vacation, also displaying a keen interest in *natural philosophy*, as reported by his younger brother, Timothy. (*Autobiography, intro. p.12*) After Daventry, and a weak start in Suffolk, he came to Nantwich in Cheshire, where, together with ministry, he established a primary school for boys and girls, gaining useful experience and material for his first academic publication on *Rudiments of English Grammar*.

Three years later he was appointed tutor at Warrington Academy, where he had one of the most fruitful periods of his whole career, establishing himself as a progressive teacher with original ideas on how third level education should be developed, ideas which would inspire the new universities of the 19th century. His tutorship was limited to language and literature. But never one to be restricted, he branched out into other spheres, especially into history, with particular emphasis on constitutional law. His *Chart of Biography*, published in 1764, earned him his doctorate from the University of Edinburgh. The tutor's post in mathematics and science would have been his first choice, but this was already filled. However, he contrived to persuade the management to bring a part-time lecturer in chemistry over from Liverpool once a week, providing himself with an invaluable post-graduate experience, which would lead him on to become one of the outstanding scientists of his time. (*p.16*)

This he supplemented with visits to London during Christmas vacations, when he made the acquaintance of members of the Royal Society and especially Benjamin Franklin, who stimulated his interest in electricity, providing him with literature and encouragement towards his first major scientific publication on *The History and Present State of Electricity*, which he supplemented with original experiments of his own, and which earned him his Fellowship of the Society in 1766. (*Autobiography, intro. p.17*)

He was ordained as a Presbyterian minister in his first year at Warrington, but whilst there he progressed, along with several of his colleagues, along the Arian, Socinian, Unitarian track, which was to dominate his theological beliefs, teaching and writing to the end of his days.

Donald Davie, in his Clark Lecture (1976), was very critical of these sectaries but allowed that "the cultural contributions of the Unitarians have been overwhelming in speculative thought, in ideas rather than images, arguments rather than fictions, chains of reasoning rather than artifacts". (*p.67*) Then he went on to say that, "It isn't a matter of setting up cold head (Unitarians) against warm heart (Methodists); that is as unfair to the redoubtably hard headed

Wesley as to the warm hearted Priestley". *(p.68)* Further on *(p.132)*, he says: "Joseph Priestley himself was perhaps a great man and a brave one".

In 1758 he moved to Leeds as a minister, but science occupied much of his spare time. He had been one of those involved in establishing a circulating library at Warrington, and now again he was similarly engaged in Leeds. Both of these libraries are still surviving.

In 1772, Lord Shelburne, the Whig politician, who was never at ease as a party man, and who was abhorred by Burke, was seeking a librarian and learned companion, who would also assist in the education of his sons. Dr. Price recommended Priestley and so a new phase in his career commenced. With his family he resided in Calne, Wiltshire, but he would spend the winter parliamentary session in London with his patron, as well as travelling abroad together. Priestley never became a politician himself, other than in the broad, general sense that anyone who involves himself with policy is a politician and, in that sense, he was certainly deeply involved, especially in the years ahead, but he never joined any particular political group. He was prepared to work with anyone who would enter into constructive dialogue, whatever other views they might have. In the end he did not find Shelburne easy to work with, but their parting was amicable, if strained.

After Calne, the Priestley's moved to Birmingham in 1780, where Joseph was minister at the New Meeting, and where they enjoyed great happiness for more than a decade. His ministry was full time, but he still found time for scientific endeavour and speculation. He wrote and published extensively on theology, on science, and on matters of public concern which were the stuff of heated controversy at that very crucial time, when the American colonists had revolted and the French were about to do so. He irritated the Establishment severely by his constant criticism of what he deemed the inappropriately close links between church and state. In particular he gave them a powerful stick with which to belabour him, when he suggested that he would use gunpowder against this edifice. *(Letter to Pitt pp.17–18)* When he later explained that the only gunpowder in question was figurative and a coded reference to logical argument, it was then too late; the damage had been done and his adversaries would not let him off the hook. In fact we know that he had consulted his friend, Josiah Wedgwood, before publication and was advised to delete the offending expression, but foolishly he had ignored the advice.

When Burke's *Reflections*, attacking Price and his associates, was published in 1790, followed by Priestley's *Letters to Edmund Burke*, early in '91, the political temperature rose steeply to flashpoint, which sparked the Birmingham Riots and disaster for Priestley among others. He and his family lost their home; his congregation its meeting house. His laboratory, library, irreplaceable manuscripts and other possessions were also destroyed. The way in which local magistrates and higher authority appear to have facilitated these evil deeds has been researched in recent years by Alderman Martineau and V. Bird in Birmingham; the evidence is damning. The losses sustained by victims were considerable, but compensation, awarded long after, was greatly scaled down. The very people conniving at such miserliness were those who would protest most loudly about similar destruction carried out by revolutionaries in France.

Priestley's years in Birmingham were the years of the Lunar Society, when he was involved with leading manufacturers, industrialists and other scientists forwarding the Industrial Revolution. Thanks to notable patrons among this group, and to other old friends, Priestley had built up one of the finest laboratories anywhere in Europe at that time. A catalogue prepared by loss assessors, giving details for compensation, is most impressive and a copy may still be found in the Birmingham and Midlands Institute.

It is a notable fact that, in Burke's *Reflections,* whereas he has numerous references to Price (at least a dozen) there is not one direct reference to Priestley. It is natural that Price should feature prominently since Burke had been spurred to action by the Old Jewry *Dissertation* of 1789, but Priestley was the more formidable adversary and Burke was well acquainted with his views. However, Priestley was not one to let matters rest on such crucial issues and so the *Letters* of 1791 constituted his response.

These dissect and analyse Burke's *Reflections* with ruthless logic, to which Burke never responded. He had several more publications on the French Revolution and related issues in his few remaining years but no *Reflections on Dr. Priestley's Letters.*

When the King was notified of the Birmingham Riots, he deprecated the disorder and destruction, no doubt remembering his own experience of the Gordon Riots, much nearer to home and little more than a decade before, but added:

"As the mischief did occur, it was impossible not to feel pleased at its having fallen on Priestley rather than another, that he might feel the wickedness of the doctrines of democracy he was propagating."

George III to Dundas

So much for Human Rights and free speech.

The Priestley family moved to London to be closer to friends and new opportunities. They were never to see Birmingham again, but nowhere in England was really safe. People feared to rent them property, traders were uneasy at dealing with them, and even domestic servants were fearful. The doctor found congenial occupation as a part-time tutor at Hackney College; one of the new institutions set up to replace the recently defunct Warrington Academy, where he had spent those happy years back in the '60s. He also succeeded to the ministry of his old friend Dr. Price at Old Jewry, after Price died that same year.

Priestley did not keep his head down; these new activities and his continuing interest in French affairs would highlight his defiance. Then in September 1792, the very month of the gruesome massacres in Paris, he was granted French citizenship, and invited to become a member of the National Convention. He accepted the citizenship, but declined election. His son, William, was also made a citizen and acclaimed in the Convention by virtue of his father's reflected glory. It is small wonder, therefore, that feelings against the family steadily worsened, until they finally decided to leave England in 1794 and emigrate to America. The general reaction in their native land was one of relief and good riddance, apart from friends and organisations which shared Priestley's views. Among messages of sympathy addressed to him on his departure was one from the United Irishmen, which would have greatly incensed Burke, if he had ever come to know of it.

Life in America was more tranquil, though politics would still haunt the family, even though he had been Franklin's friend and was known to have supported the colonists in their struggle against an oppressive British government and monarchy. But times had changed and his notions of democracy were no longer in fashion there. The family settled in Northumberland, Pennsylvania. Priestley was offered a chair of chemistry at Philadelphia but declined it. Then in 1803, he was invited to become principal of the University of Pennsylvania, but again he declined the post. He occupied his time during his remaining years mainly with writing and occasional preaching. He died peacefully in 1804, his wife and youngest son having predeceased him.

Thomas Paine, MA (1737–1809)

Like Priestley and Price he came of humble stock. Priestley's father had been a cloth dresser: Paine's was a staymaker, and Thomas followed the same career in early life. His home was at Thetford in Norfolk; his parents had a mixed marriage; his mother was Anglican, so Tom was baptised within weeks of his birth and confirmed at the age of 12. His father was a Quaker and frequently took him to meetings. This dichotomy had a notable effect, and also a bearing on his education. He attended the local grammar school, but his father would not allow him to take Latin because of its Popish associations, and so his formal education, which finished at 12, was curtailed. However, it did not make of him a dunce; in one way it sharpened his writing because, much later, he was to declare: "I scarcely ever quote; the reason is I always think". (*Rights of Man, intro. p.12*) Many an academic might ponder this statement with profit, although Paine would go on to quote liberally in his contest with Burke.

Rejecting his father's craft, he went to sea for six months on a privateer, then returning to London he immediately attended a course of scientific lectures. He soon moved on to work as an excise man and later, for a short time, as a schoolmaster, as well as being a Methodist lay preacher. He became a member of Lewes Town Council, in Sussex, and of a local discussion group called *The Headstrong Club*, which sharpened his ideas on social matters, including economics. In this setting he first encountered the ideas of John Locke about the English Revolution of 1688. Locke had asserted the indefeasible right of men to be governed by elected assemblies, and if necessary to resist, even to overthrow a non-elected tyranny. These same concepts, from *Reflections on Civil Government* by Locke, were to influence Priestley, Price, their friends and, even to some extent, Edmund Burke. Paine's experience as a Wesleyan preacher schooled him in the art of public communication, especially to the lower orders in society; the Headstrong Club was his university.

Paine's first sally into politics came with a petition, in 1773, on behalf of his fellow excise men, which was to lose him his job, but helped to establish his craft both in written presentation and in lobbying politicians. It was at this juncture that he first met and impressed Benjamin Franklin, who encouraged him to emigrate and provided him with a good reference. In presenting *The Case of the Officers of the Excise* he pointed to a significant rise in the cost of living resulting from an "increase of money in the kingdom", but the resulting inflation would only benefit those who could off load by charging higher prices to the consumer. In the case of the excisemen he pointed out that low pay would only invite corruption, and above all else he stressed

Portrait of Thomas Paine

that the rich did not know what it was like to be poor, a fact which was just as relevant in England as it was in pre-revolutionary France. It was these rich people whom he was attempting to address, with lessons which they did not wish to take on board, instinctively resisting this embryonic Trades Unionism. He remained unemployed and was forced into exile, having learned much about corrupt administration and vested interest.

Arriving in America late in 1774, his interest was in the possibilities opening up through Science. Had he been in Birmingham he would probably have become a member of the Lunar Society, but it was his humanitarian bent which now came to the fore. Philadelphia presented unexpected opportunity and soon he was engaged in journalism, espousing such causes as abolition of slavery, with rights for negroes and justice for women. But he was still at heart a monarchist, pleading for a return to "perpetual harmony between Britain and her colonies". Within the year, writing in the Pennsylvania Journal he condemned England for cruelty towards the Indians of Asia and of North America, as well as Negro slaves. He then declared: "The Almighty will finally separate America from Britain; call it Independence or what you will". *(Rights p.193)*

Now he was fully committed and, in January 1776, launched his first major pamphlet, *Common Sense*. This explained the American revolt in simple straightforward terms to the colonists, many of whom were still rather mystified as to what it was all about. Paine attacked not only George III but also the institution of monarchy itself. It is a smaller tract, but foreshadowed much that it more fully developed in his *Rights of Man*. It asserts that monarchy is wrong in principal, and harmful in practice, the hereditary principle being contrary to nature, since it denied equality among men, and even in the favoured family it could give precedence to the less gifted individual over a more promising sibling, simply through accident of birth. Burke could probably have told him that in the ancient Celtic system of tanistry, whereas power was transmitted within a dominant family, the tribe would decide which member of that family was most worthy to inherit the power. It was similar with the Old Testament patriarchs over many generations, the choice of David being a notable example, the youngest son in a large family.

Paine favoured centralised power in a democratic confederation of states, when colonists were arguing for individual autonomous states; his model was the one chosen by the Jacobins during the French Revolution. *Common Sense* sold well over 100,000 copies in several editions; George Washington hailed it for the powerful effect it was having on the morale of his followers. Thomas Jefferson was author of *The Declaration of Independence* but *Common Sense* was the model on which he based it. *(Rights p.20)*

The *Crisis Papers*, published intermittently by Paine from 1776 to '83, helped greatly by further boosting morale, to carry the Americans through their war. They explored the relationship between the politicians and their army, encouraging the colonists and taunting their adversary. He stressed that he was not being disloyal to his native land, but abhorred the greed of empire. Paine had strong views on the need for federal unity if the war was to be prosecuted successfully, which could only happen if morale in the army was good, and finance was organised on a federal basis. He helped to establish The Bank of Pennsylvania, soon to become The Bank of North America, and through it money could be borrowed against the security of post-war tax receipts. He abhorred inflation, which gives rise to "dissipation and carelessness", in place of "frugality and thrift". He could see that inflation redistributes wealth, in favour of those already wealthy, to the detriment of the wage earner and the artisan.

Paine was a man of vision when he considered national economy. He was a century and a half ahead of his time in presenting a blue-print for the Welfare State, cherishing the dispossessed and the downtrodden. These are ideas he explores in some detail in *The Rights of Man, Part II*, prophesying such provision as: children's allowance; primary education for all; old age pensions; maternity grants; a grant for funeral expenses, and inner city development.

After the war in America, Paine's scientific bent manifested itself in practical projects, such as the design of an iron bridge, but he did not remain for long out of politics or out of print. His next pamphlet was entitled, *Dissertations on the Government, the Bank and Paper Money*. He favoured sound finance leading to economic growth and national independence with democracy, together with international peace. The University of Pennsylvania crowned his considerable and worthy literary output by conferring upon him its Master of Arts degree, whilst the American Philosophical Society elected him an honorary member.

In 1787, as if on cue, Paine left America for France, but in fact it was to promote his iron bridge project. He was hampered by his poor grasp of the French language, but in spite of this made many interesting and useful contacts.

He became alarmed as relations between England and France deteriorated and, when the likelihood of war increased, he published his next pamphlet, *Prospects on the Rubicon*, hoping to dissuade England against war, realising, however, that traditional enmity over centuries was a very powerful factor. His concern was for England as much as for France. The American adventure had already increased the nation's debt considerably and a new war could only make conditions worse. But his arguments lost force in the new economic climate which came with the industrial revolution; England proved to be more resilient that he predicted.

Returning to England, Paine was received warmly by leading Whigs such as Fox, Shelburne, Vaughan and Burke, with whom he lodged for a time. Burke was impressed with Paine, describing him to John Wilkes as "The Great American". He also remarked jocularly to a mutual friend, "We hunt in pairs". *(Keane p.590)* Paine corresponded regularly with Jefferson in Paris, who was then the American ambassador. He was in England when the French Revolution started in 1789, returning to France in September, from where he wrote with enthusiasm to his old friend, George Washington, stating of himself, "A share in two revolutions is living to some purpose". Back in England the following year, he came with the key of the Bastille, which he was to send to Washington. His covering letter described this as "the first ripe fruits of American principles transplanted into Europe". This seems over-modest when it is considered that in his own *Common Sense* the American principles had been crystallised. *(Rights, intro. p.30)*

Like other liberals he was shocked and taken aback at Burke's intemperate and fierce attack on the Revolution in France in its earliest stages. This was quite unexpected in view of Burke's stance on America, and struck Paine, together with kindred spirits, as nothing short of apostasy. However, the views upon which Burke would elaborate in his *Reflections* were not new; he had expressed them in a lower key in the past and was now giving them full vent. Paine's greatest and most enduring work, *The Rights of Man*, together with Priestley's *Letters to . . . Edmund Burke*, argued most effectively the contrary case. These writings impressed a great many thinking people throughout Great Britain and Ireland, causing the king, the aristocracy and the church hierarchy, to take fright, with results that have akeady been touched upon. Paine planned to visit Ireland in 1791 but had to cancel. However, the United Irishmen of Dublin made him an honorary member. *(Keane, pp.321, 333)*

Paine's ideas were taken up enthusiastically in London by *The Society for Constitutional Information*, and similar societies began to spring up in many provincial towns. He was guest of honour at a large dinner party in November 1791, ostensibly to commemorate the anniversary of England's Revolution of 1688, just as Earl Stanhope, Dr. Price and their friends had done two years before. As the movement grew, thoughtful philosophers, well informed liberals, and articulate artisans, were joining forces to an alarming extent, from a government standpoint.

The Rights of Man, Part II came a year after *Part I*, in February 1792, and the joint work is said to have sold over 200,000 copies. By May the

Establishment had decided that enough was enough, so a Royal Proclamation was issued and on the same day Paine was charged with seditious libel, the awful crime of criticising and irritating 'the great and the good', by the exercise of free speech. His trial was put back from June to December, and meantime he had returned to France. Before the year ended he had been tried in absentia, was declared an outlaw and would never again return to England. He had been returned for Calais as representative in the National Assembly (Would Queen Mary's ghost have rejoiced?), and expected to have a part in drafting a new French constitution. But instead he was caught up in the Reign of Terror and narrowly escaped with his own life. Once he had voted against sending King Louis to the guillotine it would not be long until he himself would go to prison on a trumped-up charge, where he would remain for most of the year 1794, until the Terror had run its course and a new American ambassador would negotiate his release.

Tom Paine felt much aggrieved that the Americans, for whom he had done so much, were slow to intervene and might have allowed him to be executed. He remained in France until 1802, when he returned to America, but he was no longer a hero there; democracy was a tender plant, and freedom from British domination was enough to satisfy most, who were no longer colonials. Their struggle was already receding into history and there were many who had taken part, but this was one man who had left and returned to Europe. He had not taken part in recent affairs and they did not need him.

But there was another factor as well; his book, *The Age of Reason*, written immediately before *(Part I)*, and then *(Part II)* after imprisonment, was an attack on Christianity and had gained him a bad press on both sides of the Atlantic. It is not entirely irreligious, because he was concerned that France, where and when he wrote it, was "running headlong into atheism". *(Letter to Samuel Adams, Jan. 1803)* His own evolving creed was deism, in keeping with Robespierre's *Festival of the Supreme Being*. There is no doubt, however, that it severely damaged his reputation and only served to eclipse so many of his major achievements, including later works such as *The Decline and Fall of the English System of Finance* and *Agrarian Justice*.

Back in America Paine spent his last years in comparative neglect, although he did have a few close and remarkably faithful friends, who made every allowance for his cantankerous and anti-social moods, knowing that he suffered great pain. Critics damn him as a degenerate and disgusting alcoholic at this time, although brandy was almost his only source of relief. Prominent among these friends was one of his executors, Thomas Addis Emmett, a New York lawyer who would later become leader of the Bar in that city. Emmett was a surviving leader of the failed United Irishmen's insurrection in 1798, pardoned and allowed to emigrate after the Act of Union in 1800.

Paine died in 1809 and, having started life with the Quakers, he expressed a wish to be buried in their cemetery. Not surprisingly the Society of Friends demurred, but one Quaker friend did attend his funeral, together with Madame Bonneville and her son who had nursed him in his last illness. Also two black men were present, who wanted to acknowledge his efforts towards the abolition of slavery. Neither the United States nor France was officially represented.

It could be argued in a historical sense, that Paine might have been fortunate to have gone to the guillotine in 1793; at least he would have been spared these later miseries and indignities. In such troubled times, the survivor who is not wholly in favour with the victors is soon forgotten; had he lost his head, Paine would have been a martyr and a hero, crowning all his other accomplishments. In the event, although he has admirers still, neither Britain, America, nor France accords him the honour which he richly deserves. The same might be said of Priestley, whose reputation would not be gainsaid had he perished in the Birmingham riots.

CHAPTER III

Was Burke Inconsistent, as Alleged?

I have no man's proxy, I speak only for myself
Burke's Reflections p.3

THERE IS NO DOUBT THAT BURKE'S OPINIONS REGARDING THE REVOLU-
TION IN FRANCE HELD MANY SURPRISES, when his views and attitudes
up to that time are taken into consideration. It is also incontestable that he
upset and disappointed many former colleagues, associates and friends. Prominent among these were Charles J Fox and other leading Whigs, together with
Priestley and Paine, who had regarded him as a valued friend with similar aims
and objectives. Paine, returning from what he describes as 'my beloved America'
(intro. to RoM Pt.II – dedic. to *Lafayette),* now independent and with a brand
new constitution, even stayed with him for a time as a house guest.

As one who had a reputation for friendship and kindliness he showed little
sympathy or consideration for some of these old friends after 1789. The breach
between himself and his erstwhile leader, Fox, was never healed, not even when
Fox sought a reconciliation in the knowledge that his old friend was dying.
When Priestley, with his family, was a victim of mob violence in 1791, and
was eventually driven into exile in '94, Burke's attitude was just as hard as that
of his newly revered monarch. Paine, imprisoned in Paris during the Reign of
Terror and threatened with the guillotine, might have expected sympathy since
his plight was largely due to the fact that he had voted against the execution
of Louis XVI, but such support, let alone sympathy, was not forthcoming.

Burke has had many defenders right down to the present, and his extreme
grief following the death of his beloved and only son, is frequently evinced as
an extenuating factor, but that was not until 1794. It is also undoubtedly true
that some of the views put forward in *Reflections* were not entirely novel; some
had been stated before and others were foreshadowed. Cruise O'Brien's thesis
in *The Great Melody,* which has already been referred to above, deserves serious
consideration and carries real conviction. But in the final analysis what he
seems to be saying is that Burke had a hidden, or partly hidden, agenda
throughout much of his political career, which related to Ireland and that when
a crisis was reached that agenda outweighed other cherished objectives. It was
"the ghost which all had heard of but none had seen". *(The Great Melody*
p.81) This would help to explain why *Reflections* was such a heated and often
illogical diatribe.

Burke's major critics were men of principle and of integrity. Just because
he slighted them by ignoring their arguments it should not be assumed that

he had triumphed. They had not ignored him but had responded to his *Reflections* by analysing the case logically and in great detail. It requires considerable concentration to follow the detailed, somewhat tortuous and often repetitive, strands in Burke's presentation. By comparison, both Paine and Priestley are refreshingly lucid, even when they also are repetitive, and labour some of their arguments from time to time.

In *Reflections* Burke was responding to the arguments set out by Dr. Price in his discourse at Old Jewry in November 1789 *On the Love of our Country.* He refers to Price on numerous occasions, as might be expected, but studiously avoids any mention of his former friends, Paine and Priestley, whose views on relevant topics were well known, even though their definitive works came later, in response to *Reflections*. There is one coded reference to Priestley *(p.8)* in a side swipe which states: "The wild gas, the fixed air, is plainly broke loose". This might not be appreciated by many readers today but would certainly have been clear to their contemporaries; it focuses on Priestley the chemist, discoverer of oxygen and other gases.

Why should it be asserted still that Burke's stance was not consistent? There is no doubt that he was a creature of his time and of the privileged classes; it could certainly not be said that he was a jumped-up plebeian, toadying to his betters. The family of de Burgo came into Ireland with the Anglo-Norman invasion in the 12th century, and has remained prominent ever since. They intermarried freely with other Norman families and with the ancient Gaelic ruling clans. Edmund's mother was of similar stock: the Nagle's name was originally de Angulos, a family which had settled in North Connaught alongside the de Burgos. His mother came of a branch which had moved to Cork's Blackwater Valley. These were depressed gentry, akin to their Gaelic counterparts, suffering from harsh penal laws, which followed the Reformation, for those who failed to conform, the recusant Catholics.

It was common, at least up until the Second World War, to speak of such families as people 'of good breeding', seeming to compare them with four-legged livestock, but this is not a true analogy because the breeder of pedigree horse flesh, cattle, dogs, or any other creature, is constantly selecting for desired characteristics, and rejecting any animal from the stock which fails to measure up. Ruling families have attempted to achieve similar results but have constantly been baulked by the vagaries of human nature, and the fact that primogeniture often ensured that the individual who would be rejected by the livestock breeder was the one born to rule.

It is one of Tom Paine's major arguments against hereditary rulers, especially when primogeniture is a deciding factor, that the accepted criteria give no guarantee of quality in those individuals 'born to rule'. But, although the crudest observation bears this out, tradition has dictated against logic and common sense to persuade the masses that Plantagenets, Tudors, Stuarts, Hanoverians, Bourbons, Romanovs, some other noble family, or cross matching between them, will produce superb individuals with true quality and a divine right to rule.

Burke was a typical product of this culture, and it might also be said that families from the top of the pile, which had become depressed even despite obvious ability, and because of other factors operating at a different level, felt a deprivation of what they considered to be their birthright. Such people struggled all the harder to regain what they considered to be their rightful place. They would be even less disposed to tolerate a challenge from individuals who could be classified as upstart, coming from outside the charmed circle.

This aspect of Burke's character is crystallised in his passage on *A True Natural Aristocracy* in his *Appeal from the New to the Old Whigs. (Aug. 1791)*

"A true natural aristocracy is not a separate interest in the state, or separable from it. It is an essential integral part of any large body rightly constituted. It is formed out of a class of legitimate presumptions, which, taken as generalities, must be admitted for actual truths. To be bred in a place of estimation; to see nothing low and sordid from one's infancy; to be taught to respect one's self; to be habituated to the censorial inspection of the public eye; to look early to public opinion; to stand upon such elevated ground as to be able to take a large view of the widespread and infinitely diversified combinations of men and affairs in a large society; to have leisure to read, to reflect, to converse; to be enabled to draw the court and attention of the wise and learned, wherever they are to be found; to be habituated in armies to command and obey; to be taught to despise danger in the pursuit of honour and duty; to be formed to the greatest degree of vigilance, foresight and circumspection, in a state of things in which no fault is committed with impunity and the slightest mistakes draw on the most ruinous consequences; to be led to a guarded and regulated conduct, from a sense that you are considered as an instructor of your fellow citizens in their highest concerns, and that you act as a reconciler between God and man; to be employed as an administrator of law and justice, and to be thereby amongst the first benefactors of mankind; to be a professor of high science, or of liberal and ingenuous art; to be amongst rich traders, who from their success are presumed to have sharp and vigorous understanding, and to posses the virtues of diligence, order, constancy and regularity, and to have cultivated an habitual regard to commutative justice: these are the circumstances of men that form what I should call a natural aristocracy without which there is no nation. . . . Men qualified in the manner I have just described form in Nature . . . the leading, guiding and governing part. . . . To give, therefore, no more importance, in the social order to such descriptions of men than that of so many units is a horrible usurpation."

(p.107)

This is vintage Burke and as Utopian as anything that had come, or would come, from Priestley, Paine or any of the French philosophers. It spells out, not only a Divine Right of Kings, but also of *natural born rulers* at any level of society. It accords with what has been set out above as to Burke's origins, background and aspirations. It is the philosophy of the playing fields of Eton.

But, can he really be serious; is he so deficient in knowledge of the history of these islands, of Europe, of Israel, Judah, and their neighbours, that he can see his model of natural aristocracy as having universal application? Has he not read the Old Testament and seen how generations rise and fall; how sons of great leaders, with all the advantages he sets out can slide into degradation and ignominy, while others, without these same advantages, have shot up through the ranks? And what of all these splendid aristocrats who have seen nothing low or sordid from infancy? Where can they have been; in isolated nurseries on a distant planet?

But Burke has not always had such an elevated opinion of aristocracy; writing, in 1770, in his *Thoughts on the Present Discontents*, he tells us:

> ". . . the peers have a great influence in the kingdom, and in every part of the public concerns. While they are men of property, it is impossible to prevent it, except by such means as must prevent all property from its natural operation; an event not easily to be encompassed *while property is power*; nor by any means to be wished, while the least notion exists of the method by which the *spirit of liberty* acts, and of the means by which it is preserved. If any particular peers, by their uniform, upright, constitutional conduct, by their public and their private virtues, have acquired an influence in the country; the people on whose favour that influence depends, and from whom it arose, will never be duped into an opinion that such greatness in a Peer is the *despotism of an aristocracy*, when they know and feel it to be the effect and pledge of their own importance.
>
> "*I am no friend to aristocracy*, in the sense at least in which that word is usually understood. It were not a bad habit to moot cases on the supposed ruin of the constitution, I should be free to declare, that if it must perish, I would rather by far see it resolved into any other form, than *lost in that austere and insolent domination . . .*"
>
> *pp.35–6 (The italics in this passage are mine. P. O'B)*

Here Burke appears to be drawing a distinction between the aristocracy as a broad class and Peers, the latter, presumably, being members of the House of Lords and therefore legislators; his main thesis, in this pamphlet, is the growth of a court faction and its use to bring power with patronage back to the throne. It seems that lesser aristocracy played a significant role in this movement, but the higher nobility were not inactive; further on he refers to the Earl of Bute as 'supposed head of this extraordinary party'. (p.46) But whatever distinctions Burke draws as between grades of aristocracy, the passage just quoted sits uneasily with his view of these noble beings as set forth in his *Appeal . . . to the Old Whigs* in 1791, which again contrasts with the sentiments expressed in his *Letter to a Noble Lord* (1796), which will be discussed in a later section.

So was Burke consistent in relation to America? The answer must be yes! Like most people in Britain, and a majority in the American colonies, he did not wish to see those colonies severed from the crown. But observing how the monarchy and an obstinate government treated the American people, reluctantly, like many others, even in America itself, he came around to accepting that independence was the only answer and better soon than later. He had, after all, set his face, over many years against the ambitions of George III to claw back power and operate outside parliament to achieve his ends. Burke was realist enough to appreciate that people in a territory so far removed, could not be subdued indefinitely, by an administration, lacking both tact and compassion, which had not the wit to see that it was working against what it believed to be its own best interest.

"Was he consistent in relation to India? Were not Warren Hastings and his associates amongst those rich traders, who from their success are presumed to have sharp and vigorous understanding . . . professors of high science, of liberal and ingenuous art"? No they were not, and Burke soon learned what an evil regime was being established in that other, even more distant, part of empire. There is no cause on which Burke expended greater energy or gave more time, and although in the end Hastings was exonerated by the House of Lords, the moral victory was Burke's.

Was he not then, this doughty campaigner, this great political philosopher, also consistent with respect to France? The debate has continued for almost two centuries since his death; he has had some powerful support but in the end the verdict would seem to go against him, but the charge must be further explored. The people of the American colonies were justified in casting off rules that they found to be unjust and oppressive; having done so, they then had the right to choose their own form of government, working from the base upwards.

The people of France were revolting against an even more oppressive, arrogant, unfeeling, degrading and dehumanising establishment, which through the reigns of Louis XIV and Louis XV had considered it right for monarchy and aristocracy to strive for their own aggrandisement and wealth, whatever the consequences for the remainder of the nation. A new king was on the throne, who was very different, but who had inherited a kingdom heavily sunk in debt. He was a man of compassion, whose sympathies were more with the common people in their distress than with the sycophants who surrounded him in the court. He was not a natural leader, nor was he a master of strategy, but neither was he disposed to obstruct those who were more able and who showed greater initiative and insight.

Paine tells us: "The king was known to be a friend of the nation, . . . Perhaps no man bred up in the style of an absolute King, ever possessed a heart so little disposed to the exercise of that species of power as the present King of France." *(Rights p.69)* Priestley refers to him in terms of: "The innocent head that happens to wear it." (The crown) *(Letters to E B p.17)*

At the outset those who aimed to create a new order in France did not see abolition of the monarchy as part of their agenda and had not the king been panicked into flight there would probably have been evolution to a constitutional type monarchy somewhat on the British model, with a more peaceful transition right across the board. Among other factors, France was blessed with a leading national figure in Lafayette and an international idealist in Tom Paine who had together been through the process of change in America a short time before; they had the disposition to provide both sane advice and guidance. Lafayette was a wise and brave man whose main disadvantage was that, being of aristocratic stock, he was seen as a traitor by his peers, and not wholly trusted by his new allies. Paine's greatest problem was that, being articulate and with a superb grasp of political philosophy ahead of most contemporaries, he had failed to acquire enough French to enable him to put his ideas across with force and conviction in the councils of that nation. This meant he was unable to use his natural talent to anything like the same extent that he had done in America.

It is here that Burke comes into the picture. In spite of reservations about the reigning British monarch, he was a firm advocate for the status quo, and we have already seen his excessive reverence for aristocracy; he could tolerate the American rupture, but France was much too near home and had been associated uneasily with England over centuries; upheaval there might be contagious and there were too many elements, both at home and abroad, already showing signs of infection. Dr. Price, with his dissertation at Old Jewry, had sounded what was, for Burke, an alarm call; action must be taken. Price was addressing The Revolution Society, commemorating the English Revolution just a century earlier, an emotive base from which to appeal to many who saw need for reform, much nearer to home.

As a House of Commons man it seems strange that Burke was so besotted with the aristocracy, but it is essential to remember that the nobility were heavily involved in administration then, not so aloof as the House of Lords has since become and, apart from the years when he represented Bristol, Burke was beholden to aristocrats for his seat in the Commons.

In the early stages of the Revolution in France many British politicians, and among them William Pitt, were prepared to bide their time and hope for a peaceful outcome. Britain, in the aftermath of the American upheaval and with its considerable national debt, did not need another war and if the French king was happy to accept a new constitution, why should Britain interfere? But Burke panicked and eventually carried the Prime Minister and government with him, once they had time to absorb his *Reflections,* and subsequent contributions. They were mesmerised.

Burke's attack on the French was concentrated mortar fire and, whereas others pondered the outcome, he was never in doubt. So credit is heaped upon him for having got it right; the prophet of doom for the French was seen as Britain's saviour. But could it be that this was self-fulfilling prophecy? Pitt was never an admirer of Burke but used him for his own ends; King George, on the other hand, became a true convert; his erstwhile scourge was now firmly ranged against the regicides and His Majesty was grateful. He heartily endorsed Burke's *Reflections* and no doubt boosted sales for that 'very good book'.

What was the effect in France? That nation had its back to the wall; aristocrats fled the wrath of the common people, whom they had abused for so long and this started immediately after the Bastille fell in 1789. These families gravitated to friends and relations scattered across Europe, drumming up an anti- revolutionary backlash, and surrounding France with enemies. The new administration badly needed friends who would support the changes taking place; it looked to Britain in the belief that, having had its own most recent domestic revolution just a century earlier and having tamed its monarchy, it would understand and provide the necessary support.

The report of an English eye-witness in Paris on the original Bastille Day, regarding popular perception of Britain as a natural ally has already been quoted, and popular support there was in plenty, led by thinking people such as Drs. Price and Priestley, Tom Paine, Earl Stanhope, Horne Tooke, Benjamin Vaughan, Mary Wollstonecraft, Mrs Barbauld, and many others, but in the end Burke prevailed.

War was the last thing that either Britain or France needed, since both had only recently been engaged against one another, both across and upon the Atlantic, during the American Independence campaign. That had been a bloody and highly expensive war; so both countries should have studied to maintain peace. However, France was soon attacked by a hostile European coalition, and against all the odds France triumphed. Had Britain at that point resorted to diplomacy, supporting France and avoiding hostility, it may be argued that the course of the revolution could have been vastly different. The king's flight, with his family, to Varennes would not have taken place; he would then have remained free and not have been perceived as a threat to the nation's new leaders. Constitutional changes might then have evolved much more peacefully, avoiding the Reign of Terror, and the final bonus, not only for Britain but also for Europe as a whole would have been the absence of Napoleonic wars, with the accompanying imperial culture.

When war with France was declared in April 1793 a National Fast was appointed to influence the disposition of people in general, but many who were opposed to British policy on French affairs saw in this gesture only humbug and chauvinism, calculated to mislead. A pamphlet on the subject, *Sins of Government Sins of Nation*, appeared from the pen of Mrs Barbauld, friend and supporter of Dr. Priestley; it sought a pause for sober and cool reflection before rushing headlong into this conflict. In it she writes:

> "Of late years indeed, we have known none of the calamities of war in our own country, but the wasteful expense of it; and sitting aloof from those circumstances of personal provocation, which in some measure might excuse its fury, we have calmly voted slaughter and merchandised destruction – so much blood and tears for so many rupees, or dollars, or ingots.We devote a certain number of men to perish on land and sea, and the rest of us sleep sound, and protected in our usual occupations, talk of the events of war as what diversifies the flat uniformity of life.
>
> We should, therefore, do well to translate this word war into language more intelligible to us. When we pay our army and our navy estimates, let us set down – so much for killing, so much for maiming, so much for making widows and orphans, so much for bringing famine upon a district . . ." etc.

Aikin, Works of ALB pp.400–1

These are arguments very similar to what Paine had expressed in *Prospects on the Rubicon*, 1787. *(Ayer pp.52–3)*

Edmund Burke would surely have applauded these sentiments in the run up to the American conflict, so why not in contemplating war with France, which in the end would be more bloody and much more protracted. Paine, on the other hand, writes of: ". . . the madness of war and the wretched impolicy of two nations, like England and France, continually worrying each other, to no other end than that of a mutual increase of burdens and taxes". *(Rights, preface p.58)*

He had a firm view on war with France and stated: "There will be no lasting peace for France, nor for the world, until the tyranny and corruption of the English government be abolished, and England, like Italy becomes a sister republic". But, in spite of Paine's popularity and the extent to which his writings were taken up, this did not happen. *The Rights of Man (Part I)* had a phenomenal circulation; the original editions sold for the same amount as Burke's *Reflections*, which limited sales, but then a cheap edition was produced which soon sold at least 100,000 copies between England, Ireland and Scotland, pushing the government into a state of panic.

Paine's great work would never have excited such widespread interest had its literary quality been as poor as many of his detractors asserted. They focused on his deficit in formal education and used this to imply that he was a literary dunce, employing false logic, but there were many respected characters who testified to the contrary. One of these was the American President, Thomas Jefferson. Writing in 1821, a dozen years after Paine had died, he stated: "No writer has exceeded Paine in ease and familiarity of style, in perspicuity of expression, happiness of elucidation, and in simple and unassuming language". Democratic politics would require a literary style that was also democratic, and Keane *(p.296)* suggests that: "The point was to outflank Burke by replacing the accepted courtly standards of literary excellence with the vulgar and quotable language of common speech, without losing sight of the twin goals of publickly airing fundamental political issues in a serious way and publickly questioning a political class accountable only to itself".

So why did Burke prevail and why assert that the outcome was not just brilliantly foreseen by him, but was indeed a self-fulfilling prophecy which succeeded because the British Prime Minister and government heeded his tale of woe, and reacted accordingly. To appreciate this point a psychiatric view may help.

There has long been confusion between mental disorder and madness; a distinction which is not always appreciated even today. With mental illness thought and emotion can be disturbed, but such disturbance can persist over many years without an affected individual ever being mad or, more accurately, being *driven mad*. On the other hand perfectly sane individuals can be driven mad, a state which many of us experience to a greater or lesser degree at some time in our lives. *Madness is an emotional reaction to frustration and/or intimidation*, in a situation where an individual or a group feel they are losing control of their destiny, and become uncontrollably angry.

A simple and very apt example is the case of King George III. This unfortunate man was victim of a disorder called 'acute intermittent porphyria'. (The terms acute and intermittent were highly significant in this case.) It is due to a defect in blood chemistry and, apart from certain physical manifestations, the mental disturbance consists of confusion and emotional instability. This was the king's problem; his well attested madness was due to the manner in which the problem was handled. Confinement in a straitjacket, gagging, and other like horrors, were calculated to provoke anger and frustration even in a person not accustomed to command and expect obeisance. His Majesty cracked! He was driven mad!

Madness, as here defined, may affect not only individuals, but communities large or small, a mob, or even the greater part of a nation. The people of France, embarked upon a quite rational revolution, having the acquiescence of their king, but gradually found themselves surrounded by hostile neighbours. The one neighbour, across the channel to the north, that might have been expected to give support, soon joined the others. Is it any wonder that frustration and anger spread like wildfire through the nation, affecting rich and poor, high and low, the rulers and the ruled? Is it any wonder that there was a Reign of Terror? Could Edmund Burke stand back and say his hands were completely clean? That he merely foresaw what was inevitable? Or is it a fact that his views and his influence on Pitt's government led on to madness in the people of France? Were they driven mad?

Significantly, Dr. Priestley, in the Preface to his *Letters to . . . Burke* declares that "every successful revolt is termed a Revolution, and every unsuccessful one a Rebellion". France did succeed in many important respects and so we speak of The French Revolution, even if the success was not all that it might have been with the failures that occurred being due largely to external influences. We shall return to the question of Burke's alleged inconsistency later.

CHAPTER IV

Constitution and Human Rights

When a true genius appears in the world, you may know
him by this sign, that the dunces are all in confederacy
against him.
    Jonathan Swift (1711, from 'Thoughts on Various Subjects')

EDMUND BURKE WAS A GREAT MAN, one of the most brilliant parliamentarians of his time, with a gift for ensuring that he had more friends than enemies around him, so Swift would probably have denied him true genius.

Priestley and Paine, on the other hand, were men of great ability across a broad spectrum, sometimes appreciated, and often not, during their own lifetime. In both cases, in later years, the dunces did join forces against them, attempting to force them from the public eye, even while still alive, and succeeding to a remarkable degree once they were off the scene. The result has been that their closely argued theses have been undervalued and dismissed, even to the present day.

Burke's *Reflections*, originally intended for a young correspondent of his in Paris, were expanded to challenge Dr. Price's Discourse *On the Love of our Country*. Price, close to death, was no longer able to respond, but both Paine and Priestley rose to the challenge, Paine with his *Rights of Man* and Priestley in his *Letters to the Right Honourable Edmund Burke*. All three had further contributions after 1791, but these are of less concern, since the object of this review is to consider the early stages of the French Revolution and its potential outcome, in view of the response to ideas put forward at that stage.

Both Priestley and Paine express their surprise and disappointment at Burke's change in attitudes and action when introducing their own works. Priestley in his preface states:

"It is with very sensible regret that I find Mr Burke and myself on the two opposite sides of any important question, and especially that I must now no longer class him among the friends of what I deem to be *the cause of liberty, civil or religious*, after having, in a pleasing occasional intercourse of many years, considered him in this respectable light. In the course of his public life, he has been greatly befriended by the Dissenters, many of whom were enthusiastically attached to him; and we always imagined that he was one on whom we could depend, especially as he spoke in our favour in the business of subscription, and he made common cause with us in zealously patronising the liberty of America.

That an avowed friend of the American Revolution should be an enemy to that of the French, which arose from the same general principles, and in a great measure sprung from it, is to me unaccountable. . . . some are disposed to ascribe this change in Mr Burke's views and politics to his resentment of the treatment of the *coalition* by the Dissenters. And certainly so *sudden* an union of Mr Burke and his friends with Lord North, with whom they had been in a state of violent opposition during the whole of the American War, did fill the Dissenters . . . with horror . . . but, . . . they lamented the fall of Mr Burke, as that of a friend and a brother."

Letters pp.iii–iv

In the first of his letters, Priestley tells Burke:

"You appear to me not to be sufficiently cool to enter into this serious discussion. Your imagination is evidently heated, and your ideas confused."

(p.2)

Later he says:

"I do not judge of your usual temper and disposition from the strain of this intemperate publication. *(Reflections . . .)* I know you and I know it to be unworthy of you."

(p.46)

In another place he tells Burke that he is 'sublimely rhetorical' *(p.66)* but "you do not deal much in definitions or axioms".

(p.56)

Tom Paine in his Preface states:

"From the part Mr Burke took in the American Revolution, it was natural that I should consider him a friend to mankind; and as our acquaintance commenced on that ground, it would have been more agreeable to me to have had cause to continue in that opinion than to change it . . . . (but) when I saw the flagrant mis-representations which Mr Burke's pamphlet contains; and that while it is an outrageous abuse on the French Revolution, and the principles of Liberty, it is an imposition on the rest of the world. I am more astonished and disappointed at this conduct of Mr Burke . . . as I had formed other expectations.

When I came to France in the Spring of 1787, the Archbishop of Toulouse was then Minister, . . . I became acquainted with the Private Secretary of that Minister, . . . and found that his sentiments and my own perfectly agreed with respect to the madness of war, and the wretched impolicy of two nations like England and France, continually worrying each other to no other end than that of a mutual increase of burdens and taxes. That I might be assured I had not misunderstood him, nor he me, I put the substance of our opinions into writing and sent it to him;

subjoining a request, that if I should see among the people of England, any disposition to cultivate a better understanding between the two nations than had hitherto prevailed, how far I might be authorised to say that the same disposition prevailed on the part of France? He answered me by letter in the most unreserved manner, and that not for himself only, but for the Minister, with whose knowledge the letter was declared to be written.

I put this letter into the hands of Mr Burke almost three years ago, and left it with him, where it still remains; hoping, and at the same time naturally expecting, from the opinion I had conceived of him, that he would find some opportunity of making a good use of it, for the purpose of removing those errors and prejudices, which two neighbouring nations, from the want of knowing each other, had entertained, to the injury of both. When the French Revolution broke out, it certainly afforded to Mr Burke an opportunity of doing some good, had he been disposed to it; instead of which, no sooner did he see the old prejudices wearing away, than he immediately began sowing the seeds of a new inveteracy, as if he were afraid that England and France would cease to be enemies."

Rights pp.57–58

Human Rights

It is with Tom Paine that the expression *Rights of Man* is most notably associated, although as Priestley tells us the concept had been in existence for much longer; of England from 1688 he states:

"To vindicate this Revolution, Lord Somers, Bishop Hoadley, Mr Locke and many others, have laid it down as a maxim, that all power in any state is derived from the people, and that the great object of all government, is the public good. As a consequence from these fundamental principles, they maintain that all magistrates, being originally appointed by the people, are answerable to them for their conduct in office, and removable at their pleasure. The right of resisting an oppressive government, that is such as the people shall deem to be oppressive, they hold most sacred."

Letters to E. B. pp.22–23

In his American campaign Tom Paine has the concept clearly in focus, but he only uses the expression in the last paragraph of the Appendix to *Common Sense*, where he concludes:

"Let the names of Whig and Tory be extinct";[*] and let none other be heard among us, than those of a good citizen, an open and resolute friend,

---

[*] About a century later W S Gilbert in one of his lyrics for the Savoy Opera, *Iolanthe*, has the concluding line "Every boy and every gal born into this world alive is either a little Liberal or else a little Conservative". – *Plus ça change!* And although the labels changed in America, Gilbert's point still applies.

and a virtuous supporter of the Rights of Mankind and of the Free and Independent States of America."

C.S. p.122

These ideas had a powerful influence when it came to drafting the American Declaration of Independence. This was done by Thomas Jefferson, but Paine's influence is obvious. *Rights of Man,* when it was published in 1791, followed the *Declaration of Rights* by the French National Assembly at a time when Lafayette was presiding. He and Paine were close associates both in America at first and now in France, so again Paine's influence is obvious. In his book the *Declaration* is inserted as a separate item and its XVII clauses are set out in full. Paine comments that: "The three first articles comprehend in general terms the whole of a Declaration of Rights: All the succeeding articles either originate from them, or follow as elucidations". *(Rights p.135)* These three articles state:

I Men are born and always continue free and equal in respect of their rights. Civil distinctions, therefore, can be founded only on public utility.

II The end of all political associations is the preservation of the natural and imprescriptable *rights of man*; and these rights are liberty, property, security, and resistance of oppression.

III The nation is essentially the source of all sovereignty; nor can any Individual or Any Body of Men, be entitled to any authority which is not expressly derived from it.

Rights p.132

Paine quotes Lafayette, saying: "For a nation to love liberty, it is sufficient that she knows it, and to be free it is sufficient that she wills it". *(Rights p.67)* All men have their blind spots, and we should note Paine's comment in the Appendix to *Common Sense* that: "He who hunts the woods for prey, the naked and untutored Indian, is less a savage than the (king) of B(ritain)." *(p.114)* Paine is applauded for his defence of black slaves, and would later discover that the American Indians had their own rich culture, and long established traditions.

Burke's views, at this time, were very different from those of Priestley and Paine; in his Reflections he states:

"In the famous law of the 3rd of Charles I called the *Petition of Right*, the parliament says to the king: 'Your subjects have inherited this freedom', claiming their franchises not on abstract principles as 'rights of men', but as the Rights of Englishmen, and as a patrimony derived from their forefathers. Selden and the other profoundly learned men who drew this petition of right were as well acquainted, at least with all the general theories concerning the 'rights of men' as any of the discoursers in our pulpits, or on your tribune; full as well as Dr. Price, or as the Abbé Sieyès. But for reasons worthy of that practical wisdom which superseded their theoretic science, they preferred this positive, recorded, *hereditary* title to all which can be dear to the man and the citizen, to that vague speculative right, which exposed their sure inheritance to be scrambled for and torn to pieces by every wild litigious spirit."

Reflections pp.34–5

It seems a strange claim that contemporaries of Charles I, no matter how 'profoundly learned', should be as well versed in general theories concerning rights of men as Burke's own contemporaries, when so much discussion and elucidation had taken place in the century and a half which intervened. And what is this hereditary title which must block all further speculation and development. Burke goes on:

"In the 1st of William and Mary, in the famous statute, called the *Declaration of Right*, the two Houses utter not a syllable of 'a right to frame a government for themselves'. You will see that their whole care was to secure the religion, laws, and liberties, that had been long possessed, and had been lately endangered. . . . Then they pray the king and queen 'that it may be *declared* and enacted, that . . . the rights and liberties *asserted* and *declared* are the true *ancient* and indubitable rights of the people of this kingdom."

p.35

But what are these 'rights of the people'? Burke does not tell us. However, Paine, also commenting upon the settlement of 1688, and the construction Burke places upon it, states:

"It is somewhat extraordinary, that the offence for which James II was expelled, that of setting up power by *assumption*, should be re-acted (sic), under another shape and form, by the parliament that expelled him. It shows that the rights of man were but imperfectly understood at the Revolution; for certain it is that the right which that parliament set up by *assumption* (for by delegation it had it not, and could not have it because none could give it) over the persons and freedom of posterity forever, was of the same tyrannical unfounded kind which James attempted to set up over the parliament and the nation, and for which he was expelled."

Rights p.65

Burke states that: "Whatever each man can separately do, without trespassing upon others, he had a right to do for himself; and he has a right to a fair proportion of all which society, with all its combinations of skill and force, can do in his favour. In this partnership all men have equal rights; but not to equal things". *(Reflections p.64)* This is a good start, but it is about as far as Burke will go; he comes up against the familiar problem which has caused so much confusion in his time and ever since. All men are born equal in the sight of God, but this does not mean that all are equally endowed or have equal potential; we all have different qualities, and it is combining these for the general good that enriches life for all. One has better physique and strength, another is more dexterous; one has a sharper intellect, another is more artistic. Others again may be poorly endowed across the board, although there are few who do not excel in some respect, given the opportunity. Everyone does not have the right to whatever he fancies; we cannot all be Prime Minister, but we all have a right that consideration, care and nurture, should be available to us, if we cannot provide adequately for ourselves. It is not clear whether Burke, like many others, has failed to grasp some of these fundamentals, or whether his mind is closed to them.

Priestley claims for all:

"the secure enjoyment of such *advantages,* or *rights,* as have been usually termed *natural,* as life, liberty, and property, which men had *from nature* without societies or artificial combinations of men. Men cannot, surely, be said to *give up* their natural rights by entering into a compact for the better securing of them. And if they make a wise compact, they will never wholly exclude themselves from all share in the administration of their government, or some control over it. For without this their stipulated rights would be very insecure."

Letters to E. B. p.24

Paine declares that:

"Every generation is equal in rights to the generations which preceded it, by the same rule that every individual is born equal in rights with his contemporary".

Rights p.88

Burke, returning to the fray, scoffs as:

"chaff and rags and paltry blurred shreds of paper about the rights of man";

going on to add:

"that in this enlightened age I am bold enough to confess that we are generally men of untaught feelings; that instead of casting away all our old prejudices, we cherish them, and, to take more shame to ourselves, we cherish them because they are prejudices; and the longer they have lasted and the more generally they have prevailed, the more we cherish them."

Reflections pp.94–5

Priestley pounces on this paradoxical outburst to ridicule its author, and to explain just where his argument is taking him.

"On this principle, Sir, had you been a Pagan at the time of the promulgation of christianity, you would have continued one. You would also have opposed the Reformation. You would, no doubt, have cherished the long and deep rooted prejudice of the earth being the centre of our system, and everything that was *old;* the creed of your nurse, and of your grandmother, in opposition to everything *new.*

The spirit of free and rational enquiry is now abroad and without any aid from the powers of this world, will not fail to overturn all error, and false religion, wherever it is found, and neither the church of Rome, nor the church of England, will be able to stand before it."

Letters to E. B. pp.113–4

A final point of Burke's upon this topic comes when he is dealing with economics. He declares:

"The revenue will not be trifled with. The prattling about the rights of men will not be accepted in payment of a biscuit or a pound of gun-powder."

Reflections p.269

Was this a deliberate rubbing of salt into Priestley's wounds, because he must have been well aware of how his erstwhile friend had been pilloried, only a few years earlier, when he had used gunpowder in an equally metaphorical sense in his Letter to William Pitt.

In many of his comments Burke is scarcely rational about human rights, and resorts to sneering when he fails to have the better of an argument. If he could have accepted that to assert rights must naturally imply corresponding duties; the man who will have his own rights must allow no less to his fellow man. Burke could have been eloquent on this theme, but he missed the point. His views had changed, or been modified, over 20 years, as we can see from his *Thoughts on the Present Discontents* (1770), where he considers:

"Whether it will be right, in a state so popular in its constitution as ours, to leave ambition without popular motives, and to trust all to the opera-tion of pure virtue in the minds of Kings and Ministers, and public men, must be submitted to the judgement and good sense of the people of England."

P.D. pp.54–5

"It is not more the duty than it is the interest of a Prince to aim at giving tranquillity to his government. But those who advise him may have an interest in disorder and confusion. If the opinion of the people is against them, they will naturally wish that it should have no prevalence. Here it is that the *people must on their part show themselves sensible of their own value.* (my italics) Their whole importance, in the first instance, and afterwards their whole freedom, is at stake. Their freedom cannot long survive their importance. . . . increase of the power of the state has often been urged by artful men, as a pretext for some abridgement of the public liberty."

pp.58–9

"The King is the representative of the people; so are the Lords, so are the Judges. They are all trustees for the people, as well as the Commons; because no power is given for the sole sake of the holder; and although

Government is an institution of Divine authority, yet its forms, and the persons who administer it, all originate from the people."

p.75

These views were expressed during the crisis which arose during the efforts to prosecute John Wilkes and expel him from parliament, leading to the infamous Middlesex by-elections. The point about advisers to the king having 'an interest in disorder and confusion' explains itself in this context. It is hard to see these views, overall, as representing other than the *Rights of Man* and surprising that Paine did not make use of this significant material, coming from his opponent, but perhaps he was not aware of, or had forgotten, this earlier pamphlet.

Burke is here expressing himself as a principled democrat, free from the prejudices which later clouded his judgement during the revolution in France, but are principles to be varied when circumstances change? He would surely never have made any such claim, but his contrary opinions, expressed in two very different contexts, seem to lay him open to the charge that this was, de facto, the position in which he placed himself in the 1790s.

Constitution

There are two major elements to any constitution whether the organisation be international, national or the village debating society: the first is structural, the second is operational. The first is usually the simpler: what officers or other functionaries are required to enable it to operate in an orderly manner? Basically these will be chairman, secretary, treasurer, by whatever grandiose titles they may appear. The bigger the organisation the more complex its management will be, and subdivision may be required to carry on its business. The basic constituents of government are legislative, executive and judicial; these must be clearly defined, and provided for.

The second element is the vital one: it must set out the aims and objectives of the organisation; what meetings are required, for business or for other functions, where, when and how often. In larger organisations the members attending for business will be representatives. How are these chosen and for what duration? Are there provisions to remove, or if necessary to punish, individuals who act against the best interests of the whole body?

In the historical situation being considered here these features are absolutely vital. If France were to have a successful, constructive and peaceful revolution, how should this be achieved? How was change to operate? What examples were relevant or should be followed? The recent experience in America, as the colonies had achieved independence, was obviously the most relevant. Then what of British experience over the previous century and a half? What of European experience even further back? Was anything to be learned from classical Greece and Rome?

The revolution was not spontaneous and unplanned; much thought and discussion had been taking place over a considerable period. In its early and peaceful stage there was a large element of evolution, and recent American experience was very much to the fore; after all France had been involved in the conflict upon and across the ocean. A son of France had played an honourable part, and was now home again to play an important role in the changes that would take place. The Marquis de Lafayette was an emigré French nobleman; now Monsieur Lafayette had returned from America a democrat. (More will be said of him in a later chapter.)

Tom Paine had played an even more vital role in America and his talents were now at the disposal of France. In his *Rights of Man, Part II,* the fourth chapter is devoted entirely to the subject *of Constitutions.* He starts with the distinction between constitutions and governments:

> "A constitution is not the act of a government, but of a people constituting a government; and government without a constitution is power without a right. . . . Power . . . must be either delegated or assumed. . . . All delegated power is trust, and all assumed power is usurpation."
>
> *Rights p.207*

Following this basic declaration, he plunges straight into the American experience where he has seen new government begin. He sets out how the individual colonies became states, and then eventually formed a federal government; how this had resulted from an interstate convention, setting forth proposals which were approved and gained the authority of the people as a whole (allowing that universal suffrage was not yet established at this time). A general election was called and the convention dissolved. Then follows a crucial paragraph:

> "In this constitution were laid down, first, a declaration of rights. Then followed the form which the government should have, and the powers it should possess – the authority of the courts of judicature and of juries – the manner in which elections should be conducted, and the proportion of representatives to the number of electors – the time which each succeeding assembly should continue . . . the mode of levying, and of accounting for the expenditure, of public money – of appointing public officers, etc., etc., etc."
>
> *p.209*

Here, he comments is "a government issuing out of a constitution . . . not only as an authority, but as a law of control to the government. It was the political bible of the state. Scarcely a family was without it". *(p.209)* He goes on to relate the gradual evolution of Congress. An Act of Confederation was passed, but recognising that this body could not give power to itself the matter was passed back to the individual states. Only after the states severally agreed was the federal government properly established. Government, he concludes, "is altogether a trust. . . . It has of itself no rights; they are altogether duties". *(p.211)*

Further on he declares: "It is not for the benefit of those who exercise the powers of government, that constitutions, and governments issuing from them, are established". By contrast he states that, "In England everything has a constitution except the nation. Every society and association that is established, first agreed upon a number of articles . . . its constitution". *(p.213)* Then starting with William of Normandy he finds that, "the government of England was originally a tyranny, founded on an invasion and conquest. . . ." *(p.214)* With the Williamite take-over of 1688 came the Bill of Rights which he describes as "a bargain, which the parts of the government made with each other to divide powers, profits, and privileges." *(p.215)* ". . . From the want of a constitution in England to restrain and regulate the wild impulses of power, many of the laws are irrational and tyrannical, and the administration of them vague and problematical." *(p.217)*

It is difficult to argue against the premise that, compared with what the Americans at that time had achieved in terms of representative government, Britain had a long way to go and even half a century later with the Reform Act of 1832, the gap was not closed. Much of the problem through the 18th and into the 19th century Paine attributes to political connection with Germany which caused Britain to be "completely engrossed and absorbed by foreign affairs". *(p.218)* He rejects monarchy as a fitting model to head a government, describing hereditary government as a species of slavery. In support of this he states: "When extraordinary power and extraordinary pay are allotted to any individual in a government, he becomes the centre, round which every kind of corruption generates and forms". *(p.225)*

We have plenty of examples in the late 20th century which still bear testimony to the wisdom of this last statement, in heads of newly emerging African states and others around the world; not forgetting the heads of large national and international corporations, some of which are powerful enough to face down or bamboozle governments. This, of course, is not a new phenomenon but one which was familiar to Edmund Burke when he was striving to bring to heel the pernicious organisation of the East India Company and its chief officer, Warren Hastings.

Concluding his chapter 'Of Constitutions' Paine poses the question: "Who would have believed that a French National Assembly would ever have been a popular toast in England. . . . It shows that man, were he not corrupted by governments, is naturally the friend of man. . . . That spirit of jealousy and ferocity which the governments of the two countries inspired . . . is now yielding to the dictates of reason, interest and humanity". And finally he says: "We can foresee all Europe may form one great republic. . . ." *(pp.230–1)* This might have been characterised up to recently as part of Paine's improbable Utopia, but suddenly we have a European Community which is growing ever larger and stronger. We can only hope that it measures up to the dream. But would Paine have been surprised to know of Britain's great reservations and reluctance, together with some strange posturing on the part of the French?

Paine has comments, also in *Part I* of his book; some of these add to what is above, for example,

"The French constitution distinguishes between the king and the sovereign. It considers the station of king as official, and places sovereignty in the nation. . . . The representatives of the nation, who compose the National Assembly, and who are the legislative power, originate in and from

Gillray Cartoon of Paine "A Good Constitution sacrificed for a Fantastik Form."

the people by election. . . . Those same matters which in France are now held as rights in the people . . . are held in England as grants from what is called the crown. . . . The House of Commons did not originate as a matter of right in the people to delegate or elect, but as a grant or boon".

(Rights p.111)

We might add: with great reluctance on the part of the monarchy.

Next he sets out the influence which Lafayette, with his American experience, has had in resurrecting the States General (a vital stage in the Revolution) and the establishment of a new constitution. *(pp.120–31)* Turning to England he recalls a speech by the Earl of Shelburne in the House of Lords when the Earl was Prime Minister and in the context of peace-making with America. He gives this from memory:

"That the form of government was a matter wholly at the will of a nation, at all times; that if it chose a monarchical form, it had a right to have it so, and if it afterwards chose to be a Republic, it had a right to be a Republic, and to say to a King, We have no longer any occasion for you." Paine, himself, adds that: "Government with insolence is despotism; but when contempt is added, it becomes worse; and to pay for contempt, is the excess of slavery".

And then from Lafayette:

"For a nation to be free, it is sufficient that she wills it".

(pp.142–3)

Paine dismisses the hybrid, which is mixed government, by which he means one that combines the hereditary element with the representative, declaring: "It is an imperfect everything, cementing and soldering the discordant parts together by corruption". Chief among these corruptions he mentions places and pensions at the disposal of ministers. *(pp.162–3)* One wonders how he would rate many of our present 'democratic' governments, not least among them his darling America, and Britain, somewhat reformed since 1832.

Price, in his *Discourse*, had far less to say about government and constitution than Paine and confines himself to broad generalisations. Looked at overall, it is surprising that Burke should have reacted so vehemently except that Price had dared to comment favourably on events in France, on kings as servants of the people, and against flawed representation. On general principles he stated that:

"Civil government is an institution of human prudence for guarding our persons, our property, and our good name, against invasion; and for securing to the members of a community that liberty to which all have an equal right, as far as they do not . . . use it to injure the liberty of others. Civil laws are regulations agreed upon by the community for gaining these ends and civil magistrates are officers appointed by the community for executing these laws."

Discourse pp.20–21

He condemns adulation and servility, saying:

"It has oftener happened that men have been too passive than too unruly, and the rebellion of Kings against their people has been more common, and done more mischief, than the rebellion of people against their Kings. . . . The potentates of this world are sufficiently apt to consider themselves as possessed of an inherent superiority, which gives them a right to govern, and makes mankind their own, and this infatuation is almost everywhere fostered in them by the creeping sycophants about them, and the language of flattery which they are continually hearing.

Civil governors are properly the servants of the public, and a King is no more than the first servant of the public, created by it, maintained by it, and responsible to it. . . . His sacredness is the sacredness of the community."

(pp.22–3)

Price goes on to comment that: "The tendency of every government is to despotism; and in this the best constituted governments must end, if the people are not vigilant, . . . and determined to resist abuses as soon as they begin". *(p.28)* There is no question here of excluding any new form of government arising in France, or which might follow in Britain. He does not share the Utopian vision of Paine and Priestley. His comments on representation are also relevant and very much to the point. He says:

"The most important instance of the imperfect state in which the Revolution (1688) left our constitution, is the INEQUALITY of our REPRESENTATION. I think, indeed, this defect of our constitution so gross and so palpable, as to make it excellent chiefly in form and theory . . . . Representation in the legislature of a kingdom is the basis of constitutional liberty, and of all legitimate government; and that without it a government is nothing but an usurpation. . . . When representation is partial, a kingdom possesses liberty only partially; and if extremely partial, it only gives a semblance of liberty, but if not only extremely partial, but corruptly chosen, and under corrupt influence after being chosen, it becomes a *nuisance* and produces the worst of all forms of government – a government by corruption – a government carried on and supported by spreading venality and profligacy through a kingdom. . . . It is the point of depravity to which abuses under such a government as ours naturally tend, and the last stage of national unhappiness."

(pp.39–40)

In his final *Nunc Dimittis* Dr. Price concludes:

"I have lived to see the rights of men better understood . . . and nations panting for liberty. . . .After sharing in the benefits of one Revolution, I have been spared to be a witness to two other Revolutions – both glorious. And now, methinks, I see the ardour for liberty catching and spreading;

a general amendment beginning in human affairs; the dominion of kings changed for the dominion of laws"

(pp.49–50)

Within a year and a half he was dead, his Lord had let him 'depart in peace'; he was spared the bitterness of witnessing the reversals, which were gall for Priestley and Paine, but less so for Burke who had predicted and to some extent provoked them, and gloried in his gift of prophesy!

Dr. Priestley, in his *Letters to Edmund Burke*, is more concerned with the close relationship between church and state, but the first five of his 14 letters do address the purely secular issues. In the first he tells Burke that,

"A nation is not to be condemned for endeavouring to better (its condition). Consequently, if they find their form of government to be a bad one, whether it was so originally, or became so through abuse or accident, they will do very well to change it for a better".

Letters to E.B. p.3

Moving on to developments in France he writes:

"If law and liberty were wanting in the old constitution, the peccant part must have been the very foundation of it; so that nothing effectual could have been done short of taking down the whole. . . . You should blame not the framers of the new government, but the wretched state of the old one, and those who brought it into that state."

(p.4)

Commenting on the new order:

"It is the acquiescence of the people that gives any form of government its proper sanction and that legalises it."

(p.6)

He points out that America has survived its upheaval in spite of the prophets of doom. In his second letter he takes Burke up on his strictures upon members of the French National Assembly, stating that:

"Of whomsoever the National Assembly of France consists, there cannot well be doubt of there being a truer representation of the French nation than our House of Commons is of ours; because there cannot well be a worse, . . ."

(p.13)

Burke has complained of the preponderance of lawyers of inferior quality in the French administration. Priestley reminds him that:

"The first American Congress . . . was said to consist chiefly of lawyers who have the talent and the habit of speaking in public, being generally conspicuous characters in all places. The study of the law, moreover, leads them to understand the constitution of the country, and their profession gives them a knowledge of mankind, and the habits of business. If the lawyers of France do as well as the lawyers of America, they will soon wipe away the reproach they may now lie under, and become the object of respect, perhaps of dread, to those who at present despise them."

(p.14)

It is remarkable that he forbears to remind Burke that his own training and background was in the law, but he goes on *(p.15)* to quote Dr. Ramsay's *History of the American Revolution,* where he noted that half the deputies in the Continental Congress of 1774 were lawyers, who, "Professionally taught the rights of the people, . . . were among the foremost to decry every attack made upon their liberties, (and) bred in the habits of public speaking, they made a distinguished figure in the meetings of the people."

Ramsay, vol. 1, p.134

He is most severe with Burke when he points out that:

"Taking for granted *(p.209),* that the present members of the National Assembly are not eligible into the next, you deduce many alarming consequences, from such an ill judged measure."

"But the measure, I am informed, is your own, not theirs; the present members being as eligible as any others, and, it is generally supposed, that a great majority of them have given so much satisfaction to their constituents, that they will not fail to be re-elected. As you took so much time in preparing your publication for the press, you would have done well to have employed part of it in procuring better information."

Letters to EB. p.16

Burke has condemned some of the occasional and spontaneous outrages which occurred in the early stages of the French Revolution and for which he appears to blame the National Assembly, but also smearing Richard Price. Priestley writes:

"In the same rash and indiscriminate manner you describe Dr. Price as exulting in the above mentioned horrid outrages, which, I dare say, give him much more serious concern than they do you, and for an obvious reason. He wishes to recommend the revolution, and therefore is sorry for everything that disgraces it; whereas you wish to discredit it, and are evidently not displeased with any circumstance that favours your purpose. Dr. Price rejoices in the *good,* and you most uncannily represent him as rejoicing in the *evil* that has necessarily accompanied it."

(pp.21–2)

Priestley's third letter deals mainly with monarchy, which remains to be dealt with later. In the fourth, he compares, "the late Revolution in France with the English Revolution of 1688, which had Burke's approval, but:

"The promoters of the English Revolution, you would have us understand, were not guided by any view of the *natural* (or as you affect to call them, the *chimerical) rights of men,* but were influenced by a regard to rights sanctioned by *ancient possession,* and consequently that their example furnishes no authority for any people to chuse their own governors, or to dismiss them for misconduct."

(p.34)

Burke has appealed to Lord Somers, but Priestley quotes this authority against him where he asserts that "all magistrates and governors proceed from the people" and that the people, when oppressed, "are justifiable in relieving themselves by a change of their governors, or of their government", and dismissing the concept "of passive obedience and loyalty". *(p.35)* Burke appears to be caught out in using this source selectively for his own ends, then building on this to declare that:

"So far is it from being true if we had possessed it before, the English nation did at that time most solemnly renounce and abdicate it for themselves and for their posterity for ever."

Reflections p.21

But, Priestley challenges:

"Could they seriously mean to bind their posterity from ever doing again what they themselves then did? Did they not, by changing the natural succession of the kings of this realm, actually exercise the right of chusing kings, declaring what description of persons should from that time succeed to the crown? And what any one parliament did, a succeeding one might, no doubt, undo."

Letters to E. B. pp.35–6

Priestley goes on to consolidate his point by appealing to two Acts, made in the time of Queen Anne, and taunting Burke that under these he was guilty of high treason, quoting directly from the Acts:

"If any person shall, by writing or printing, maintain and affirm that the kings and queens of this realm, with and by the authority of parliament, are not able to make laws and statutes of sufficient validity, to limit the crown and the descent, inheritance and government thereof, every such person shall be guilty of high treason."

(p.36)

We cannot wonder that Burke from 1791 never made any serious attempt to refute the arguments of either Priestley or Paine, not can we be surprised at Priestley's comment, in his third letter, when quoting Burke's most admired passage which begins "the age of chivalry is gone!" He writes: "It appears to me, that in a great pomp of *words,* it contains but few *ideas,* and some of them inconsistent and absurd." *(p.29)*

Priestley does not mince words when he considers the succession in 1688:

"A king had abused his trust, and, in the construction of the remaining governing powers of the country, as well as of the people, had virtually *abdicated the government.* According to the established rule of succession, his son should have succeeded him, but they apprehended the same evils from the son, . . . and likewise from all princes of the same description with the father, that is all who should profess the Roman Catholic religion. They therefore made a law to exclude all such princes, and fixed the succession in the nearest Protestant line. But, in conjunction with the first of this line, they chose a person entirely foreign to it, who had no legal pretensions to the crown at all, being only the husband of Queen Mary . . . and on the failure of issue, by his wife Mary and the Princess Anne, they gave the crown to the heirs of the body of the Prince of Orange."

(p.37)

Priestley does not quarrel with deposing the Catholic James II, since throughout his life he was always opposed to the Catholic religion and to Catholics in power, whether it were Papal or national, and more vehemently, if that were possible, than his opposition to the Anglican establishment. But, he would not otherwise deny them human rights, in particular free speech and freedom of association. This he demonstrated very clearly, in 1780, following the Gordon riots, in a pamphlet which he published condemning the prejudice which had triggered these riots and the harsh Penal Laws in operation against them. He did have individual Catholic friends and among them around 1790 was the Rev. Joseph Berington who lived close to Birmingham and whose pamphlet on *The Rights of Dissenters from the Established Church in relation principally to English Catholics* (1789) he commends to Burke. *(p.141)*

Priestley takes the American example to justify radical constitutional change as he writes:

"When America was driven, as you will allow (for at that time you were very active in the business, and many a time have I, with singular satisfaction, heard you plead the cause of American liberty) by the oppression of this country, to break entirely from it, the Americans, sensible of more evils attending their former government, than our ancestors at the Revolution, ventured to do a great deal more, and set a glorious example to France, and to the world. They formed a completely new government on the principles of *equal liberty*, and the *rights of men*, 'without nobles', as Dr. Price, expressively and happily said, 'without bishops and without a king', which, indeed, the Dutch, after their separation from the Spanish monarchy, did in a great measure before them. If arbitrary princes tremble at these great *examples*, (at the very idea of which you yourself, as if you were a part of royalty, and appertaining to it, tremble also) it is time that they who have so long made others tremble, should, in their turn, tremble themselves. But let the *people* rejoice. It will either make their princes keep within bounds, or encourage them to hope that the time of their deliverance is at hand."

(pp.39–40)

Priestley goes on to quote extensively from Paley's *Principles of Moral and Political Philosophy*, on the theme that constitutions are not immutable. *(pp.40–*

42) In his fifth letter he comments on Burke's outburst against Dr. Price and the Revolution Society, condemning their audacity in congratulating the French National Assembly, "without the express authority of the (British) government." Burke is purporting to believe that the naive French might perceive this society to be "some sort of corporate body, acknowledged by the laws of the kingdom, and authorised to speak the sense of some part of it". He goes on to say: "It is a policy that has very much the complexion of a fraud".

(Reflections pp.6–7)

Priestley pours scorn on this feigned indignation and in the course of his detailed argument writes that:

"The founders of a new system of government in France, which has hitherto been considered *the natural enemy of England,* they might think it wise to embrace the first opportunity of shewing that they were disposed to be our *friends,* and that they took it kindly, that any number of respectable individuals in this country should approve of their proceedings . . ."

"The members of the French Assembly would judge of the *extent* of the friendly disposition of this country towards them, by the names of the persons who promoted the measure; and when they saw that of *Dr. Price,* so well known, and so favourably known, for true patriotism, disinterested benevolence, and public spirit, both in France and America, they would naturally, and justly, conclude, that, though no great part of the English nation was present, those who were spoke the sentiments of great numbers, and those the most respectable in the country. . . . Where is the great impropriety of a nation receiving even advice, and much more accepting congratulations, from single men of eminent wisdom and virtue?"

(Letters to E.B. pp.44–5)

Priestley believed that had Burke been present to hear Dr. Price he would:

"have been both a wiser and a better man than you now are, wise and good as you, nevertheless, may be; for I do not judge of your usual temper and disposition from the strain of this most intemperate publication. I know you and I know it to be unworthy of you."

(p.46)

The passages are included to stress, once again, the negative influence which Burke came to exert upon Anglo-French relations, in contrast with what might have emerged had the British establishment heeded the opinions and advice of such men as Priestley, Price, Paine and their many friends, men and women of peace and good sense who had the best interest of both nations at heart. Nevertheless, once William Pitt and his government had been swayed by Burke's *Reflections,* and the thunder of the Anglican establishment, it is no longer any surprise that Priestley, Paine and many others of like view were so abominably treated.

Many of *Burke's* views on constitution have been dealt with already in the comments of his adversaries, but there are some points remaining where he must speak for himself. Paine Complained that "Burke had *voluntarily* declined going into comparison of the English and French constitutions", and therefore, "whether there is not some radical defect in what is called the English constitution, that made it necessary for Mr Burke to suppress the comparison". *(Rights pp.114–5) In his Letter to a Member of the National Assembly (1791) (p.281)* Burke castigates people who are 'reason proof'. On close consideration it is almost impossible to find an individual who is not reason proof on some particular issue, and Burke, like most of us, when he does not wish to consider the arguments of an adversary, dodges the issue as Paine has stressed.

In *Reflections,* Burke tells his correspondent in Paris: "Your leaders in France began by affecting to admire, . . . the British Constitution; but as they advanced they came to look upon it with a sovereign contempt". *(p.60)* Further on he states that a new French government "well deserved to have its excellences heightened, its faults corrected, and its capacities improved into a British constitution". *(p.144)* One could never see the National Assembly copying slavishly the British model, but with support and encouragement from Westminster they might have selected and adapted some of its best elements.

In one of his more flowery passages Burke states:

"Old establishments are tried by their effects. If the people are happy, united, wealthy and powerful, we presume the rest. We presume that to be good from whence good is derived. In old establishments various correctives have been found for their aberrations from theory. Indeed they are the results of various necessities and expediencies. They are not often constructed after any theory; theories are rather drawn from them. In them we often see the best end obtained where the means seem not perfectly reconcilable to what we may fancy was the original scheme. The means taught by experience may be better suited to political ends than those contrived in the original project. They again react upon the primitive constitution, and sometimes improve the design itself, from which they seem to have departed. I think all this might be exemplified in the British constitution."

(Reflections pp.190-1)

So what does all this mean? Basically it is that evolution takes place, but it is better that it should merely happen, than that any element of speculation should be involved. We must not criticise Burke for not having the same appreciation of evolution which has come into much sharper focus since his time. We can now see clearly that in the natural world evolution can throw up some quite defective examples at one extreme and near perfection at the other. It is no different when we consider the organisations we contrive for ourselves, but in the animal kingdom defective strains are soon weeded out by natural selection, whereas in the ways we organise ourselves, if bad models emerge, introduced by men with selfish and sometimes evil motives, they can persist for long periods, often for several generations. Defective representation in the British system, so greatly cherished by Burke, is a good example. His great distrust of any speculative element employed to

Statue of Edmund Burke in front of Trinity College, Dublin.

improve that system manifests itself again. Glossing over these problems of representation he states:

> "With us the king and lords are several and joint securities for the equality of each district, each province, each city. When did you hear in Great Britain of any province suffering from the inequality of its representation; what district from having no representation at all? Not only our monarchy and our peerage secure the equality on which our unity depends, but it is the spirit of the House of Commons itself. The very inequality of representation, which is so foolishly complained of, is perhaps the very thing which prevents us from thinking or acting as members for districts. Cornwall elects as many members as all Scotland. But is Cornwall better taken care of than Scotland?"
>
> *(p.208)*

Earlier he has stated:

> "It would require a long discourse to point out . . . the many fallacies that lurk in the generality and equivocal nature of the terms 'inadequate representation'. I shall only say here, in justice to that old-fashioned constitution, under which we have long prospered, that our representation has been found perfectly adequate to all the purposes for which a representation of the people can be desired or devised."
>
> *(p.61)*

What extraordinary arguments! Because of flagrant inequality, people are deterred from thinking of their own territory and this has got to be good, because Burke says so. Never mind if the House of Commons is not truly representative, the aristocracy will look after the people, and never mind that large towns, such as Birmingham, Sheffield and Manchester, soon to be leading cities, have no representation. These are merely the nation's sweat-shops on which the industrial revolution is being founded. They represent new growth, with little history or tradition to speak of; the very paternal mill owners and other bosses will look out for them; they should not concern themselves about trivial matters such as the rights of man!

But Burke was mistaken, as was soon to be shown in the interest that so many of these wretches took in Tom Paine's book; the *articulate artisan* was not to be under-rated. Even then Burke and so many others of the establishment, who were to follow his lead, could only believe that these people were grossly misled by the bad example emanating from France. Burke has no doubts on this score; he tells his audience:

> "I wish my countrymen rather to recommend to our neighbours the example of the British constitution, than to take models from them for the improvement of our own. In the former they have got an invaluable treasure. They are not, I think, without some causes of apprehension and complaint; but these they do not owe to their constitution, but to their own conduct. I think our happy situation owing to our constitution; but

owing to the whole of it, and not to any part singly; owing in a great measure to what we have left standing in our several reviews and reformations, as well as to what we have altered or superadded. Our people will find employment for a truly patriotic, free and independent spirit in guarding what they possess from violation. I would not exclude alteration neither; but even when I changed, it would be to preserve. I should be led to my remedy by a great grievance. In what I did I should follow the example of our ancestors. . . . Not being illuminated with the light of which the gentlemen of France tell us they have got so abundant a share, they acted under a strong impression of the ignorance and fallibility of mankind. . . . Let us add, if we please, but let us preserve what they (our ancestors) have left; and standing on the firm ground of the British constitution, let us be satisfied to admire, rather than attempt to follow in their desperate flights the aëronauts of France."

Reflections pp.273–4

One can only feel a sense of desperation in even attempting to argue with an advocate who can so delude himself; even when he changes it must be to preserve, by following the example of his ancestors. Let us add, but let us preserve the status quo. What can all this mean? No wonder his erstwhile friends, Priestley and Paine, are so scornful; no wonder his former Whig party colleagues are so dispirited by his defection and change of heart. How can his supporters maintain that he has not changed radically? He did not write or speak like this during the American revolt, or in 1770.

Britain still prides itself on having an unwritten constitution, giving a flexibility to governments with which they can play fast and loose when awkward situations arise. With a written constitution certain changes cannot be made without direct reference to the electorate as a whole. Since his time many governments must have been indebted, consciously or otherwise, to Edmund Burke for this continuing boon!

CHAPTER V

The Commons

Bow, bow, ye lower middle classes!
Bow, bow ye tradesmen, bow ye masses!

from 'Iolanthe', W S Gilbert (triumphant entry of Peers)

ON THE ELEMENTS OF GOVERNMENT BURKE COMMENTS: "We have an inheritable crown; an inheritable peerage; and a House of Commons, and a people inheriting privileges, franchises, and liberties from a long line of ancestors". *(Reflections p.35)* How can he equate the Commons with the monarchy and the aristocracy? As we know it the Commons, as an effective arm of government, only dates from the Cromwellian period, any predecessor was a rather toothless creature. Comparing the French Tiers État with the British House of Commons, he comments:

"After I had read over the list of persons and descriptions elected into the Tiers État, nothing which they afterwards did could appear astonishing. Among them, indeed, I saw some of known rank; some of shining talents; but of any practical experience in the state, not one man was to be found. The best were only men of theory. . . . If an assembly is viciously or feebly composed . . . nothing but such a supreme degree of virtue as very rarely appears in the world . . . will prevent men of talents disseminated through it from becoming only the expert instruments of absurd projects!"

(Reflections, p.44)

Such an argument might just as well have been applied to the House of Commons in its early days, and perhaps with some justification, but this assembly is now hallowed in Burke's estimation because it has survived for about a century and a half. Might not the French be allowed to embark on a new venture even if the new assembly was apt to make mistakes in the beginning, without the censure of Mr Burke. Going on to criticise the preponderance of lawyers in that new assembly, he tells his readers that:

"In that military kingdom, no part of the profession had been much regarded, except the highest of all, who often united to their professional offices great family spleandour, and were invested with great power and authority. These certainly were highly respected, and even with no small degree of awe. The next rank was not much esteemed; the mechanical part was in a very low degree of repute."

(p.46)

He then goes on to complain of the,

"composition of the Tiers État in the National Assembly; in which was scarcely to be perceived the slightest traces of what we call the natural landed interest of the country. We know that the British House of Commons, without shutting its doors to any merit in any class is, by the sure operation of adequate causes, filled with everything illustrious in rank, in descent, in hereditary and in acquired opulence, in cultivated talents, in military, civil, naval and political distinction that the country can afford."

(pp.46–8)

Once again Burke is back to his favourite theme of natural aristocracy, inherited greatness, and landed gentry, but does the history of any nation bear out his thesis that such a combination must guarantee excellence? Not then, not now, to the extent that such phenomena still prevail, and not ever in human history; in individual cases perhaps, but not as a general rule. Apart from lawyers he also complains that these were joined by "a pretty considerable proportion of the faculty of medicine", whose qualifications he could not accept because "the sides of sick-beds are not the academies for forming statesmen and legislators". *(p.47)* Could he not see that these were among the better educated in the community, might be gifted with some compassion and a desire to see more humane conditions throughout the community as a whole. For us today, in retrospect, it must be realised that the medical men of that era would have more time to spare since there was so much less that they could then provide for their patients, and thus pressures were considerably less, making those among them with an aptitude for politics more available.

What does Burke mean by "the sure operation of adequate causes" which seem to ensure that representation in the House of Commons is constituted as it should properly be, in the minds of himself and those like him, whether they be Whigs or Tories. Oh yes, it does allow the occasional trouble-maker like John Wilkes to slip through the net, but it has shown that it could operate to exclude him or in the long run to tame him.

Burke rejoices that the House of Commons is,

"circumscribed and shut in by the immovable barriers of law, usages, positive rules of doctrine and practice, counterpoised by the House of Lords, and every moment of its existence at the discretion of the Crown to continue, prorogue, or dissolve us."

(p.48)

But he does not acknowledge that the French assembly, the *States General*, started out with a body of nobles and clergy, equal between them to the strength of the Commons, and that this arrangement had failed because so many of the aristocracy, both lay and clerical, had voted with their feet, instead of with their brains and abandoned their beleaguered nation. He does criticise the clergy representation however, complaining that:

"election was so contrived as to send a very large proportion of mere country curates to the great and arduous work of new-modelling a state; . . . men who knew nothing of the world beyond the bounds of an obscure village; who, immersed in hopeless poverty, could regard all property, whether secular or ecclesiastical, with no other eye than that of envy; among whom must be many, who, for the smallest hope of the meanest dividend in plunder, would readily join in any attempts upon a body of wealth, in which they could hardly look to have any share, except in a general scramble. Instead of balancing the power of the active chicaners in the other assembly, these curates must necessarily become the active coadjutors, or at best the passive instruments of those by whom they had been habitually guided in their petty village concerns."

(p.50)

One small point, in describing them as curates, he is loosely translating the French word *curé*, which in Britain is the equivalent of parish priest. However, this makes little difference since it is the lowly status of these men that is being highlighted. But, dear Mr Burke, can you not see that what you have put your finger upon is a primary reason for revolution; if both church and state have so degraded their functionaries at this basic level, only radical change will suffice; it is the management of this change which is vital and your influence was soon to persuade your own government to oppose strongly the tendencies of the French nation, driving it to extremes – driving it mad!

Burke's reasoning is very diffuse and tends to contradiction as often as not; for instance he states:

"that from Magna Charta to the Declaration of Right, it has been the uniform policy of our constitution to claim and assert our liberties, as an *entailed inheritance* derived to us from our forefathers, and to be transmitted to our posterity; as an estate specially belonging to the people of this kingdom, without any reference whatever to any other more general or prior right. By this means our constitution preserves an unity in so great a diversity of its parts. We have an inheritable crown; an inheritable peerage, and a House of Commons and a people inheriting privileges, franchises and liberties, from a long line of ancestors. The policy appears to me to be the result of profound reflection; or rather the happy effect of following nature, which is wisdom without reflection and above it."

(pp.35–6)

What does he mean by "an estate specially belonging to the people . . . without any reference . . . to any other more general or prior right"? To what people is he referring? Is it not clear that those inheriting are the monarch and the aristocracy and that the common people at the base of the feudal pile have few, if any, privileges, limited liberties, and a share in franchise which is but a mockery? So this has to be justified by an ethereal "wisdom without reflection". Overall, there can be little doubt that at this stage of his life Burke has little patience with reflection or speculation as a basis for progress in the affairs of state. His philosophy has virtually degenerated to advising those of inferior status to *trust nanny*, or as Belloc was later to express it: "Be sure of holding on to nurse, for fear of finding something worse".

Another strange example is to be found in his *Letter to a Member of the National Assembly*, dated January 1791. Having decided that a House of Peers on the British model is not suited to the situation in France because "it would destroy your true natural nobility", he goes on to state:

> "If you are not in a condition to frame a House of Lords, still less are you capable . . . of framing anything which virtually and substantially could be answerable . . . to our House of Commons. That house is within itself, a much more subtle and artificial combination of parts and powers, than people are generally aware of. What knits it to the other members of the constitution; what fits it to be at once the great support, and the great control of government; what makes it of such admirable service to that monarchy, which, if it limits, it secures and strengthens, would require a long discourse, belonging to the leisure of a contemplative man, not to one whose duty it is to join in communicating practically to the people the blessings of such a constitution."

> "Your Tiers État was not in effect and substance a House of Commons. You stood in absolute need of something else to supply the manifest defects in such a body as your tiers état. On a sober and dispassionate view of your old constitution, as connected with all the present circumstances, that the crown, standing as things have stood . . . was and is incapable, alone and by itself, of holding a just balance between the two orders, and at the same time of effecting the interior and exterior purposes of a protecting government."

> *(Letter to a Member, pp.316–7)*

Why is Burke so vehement in his opinion that the French Tiers État cannot become an effective House of Commons? And why should the crown be incapable of holding the balance between the two orders? We have already seen that it was the virtual abdication of the nobility, lay and clerical, from the process of government, when they could not get their own way by force and intrigue, that destroyed any balance there might have been. Burke could not bring himself to acknowledge this, but is right to the extent that some balance between traditional rulers and the new incumbents might have softened the transition, leading to a state of affairs closer to that which had been achieved in America. But Burke and the British administration did nothing to encourage more enlightened, patriotic and responsible behaviour on the part of the old ruling classes in France; instead Britain, led by Burke, fanned their paranoia, driving them into the arms of the many hostile elements surrounding that beleaguered land.

Why also, with recent experience in America, was Burke so dismissive of the potential of the *Commons* in France? America had been successfully governed without a king or a House of Lords for more than a decade and democratic evolution was proceeding smoothly. Could the French nation not be trusted to achieve as much success, whether on a similar pattern, or with a constitutional monarchy, as in Britain? Again, the answer lies more with the hostile forces threatening France, than with emerging democracy.

While Burke is addressing himself urgently to the problems of a newly emerging French government and moved to pontificate upon the subject, it does not suffice to state that the British House of Commons is "a much more subtle and artificial combination of parts and powers than people are generally aware of" and having posed this mystery then to go on and plead that a long discourse would be required which he implies is beyond his powers at that time. One can only comment that this is not the Burke of former conflicts: in defence of the American rebels, in opposition to Warren Hastings, and other great causes, the Burke who was never stuck for words. Can it be that the long discourse is not forthcoming because the argument cannot be sustained? Here again he is to a large extent belying himself when we look back to his *Thoughts on the Present Discontents* where he expresses remarkably democratic views on representation and on the Commons:

"The power of the people, within the laws, must show itself sufficient to protect every representative in the animated performance of his duty, or that duty cannot be performed. The House of Commons can never be a control on other parts of the Government, unless they are controlled themselves by their constituents; and unless these constituents possess some rights in the choice of that House, which it is not in the power of that House to take away. If they suffer this power of arbitrary incapacitation to stand they have utterly perverted every other power of the House of Commons."

(Thoughts on the Present Discontents, 1770, p.88)

This statement must be viewed in the context of the quarrel with John Wilkes MP, and the ruling on the outcome of the Middlesex by-election, in which although Wilkes was returned by a large majority he was declared to be incapacitated, and therefore his heavily defeated opponent was declared elected. Burke comments further:

". . . an attempt to turn the right of election into such a farce and mockery as a fictitious fine and recovery, will, I hope, have another fate; because the laws which give it are infinitely clear to us, and the evasion is infinitely contemptible."

"The people indeed have been told, that this power of discretionary disqualification is vested in hands they may trust, and who will be sure not to abuse it to their prejudice. Until I find something in this argument differing from that on which every mode of despotism has been defended, I shall not be inclined to pay it any great compliment."

(p.91)

"The very desire of that body (House of Commons) to have a trust contrary to law reposed in them, shows that they are not worthy of it. They will certainly abuse it; because all men possessed of an uncontrolled

discretionary power leading to the aggrandisement and profit of their own
body have always abused it."

(pp.92–3)

However, there are deeper issues at stake in this contest which he then goes
on to explore:

"But we must purposely shut our eyes, if we consider this matter merely
as a contest between the House of Commons and the Electors. The true
contest is between the Electors of the Kingdom and the Crown; the Crown
acting by an instrumental House of Commons. It is precisely the same,
whether the Ministers of the Crown can disqualify by a dependent House
of Commons, or by a dependent court of *Star Chamber,* or by a dependent
court of King's Bench. If once Members of Parliament can be practically
convinced that they do not depend on the affection or opinion of the
people for their political being, they will give themselves over, without
even an appearance of reserve, to the influence of the Court."

"Indeed a parliament unconnected with the people, is essential to a
Ministry unconnected with the people; and therefore those who saw
through what mighty difficulties the interior ministry waded, and the
exterior were dragged, in this business, will conceive of what prodigious
importance, the new corps of *King's men* held this principle of occasional
and personal incapacitation, to the whole body of their design."

"When the House of Commons was thus made to consider itself as
the master of its constituents, there wanted but one thing to secure that
House against all possible deviation towards popularity; an unlimited fund
of money to be laid out according to the pleasure of the Court."

(pp.93–4)

So here we have the real burden of his complaints, the true cause of the *Present
Discontents;* it is the subordination of parliamentary democracy to the whims
of a Cabal created within a Court circle. He goes on, in his next section, to
explain how the Civil List is being manipulated to achieve those ends. Later
he tells us that:

"A restoration of the right of free election is a preliminary indispensable
to every other reformation."

(p.103)

"Until a confidence in Government is re-established, the people ought to
be excited to a more strict and detailed attention to the conduct of their
Representatives. Standards, for judging more systematically upon their
conduct, ought to be settled in the meetings of counties and corporations.
Frequent and correct lists of the voters in all important questions ought
to be procured."

(p.109)

". . . It ought to be the electors' business to look to their Representatives.
. . . The notorious infidelity and versatility of Members of Parliament, in

their opinions of men and things ought in a particular manner to be considered by the electors in the inquiry which is recommended to them."

(p.113)

It is difficult to reconcile these forthright and outspoken views of Burke with his determined resistance to constitutional reform and especially electoral reform, twenty years later. We can only conclude that he has become a hostage to the corrupt system, in which a small handful of electors, beholden to a patron, can send a member of parliament, while thousands of other citizens in the large emerging cities of the industrial revolution can be wholly deprived of representation. Never mind that the growing and future wealth of the nation is in the hands of such people.

Winston Churchill in his *Age of Revolution* devotes a significant section *(pp.136–40)* to the Wilkes crisis and is more explicit than Burke, especially where he states:

"If a Minister of the Crown ordered something to be done which was unlawful, then both he and his servants must answer for it in the ordinary courts of law in exactly the same way as a private person. The Under Secretary who entered Wilkes' house and took away his papers and the King's Messengers who arrested the printer were mere trespassers and were liable as such. They were guilty of false imprisonment, and the judges refused to interfere when juries awarded large sums by way of compensation. . . . the small injury done to the plaintiff (said the Chief Justice) or the inconsiderableness of his station and rank in life, did not appear to the jury in that striking light in which the great point of law touching the liberty of the subject appeared to them at the trial."

(p.138)

Paine has less to say about the *Commons*, being more concerned to discuss monarchy and aristocracy, but he does have a few pithy comments, for instance:

"The constitution of France says,'That every man who pays a tax of sixty sous per annum (quite a small amount) is an elector'. – What article will Mr Burke place against this? Can anything be more limited, and at the same time more capricious, than the qualifications of electors are in England? Limited, because not one man in a hundred is admitted to vote: Capricious – because the lowest character that can be supposed to exist, and who has not so much as the visible means of an honest livelihood, is an elector in some places; while in other places the man who pays very large taxes, and has a known fair character . . . is not admitted to be an elector. . . . William the Conqueror and his descendants parcelled out the country . . . and bribed some parts of it by what they called Charters, to hold the other parts of it the better subjected to their will. This is the reason why so many of those charters abound in Cornwall, the people were averse to the government established at the Conquest, and the towns were garrisoned and bribed to enslave the country. All the old Charters are the badges of this conquest, and it is from this source that the capriciousness of elections arises."

"The French constitution says, that the number of representatives for any place shall be in a ratio to the number of taxable inhabitants or electors. What article will Mr Burke place against this? The county of Yorkshire, which contains near a million of souls, sends two county members; and so does the county of Rutland, which contains not an hundredth part of that number. The town of Old Sarum which contains not three houses, sends two members; and the town of Manchester, which contains upwards of sixty thousand souls, is not admitted to send any. Is there any principle in these things? Is there anything by which you can trace the marks of freedom, or discover those of wisdom? No wonder then, Mr Burke has declined the comparison, and endeavoured to lead his readers from the point by a wild unsystematical display of paradoxical rhapsodies."

(Rights, pp.95–6)

He has some further significant comments on the foundation and make up of the lower house in parliament:

"The parliament in England, in both its branches, was erected by patents from the descendants of the Conqueror. The House of Commons did not originate as a matter of right in the people to delegate or elect, but as a grant or boon."

(p.111)

"Mr Pitt . . . introduced himself to the public notice by a proposed Reform of Parliament, which in its operation would have amounted to a public justification of corruption. The nation was to be at the expense of buying up the rotten boroughs, whereas it ought to punish the persons who deal in the traffic."

(p.151)

"With respect to the House of Commons, it is elected but by a small part of the Nation; but were the election as universal as taxation, which it ought to be, it would still be only the organ of the Nation, and cannot possess inherent rights. – When the National Assembly of France resolves a matter, the resolve is made in right of the Nation; but Mr. Pitt on all national questions, so far as they refer to the House of Commons, absorbs the right of the Nation into the organ, and makes the organ into a Nation, and the Nation itself into a cypher."

(p.152)

Paine is well aware that the issue of rotten boroughs is an Achilles Heel for the state, but one which would survive for nigh on half a century more before it disappeared. As he is responding to Burke's *Reflections* it is surprising that he does not emphasise his personal vulnerability on this score. Also Burke defended the American revolt on the grounds of "taxation without representation" but he does not extend the same principle to Britain itself.

Paine does not quote extensively from Burke's *Reflections* but if he did, he would have answered his own rhetorical question about representation with the remarkable passage already quoted which concludes: "But is Cornwall better taken care of than Scotland?" *(p.208)* No doubt Burke would have argued that this statement should have answered Paine's anxieties about representation.

Winston Churchill has some interesting comments on calls for reform in the late 18th century, which include reflections on the role of Edmund Burke, as well as the influence of Tom Paine:

"Demand for some reform of the representation in Parliament began to stir; but the agitation was now mild and respectable. The main aim of the reformers was to increase the number of boroughs which elected Members of Parliament, and thus reduce the possibilities of government corruption. There was even talk of universal suffrage and other novel theories of democratic representation. But the chief advocates of reform were substantial landowners or country clergymen like Christopher Wyvill, from Yorkshire, or mature, well established politicians like Edmund Burke. They would all have agreed that Parliament did not and need not precisely represent the English people. To them Parliament represented, not individuals, but *interests* – the landed interest, the mercantile interest, even the labouring interest, but with a strong leaning to the land as the solid and indispensable base of the national life. These well-to-do theorists were distressed at the rapid spread of political corruption.

This was due partly to the Whig system of controlling the Government through the patronage of the Crown, and partly to the purchase of seats in Parliament by the new commercial and industrial classes. The *Nabobs* of the East India interest, as we have seen, appeared at Westminster, and the incursion of the money power into politics both widened the field of corruption and threatened the political monopoly of the landowning classes.

Thus the movement in governing circles was neither radical nor comprehensive. It found expression in Burke's Economic Reform Act of 1782, disfranchising certain classes of Government officials who had hitherto played some part in managing elections. This was a tepid version of the scheme Burke had meant to introduce. No general reform of the franchise was attempted, and when people talked about the rights of Englishmen they meant the sturdy class of yeomen vaunted as the backbone of the country, whose weight in the counties it was desired to increase. Many of the early reform schemes were academic attempts to preserve the political power and balance of the rural interest. The individualism of 18th century England assumed no doctrinaire form. The enunciation of first principles has always been obnoxious to the English mind. John Wilkes had made a bold and successful stand for the liberty of the subject before the law, but the whole controversy had turned on the narrow if practical issue of the legality of general warrants. Tom Paine's inflammatory pamphlets had considerable circulation among certain classes, but in

Parliament little was heard about the abstract rights of man. In England the revolutionary current ran underground and was caught up in provincial eddies."

(W. S. C. The Age of Revolution pp.197–8)

Paine has criticised the way in which Britain appeared to have hamstrung itself by apparently binding generations yet unborn. In contrast he describes the rapid evolution taking place in France, from summoning the States General to the emergence of a new National Assembly. At this stage he was living in Paris, but was not more than an observer. He describes how powerful leaders such as Monsieur D'Artois (the future King – Charles X) and de Broglie, an intended Minister in the new Assembly, with a force of 30,000 troops set out to frustrate this very Assembly, which they were assumed to support. An attempt was made to prevent the Assembly meeting by barring it from its chamber, but it found another venue in a nearby covered tennis court, where members took an oath not to separate until a new constitution was established. D'Artois and de Broglie attempted to frustrate this aim by intimidation and force, but before their plan could mature the Bastille was taken; the conspirators panicked and fled, which was the real triumph of July 14th.

Paine has set out how the new assembly had taken shape:

"The national representatives . . . sent an invitation to the two chambers, to unite with them . . . . A majority of the clergy, chiefly of the parish priests, withdrew from the clerical chamber, and joined the nation; and forty-five from the other chamber joined in like manner. There is a sort of secret history belonging to this last circumstance, which is necessary to its explanation: It was not judged prudent that all the patriotic members of the chamber styling itself the Nobles, should quit it at once; and in consequence of this arrangement, they drew off by degrees, always leaving some, as well to reason the case, as to watch the suspected. In a little time, the numbers increased from forty-five to eighty, and soon after to a greater number; which with a majority of the clergy, and the whole of the national representatives, put the malcontents in a very diminutive condition."

"The King, who very different from the general class called by that name, is a man of good heart, showed himself disposed to recommend an union of the three chambers, on the ground the National Assembly had taken; but the malcontents exerted themselves to prevent it, and began now to have another project in view. Their numbers consisted of a majority of the aristocratic chamber, and a minority of the clerical chamber, chiefly bishops and high-beneficed clergy; and these were determined to put everything to issue, as well by strength as by stratagem. They had no objection to a constitution; but it must be such a one as themselves should dictate, and suited to their own views and particular situations. On the other hand the Nation disowned knowing anything of them but as citizens, and was determined to shut out all such upstart pretensions. The more aristocracy appeared, the more it was despised; there was a visible imbecility and want of intellect in the majority, a sort of *je ne sais quoi,* that while it affected to be more than citizen, was less than man. It lost ground from contempt more than from hatred; and was rather jeered at as an ass, than dreaded as a lion."

(Rights pp.127–8)

Conspiracy ripened as we have seen and was then overthrown. Paine rejoices in the aftermath, telling us:

"It is worth remarking, that the National Assembly neither pursued those fugitive conspirators, nor took any notice of them, nor sought to retaliate in any shape whatever. Occupied with establishing a constitution founded on the Rights of Man and the Authority of the People, the only authority on which Government has a right to exist in any country, the National Assembly felt none of those mean passions which mark the character of impertinent governments, founding themselves on their own authority, or on the absurdity of hereditary succession."

(p.131)

Whatever we may think of Paine's comments it must never be forgotten that he is reporting here as a concerned eye-witness and not as some remote philosopher, or journalistic commentator. Also he is dealing with matters which are immediate, and not reflecting on events which had already passed into history, but before the *Reign of Terror.*

CHAPTER VI

Aristocracy – The House of Lords

We are Peers of highest station
Paragons of legislation,
Pillars of the British Nation! Tantara! Tzing! Boom!

WS Gilbert, Iolanthe

THE SECOND ELEMENT IN THIS BRITISH CONSTITUTION IS THE HOUSE OF LORDS and Burke has some striking points to make:

"The House of Peers . . . is wholly composed of hereditary property and hereditary distinction; and made therefore the third of the legislature; and in the last event the sole judge of all property in all its subdivisions . . . though hereditary wealth and the rank which goes with it, are too much idolised by creeping sycophants, and the blind abject admirers of power, they are too rashly slighted in shallow speculations of the petulant, assuming, short sighted coxcombs of philosophy. Some decent regulated pre-eminence, some preference (not exclusive appropriation), given to birth, is neither unnatural, nor unjust, not impolitic."

(Reflections, p.56)

He does admit that there are blemishes, and those he mentions are not entirely trivial, but the clear and ultimate message is: hands off! – and no reference to the grabbing and enclosure of common land which had been going on for generations, right up to his own time, causing great distress and resentment among the common people. It has been ever so. Was Burke not familiar with the story of Ahab who coveted Naboth's vineyard, and seized it with the connivance of his evil queen Jezebel, whose name has remained odious for all time? *(I Kings, 21) Plus ça change, plus c'est la même chose!*

But he is concerned for Britain, which might soon be contaminated by the dangerous disease which is sweeping France. He asks: "Is our monarchy to be annihilated? . . . Is the House of Lords to be voted useless? Is episcopacy to be abolished? Are church lands to be sold to Jews and jobbers?" *(p.59)* There is here a marked taint of anti-semitism which crops up in Burke's writings from time to time, but in this he is only reflecting the attitude of the society in which he lives; it is no special prejudice of his own.

Burke, who professes such disdain for philosophers, especially if they are French, when he shows a philosophical bent himself, does not appreciate how he is apt to trip himself, as when he muses on history, which he tells us:

"consists, for the greater part, of the miseries brought upon the world by pride, ambition, avarice, revenge, lust, sedition, hypocrisy, ungoverned zeal and all the train of disorderly appetites, which shake the public with the same . . . troublous storms that toss the private state and render life unsweet."

(p.155)

Are these brought upon humanity by the uncouth lower classes? Or is it not his beloved aristocracy which makes the historical record? And are these, therefore, the vices which *they* bring upon society?

Chesterton has another view of this nation's history which is not greatly at variance, but would scarcely have pleased Burke, when he writes:

"The history of the English can be most briefly summarised by taking the French motto of *Liberty, Equality and Fraternity* and noting that the English have sincerely loved the first and lost the other two."

(A Short History of England, p.84)

Unlike Burke, Chesterton does not overlook the enclosures:

"Parliament was passing bill after bill for the enclosure, by the great landlords, of such of the common lands as had survived out of the great communal system of the Middle Ages. It is much more than a pun, it is the prime political irony of our history, that the Commons were destroying the commons. The very word *common* . . . lost its great moral meaning, and became a mere topographical term for some remaining scrap of scrub or heath that was not worth stealing."

(p.213)

Commenting upon the changes taking place in France, and on French reflections upon the British constitution, Burke assures his audience:

"I shall only say here, in justice to that old fashioned constitution, under which we have long prospered, that our representation has been found perfectly adequate to all the purpose for which a representation of the people can be desired or devised." (But) "The enemies of our constitution . . . the revolutionists . . . consider our House of Commons as only 'a semblance', 'a form', 'a theory', 'a mockery', perhaps 'a nuisance'. . . their principle . . . goes much further than to an alteration in the election of the House of Commons for, if popular representation or choice is necessary to the legitimacy of all government the House of Lords is, at one stroke, bastardised and corrupted in blood. That House is no representative of the people at all, even 'in semblance or in form'. The case of the crown is altogether as bad."

(Reflections pp.61–2)

Here, as in so many other instances, he is shroud waving, but there is more truth in these opinions, which he castigates as being French, and therefore hostile, than he would ever be prepared to acknowledge. Further on he comments on what has been achieved in France and has this criticism:

"Your all sufficient legislators, in their hurry to do everything at once, have forgot one thing that seems essential. . . . They have forgot to constitute *a senate*, or something of that nature and character. Never, before this time, was heard of a body politic composed of one legislative and active assembly, and its executive officers, without such a council; without something to which foreign states might connect themselves, and something to which, in the ordinary detail of government, the people could look up; something which might give a bias and steadiness, and preserve something like consistency in the proceedings of the state. Such a body kings generally have as a council. A monarchy may exist without it, but it seems to be in the very essence of a republican government. It holds a sort of middle place between the supreme power exercised by the people, or immediately delegated from them, and the mere executive, of this there are no traces in your constitution. . . ."

(pp.219–20)

It is not clear whether Burke has in mind a House of Lords or a Privy Council, when he says that, "such a body kings generally have as a council". But again, we must remember that Burke's *Reflections* were published in 1790, that there was considerable agitation, and that evolution to a new constitution was at a very early stage. On the one hand he is criticising the French legislators for their haste "to do everything at once", and then he is belabouring them for having forgotten something which he considers essential. Nor does he take into account the cowardly defection of so many of the nobility.

In the following year (1791), in his *Letter to a Member of the National Assembly*, Burke writes:

"I do not advise a House of Lords to you. Your ancient course by representatives of the noblesse appears to me rather a better institution. I know that with you, a set of men of rank have betrayed their constituents, their honour, their trust, their king, and their country, and levelled themselves with their footmen, that through this degradation they might afterwards put themselves above their natural equals. Some of these persons have entertained a project that, in reward for this their black perfidy and corruption, they may be chosen to give rise to a new order, and to establish themselves into a House of Lords. Do you think that, under the name of a British Constitution, I mean to recommend to you such lords, made of such kind of stuff? . . ." "If you were now to form such a House of Peers, it would bear, in my opinion, but little resemblance to ours in its origin, character, or the purposes which it might answer, at the same time that it would destroy your true natural nobility."

(Letter to a Member . . ., pp.315–6)

The men of rank he is criticising are those who had surrendered their titles, or as he would have it "levelled themselves with their footmen"; who had thrown in their lot with their fellow countrymen and were, in fact, exhibiting true nobility with some prospect of retaining that very balance which he considered so vital. The "true natural nobility', to whom he refers, are obviously those who had turned tail and fled, because so many of them were damned by their past. In his *Thoughts on French Affairs,* dated December 1791, Burke has some further comments on French as compared with English nobility.

"As to the monied men – whilst the monarchy continued, there is no doubt that merely as such, they did not enjoy the *privileges* of nobility; but nobility was of so easy an acquisition, that it was the fault or neglect of all of that description, who did not obtain its privileges, for their lives at least, in virtue of office. It attached under the royal government to an innumerable multitude of places, real and nominal, that were vendible; and such nobility were as capable of everything as their degree of influence or interest could make them, that is, as nobility of no considerable rank or consequence. M. Necker, so far from being a French gentleman, was not so much as a Frenchman born, and yet we all know the rank in which he stood on the day of the meeting of the states."

(Thoughts on French Affairs, 1791, p.334)

This last comment is quite extraordinary, if M. Necker is to be scorned because he is "not a Frenchman born" what of those Dutch gentlemen who came with King William, or the Hanoverians who came with George I, and who were soon slotted into the British peerage, not to mention the multitude of Normans who came with the first William, providing the largest crop ever of new aristocracy; that group which Tom Paine would never let us forget. But Burke would not even dream of questioning these; their nobility has been endorsed over many generations with the seal of primogeniture. But he has some further consideration to bestow in this matter:

"As to the mere matter of estimation of the mercantile or any other class; this is regulated by opinion and prejudice. In England, a security against the envy of men in these classes is not so very complete as we may imagine. . . . It is the natural operation of things where there exists a crown, a court, splendid orders of knighthood, and an hereditary nobility; – where there exists a fixed permanent, landed gentry, continued in opulence and greatness by the law of primogeniture, and by a protection given to family settlements; – where there exists a standing army and navy; – where there exists a church establishment, which bestows on learning and parts an interest combined with that of religion and the state; – in a country where such things exist, wealth, new in its acquisition, and precarious in its duration, can never rank first, or even near the first; though wealth has its natural weight further than as it is balanced and even preponderated amongst us, as among other nations, by artificial institutions and opinions growing out of them. At no period in the history of England have so few peers been taken out of trade, or from families newly created by commerce. In no period has so small a number of noble families entered into the counting house . . . . (But) it appears plain to me,"that envy and ambition may, by art, management and disposition, be as much excited among these descriptions of men in England, as in any other country; and that they are just as capable of acting a part in any great change."

(Thoughts, pp.334–5)

This is another remarkable and extraordinary passage which reveals much about the mind of Burke, his attitudes and those of his many admirers. The first point to note, once again, is the reverence and respect with which he treats the long established aristocracy, and now he combines this with deep suspicions of *the yuppie* (upstart) classes, who are capable of dangerous thought, and in their naivety may be influenced by even more radical thinkers, leading them into dangerous political paths. The latter part of this argument is cloaked in careful and deliberately obtuse language, but closer analysis clarifies the drift. As ever with Burke, in this phase of his political life, it is the *status quo ante* which must be preserved and protected at all costs, ignoring the fact that this very status has resulted from a long and gradual process of evolution, which will continue despite Edmund Burke and all those whom he renders fearful of change.

Chesterton has some relevant comment on Burke and his erstwhile beloved party:

"The French Revolution was the challenge that really revealed to the Whigs that they must make up their minds to be really democrats, or admit that they were really aristocrats. They decided, as in the case of their philosophic exponent Burke, to be really aristocrats; and the result was the White Terror, the period of Anti-Jacobin repression which re-vealed the real side of their sympathies more than any stricken fields in foreign lands. Cobbett, the last and greatest of the yeomen, of the farming class which the great estates were devouring daily, was thrown into prison merely for protesting against the flogging of English soldiers by German mercenaries. . . . the name of Cobbett is very important here; indeed it is generally ignored because it is important. Cobbett was the one man who saw the tendency of the time as a whole, and challenged it as a whole; consequently he went without support. It is a mark of our whole modern history that the masses are kept quiet with a fight. They are kept quiet by the fight because it is a sham fight; thus most of us know by this time that the Party System has been popular only in the same sense that a football match is popular."

(Short History, pp.213–4)

Cobbett overlapped with Paine and Priestley not only in time but largely in sentiment; like them there could be no place for one with such advanced views in the Parliamentary System as it then existed, but he lived on to see the Reform Act of 1832, and was finally able to achieve election to the Commons right at the end of his life. His *History of the Reformation* is as searching in its analysis of the Church and State establishment as anything that came from Priestley or

Paine, and that from one who boldly states that he is himself a member of the Established Church.

Thomas Paine, in his attitudes to aristocracy and monarchy, with inherited wealth and power, provides a complete contrast to Burke's reverence for the status quo. He has experienced at first hand the upheaval in America, which is now moving ahead, having shed the sacred elements of established society so dear to the heart of Burke. Furthermore, he is already involved in the early stages of recent evolution in France, which is indebted to him for his thinking and writing on human rights and which has already included an extended *Declaration of the Rights of Man and of Citizens* by the National Assembly, in its constitution. *(Rights, pp.132–4)* On the theme of aristocracy, nobles, lords, peers, inheritance, wealth and a House of Lords, he has much to contribute and to criticise. To start on a high note:

> "The French constitution says, *There shall be no titles*; and of consequence all that class of equivocal generation, which in some countries is called *aristocracy* and in others *nobility* is done away, and the *peer* is exalted into MAN."
>
> "Titles are but nicknames, and every nickname is a title. The thing is perfectly harmless in itself; but it marks a sort of foppery in the human character, which degrades it. . . . A certain writer, of some antiquity, says,'When I was a child, I thought as a child; but when I became a man, I put away childish things.' . . . It is properly, from the elevated mind of France, that the folly of titles has fallen. It has outgrown the baby-clothes of *Count* and *Duke*, and breeched itself in manhood."
>
> *(p.102)*

It is notable that, in his quotation, he cannot bring himself to name the Christian disciple Paul, which marks an advanced stage in his own personal evolution from the days of *Common Sense* to a time much nearer to his *Age of Reason*. He continues:

> "Is it then any wonder that titles should fall in France? Is it not a greater wonder that they should be kept up anywhere? What are they? What is their worth and what is their amount? When we think or speak of a *Judge* or a *General*, we associate with it the ideas of office and character; we think of gravity in the one, and bravery in the other: but when we use a word *merely as a title*, no ideas associate with it."
>
> *(p.103)*

Developing his theme and exploring the origins of this phenomenon which he abhors, he goes on:

> "That, which is called aristocracy in some countries, and nobility in others, arose out of the governments founded upon conquest. It was originally a military order, for the purpose of supporting military government; and to keep up a succession of this order for the purpose for which it was

established, all the younger branches of those families were disinherited, and the law of primogenitureship set up."

"The nature and character of aristocracy shows itself to us in this law. It is a law against every law of nature, and Nature herself calls for its destruction. Establish family justice and aristocracy falls. By the aristocratical law of primogenitureship in a family of six children, five are exposed. Aristocracy has never more than *one* child. The rest are begotten to be devoured. They are thrown to the cannibal for prey, and the natural parent prepares the unnatural repast."

(p.104)

This is strong language; a rather extreme and exaggerated view, but the point is well taken and he goes on to consider the practical consequences:

"As everything which is out of nature, affects . . . the interest of society, so does this. All the children which the aristocracy disowns (all except the eldest) are in general, cast like orphans upon a parish, to be provided for by the public, but at a greater charge. – Unnecessary offices, and places in governments and courts are created, at the expense of the public to maintain them."

"With what kind of parental reflections can the father or mother contemplate their younger offspring. By nature they are children, and by marriage they are heirs; but by aristocracy they are bastards and orphans. . . . Here then lies the monster; and Mr Burke, if he pleases, may write the epitaph."

(p.104)

So Paine is now being more practical: all children, other than the first, are not, in fact *begotten to be devoured*, but instead they become a burden upon society for whom places must be provided, irrespective of merit. Going on to deal with the former state in France and contrasting this with England, he continues:

"In France aristocracy has one feature less in its countenance, than what it has in some other countries. It did not compose a body of hereditary legislators. It was not *a corporation of aristocracy* for such I have heard M. de Lafayette describe an English House of Peers. Let us then examine the grounds upon which the French constitution has resolved against having such a House in France."

"Because, in the first place . . . aristocracy is kept up by family tyranny and injustice. Secondly, Because there is an unnatural unfitness in an aristocracy to be legislators for a nation. Their ideas of *distributive justice* are corrupted at the very source. They begin life by trampling on all their younger brothers and sisters, and relations of every kind; and are taught and educated so to do. With what ideas of justice or honour can that man enter a house of legislation, who absorbs in his own person the inheritance of a whole family of children, or doles out to them some pitiful portion with the insolence of a gift?"

"Thirdly, Because the idea of hereditary legislation is as inconsistent as that of hereditary judges or hereditary juries; and as absurd as an hereditary mathematician, or a hereditary wise man, or as ridiculous as an hereditary poet laureat."

"Fourthly, Because a body of men holding themselves accountable to nobody, ought not to be trusted by anybody."

"Fifthly, Because it is continuing the uncivilised principle of governments founded in conquest, and the base idea of man having property in man, and governing him by personal right."

"Sixthly, Because aristocracy has a tendency to degenerate the human species. – By the universal economy of nature it is known, and by the instance of the Jews it is proved, that the human species has a tendency to degenerate, in any small number of persons, when separated from the general stock of society, and intermarrying constantly with each other. It defeats even its pretended end, and becomes in time the opposite of what is noble in man."

(p.105)

Paine is sometimes belaboured for his populist style, which is far removed from that of Burke and even from that of Priestley with whom he has so much more in common, but in a passage, such as this, he demonstrates his fine capacity for analysis and clear exposition of a complex problem. Aristocracy is still a topic on which there is a good deal of bias and prejudice, but many professional historians would subscribe to Paine's analysis. He has a rather cynical view of the relationship between monarchy and the rest of aristocracy, when he writes:

"*Notwithstanding appearances, there is not any description of men that despise monarchy so much as courtiers* . . . The difference between a republican and a courtier with respect to monarchy, is, that the one opposes monarchy, believing it to be something, and the other laughs at it knowing it to be nothing."

(p.113)

Towards the end of his book Paine says of Burke that he has the "fawning character of a courtier". *(p.160)* On the House of Peers, in relation to the Regency crisis he has this to say:

"What is called the Parliament, is made up of two Houses, one of which is more hereditary, and more beyond the control of the Nation, than what the Crown is supposed to be. It is an hereditary aristocracy, assuming and asserting indefeasible, irrevocable rights and authority, wholly independent of the Nation. Where then was the merited popularity of exalting this hereditary power over another hereditary power less independent of the Nation than what itself assumed to be, and of absorbing the rights of the Nation into a House over which it has neither election nor control?"

(p.152)

Paine's most concentrated attack on the evils flowing from aristocracy and the House of Lords comes late in Part II of his *Rights of Man* and is of considerable length. A few extracts will serve to make his case; as for instance:

"What is called the House of Peers, is constituted on a ground very similar to that, against which there is a law in other cases. It amounts to a combination of persons in one common interest. No reason can be given, why an house of legislation should be composed entirely of men whose occupation consists in letting landed property, than why it should be composed of those who hire, or of brewers, or bakers or any other separate class of men."

"Mr Burke calls this house 'the great ground and pillar of security to the landed interest' . . . What pillar of security does the landed interest require more than any other interest in the state, or what right has it to a distinct and separate representation from the general interest of a nation? The only use to be made of this power (and which it has always made) is to ward off taxes from itself, and throw the burden upon such articles of consumption by which itself would be least affected."

(p.246)

"Why does Mr Burke talk of his House of Peers, as the pillar of the landed interest? Were that pillar to sink into the earth, the same landed property would continue, and the same ploughing, sowing and reaping would go on. The aristocracy are not the farmers who work the land, and raise the produce, but are the mere consumers of the rent; and when compared with the active world are the drones; a seraglio of males, who neither collect the honey nor form the hive, but exist only for lazy enjoyment."

"Mr Burke, in his first essay, called aristocracy, *the Corinthian capital of polished society*. Towards completing the figure he has now added the *pillar;* but still the base is wanting; and whenever a nation choose to act a Samson, not blind, but bold, down go the temple of Dagon, the Lords and the Philistines."

"If a house of legislation is to be composed of men of one class, for the purpose of protecting a distinct interest, all the other interests should have the same. The inequality, as well as the burden of taxation, arises from admitting it in one case, and not in all. Had there been a house of farmers, there had been no game laws; or a house of merchants and manufacturers, the taxes had neither been so unequal nor so excessive. It is from the power of taxation being in the hands of those who can throw so great a part of it from their own shoulders, that it has raged without a check."

"Men of small but moderate estates are more injured by the taxes being thrown on articles of consumption than they are eased by warding it from landed property, for the following reasons:

"First, they consume more of the productive taxable articles, in proportion to their property, than those of large estates. Secondly their residence is chiefly in towns, and their property in houses; and the increase of the poor-rates, occasioned by taxes on consumption, is in much greater proportion than the land-tax has been favoured. In Birmingham the poor-rates are not less than seven shillings in the pound. From this . . . the aristocracy are in a great measure exempt."

(p.249)

"These are but a part of the mischief flowing from the wretched scheme of an House of Peers. As a combination it can always throw a considerable portion of taxes from itself; and as an hereditary house, accountable to nobody, it resembles a rotten borough, whose consent is to be courted by interest. There are but few of its members who are not in some mode or other participators, or disposers of the public money. One turns a candle holder, or is a lord in waiting; another a lord of the bed chamber, a groom of the stole, or any insignificant nominal office to which a salary is annexed, paid out of the public taxes, and which avoids the direct appearance of corruption. Such situations are derogatory to the character of man; and where they can be submitted to, honour cannot reside."

(p.250)

"To all these are to be added the numerous dependants, the long list of younger branches and distant relations, who are to be provided for at the public expense: in short, were an estimate to be made of the charge of aristocracy to a nation, it will be found nearly equal to that of supporting the poor. The Duke of Richmond alone takes away as much for himself as would maintain two thousand poor and aged persons. Is it then, any wonder, that under such a system of government, taxes and rates have multiplied to their present extent."

(p.250)

"Mr Burke, in speaking of the aristocratical law of primogeniture, says, 'It is the standing law of our landed inheritance; and which, without question, has a tendency . . . to preserve a character of weight and con-sequence.

"As to its preserving a character of *weight and consequence*, the case appears to me directly the reverse. It is a taint upon character; a sort of privateering of family property. It may have weight among dependent tenants, but it gives none on a scale of national, and much less of universal character. Speaking for myself, my parents were not able to give me a shilling, beyond what they gave me in education; and to do this they distressed themselves. Yet, I possess more of what is called consequence in the world, than anyone in Mr Burke's catalogue of aristocrats."

(p.251)

Paine has been quoted at length on this topic, and in the next section has even more to say on monarchy, but it is difficult to do him justice by shortening his argument any further than has been done; it has a flow and a logic which should not be stemmed. If Edmund Burke had deigned to reply, he would probably have pleaded that the aristocracy was led by many fine characters who had the nation's best interest at heart, as well as the interest of their own tenants, but any such attempt would have been feeble in face of the heavy barrage which Paine has mounted. Burke knew this and so did many other people, at all levels of society, and so whereas he responded to French correspondents, he did not pick up the gauntlets thrown down by Paine or Priestley.

However, a few years later, Burke himself was to suffer an extremely rude and unjustified rebuff from some leading members of this cherished aristocracy, but retaliated with vigour. This related to his long campaign on Indian affairs (1781–95) which culminated in the impeachment of Warren Hastings, who had been Governor General there. Great abuses were rife, and many British officials were involved, but the overall responsibility rested with Hastings. In 1787 Burke persuaded the House of Commons that this official should be impeached; it was a moment of great triumph, as there was strong opposition. The case now moved to the House of Lords where the trial opened early in 1788; Burke took charge of the prosecution case on behalf of the Commons. It was an uphill battle from the start, as Hastings had many powerful friends in high places; and none more powerful than the Lord Chancellor, Thurlow, who had been a fellow scholar at Westminster with Hastings, and who, of course, presided.

With long lapses the case was allowed to drag on until 1794, when events in France were occupying the public mind, and Indian affairs had been allowed to become something of a bore. Burke's closing speech was a marathon, but did not avail in the end; he accepted the Stewardship of the Chiltern Hundreds, a fictitious office of profit under the Crown, which allowed him to retire from parliament; he was apparently offered a peerage but declined. His only son, Richard, died in the same year and left him grief stricken. In 1795 Warren Hastings was acquitted by the Lords, and granted an annuity of £4,000 by the East India Company; the Lords also awarded him colossal costs. In contrast Burke was voted a pension of £1,200 per annum; but critics, in his own Whig party, pretended to be outraged at this unexpected *generosity*, led by the Earl of Lauderdale and the Duke of Bedford; they were opposed to him because of their own stance on the French Revolution and the war with France. Lauderdale suggested that Burke's *Reflections . . .* in 1790 was written in hopes of this pension. Burke was outraged and produced his *Letter to a Noble Lord.*

This *Letter* was addressed to the Duke of Bedford, a member of the Whig leadership, who was the more vulnerable; his family, the Russells, having enjoyed Crown patronage, on a colossal scale, since his ancestor was ennobled by Henry VIII. The pseudonymous letter writer Junius had said of this *Noble Lord* many years before: "I dare say he has bought and sold more than half the representative integrity of the nation"; but at that time Burke was not listening. Now, however, his focus is sharp and he lets fly:

> "I was not, like his Grace of Bedford, swaddled and rocked and dandled into a legislator. . . . I was not made for a minnion or a tool . . . . I was obliged to show my passport, and again and again to prove my sole title

to the honour of being useful to my country . . . I have supported with very great zeal . . . these opinions, or, if his Grace likes another expression better, those old prejudices, which buoy up the ponderous mass of his nobility, wealth and titles. I have omitted no exertions to prevent him and them from sinking to that level to which the meretricious French faction his Grace at least coquets with omit no exertion to reduce both. I have done all I could do to discountenance inquiries into the fortunes of those who hold large portions of wealth, without any apparent merit of their own. I have strained every nerve to keep the Duke of Bedford in that situation which alone makes him my superior."

"Homer nods, and the Duke of Bedford may dream; and as dreams are apt to be ill pieced and incongruously put together, his Grace preserved his idea of reproach to me, but took the subject matter from the crown grants *to his own family.* . . . The grants to the House of Russell were so enormous as not only to outrage economy, but even to stagger credibility. The Duke of Bedford is the leviathan among all the creatures of the crown. He tumbles about his unwieldy bulk, he plays and frolics in the ocean of royal bounty. Huge as he is, and whilst 'he lies floating many a rood', he is still a creature. His ribs, his fins, his whalebone, his blubber, the very spiracles through which he spouts a torrent of brine against his origin, and covers me all over with the spray, everything of him and about him is from the throne."

". . . It would not be gross adulation, but uncivil irony, to say that he has any public merit of his own to keep alive the idea of the services by which his vast landed pensions were obtained. My merits, whatever they are, are original and personal, his are derivative. It is his ancestor, the original pensioner, that has laid up this inexhaustible fund of merit which makes his Grace so very delicate and exceptious about the merit of all other grantees of the crown."
(Extracts from Letter to a Noble Lord (1796) taken from 'The Great Melody' pp.537–9)

The attack is grossly personal; the hurt is palpable, and Burke's anger is great; he is carried away and seems to forget all the grand sentiments of former times regarding his cherished aristocracy. Like a house of cards the whole edifice has come tumbling down and with it goes also heredity. How his adversaries must have chuckled!

He did not dare even to consider Paine's taunt that the House of Peers, as an hereditary institution was accountable to nobody and thus resembled a rotten borough; this arrow came straight for his Achilles heel and struck home devastatingly!

Again Chesterton has a view of aristocracy which accords with this great outburst of Burke's, but would not necessarily have pleased him:

"The great gentry were more in the position of Napoleonic marshals than of Norman knights, but their position was worse; for the marshals might be descended from peasants and shopkeepers; but the oligarchs were descended from usurers and thieves. That for good or evil was the paradox of England; the typical aristocrat was the typical upstart."

(Short Histoy, p.212)

And what of our latest upstart aristocracy in the late 20th century?

CHAPTER VII

Monarchy

When my father was a king, he was a king who knew exactly what he
knew.
Shall I then be like my father and be willfully immovable and strong?
. . . it puzzles me to learn that tho' a man may be in doubt of what he
know,
Very quickly will he fight; he'll fight to prove that what he does not know
is so!
　　King's Soliloquy – The King and I – (Rodgers) and Hammerstein

MONARCHY IS THE LAST AND SUPREME ELEMENT IN BURKE'S PRECIOUS CONSTITUTION; in 1790 he is professing an amazing reverence for this institution, which had previously given him a great deal of concern in the way it operated. He had been severely critical of its incumbent, George III, who at an earlier stage appeared to be clawing back some of the absolute power, which had been lost to his two predecessors in the Hanoverian dynasty, more interested in their Germanic base than in Great Britain. Now, however, the king and his critic fall into a mutually supportive league. Burke's change of heart is remarkable and strange, but not inexplicable; for a start the king is now a much weakened individual, since defeat in America and the onset of his mental illness; thereafter, the perceived threat to the British establishment posed by developments in France suddenly becomes paramount. The combination of these factors makes it politic for him to give his wholehearted support to this threatened institution. His perception of an incipient threat to Catholic Ireland, as outlined by Conor Cruise O'Brien, is yet one more factor. Priestley and Paine have totally different ideas and attitudes, highly critical.

About 20 years earlier, Dr. Priestley, then a minister in Leeds addressing a group of younger members of his congregation advised them:

"Submit to those who are invested with the supreme power in your country, as your lawful civil magistrates; but if they would prescribe to you in matters of faith, say that you have but one Father, even God, and one Master, even Christ, and stand fast in the liberty with which he has made you free. *Respect a parliamentary king* (my italics) and cheerfully pay all parliamentary taxes, but have nothing to do with a parliamentary religion or a parliamentary God."

This is the man who during the French Revolution gets the label of regicide and troublemaker, but, in fact he had no problem with accepting a constitutional monarchy, any more in the 1790s than he had in the '70s; it was his rejection of "a parliamentary religion" which damned him with the establishment, a theme which has yet to be addressed, and where his true opposition will be fully revealed.

In the first of his Letters to Burke he tells him:

"That some very material change was wanting in the old government of France, you cannot deny, after allowing *(Reflections, p.145)* that 'in that country the unlimited power of the sovereign over the persons of his subjects was inconsistent with law and liberty'. If law and liberty were wanting in the old constitution, the peccant part must have been the very foundation of it; so that nothing effectual could have been done short of taking down the whole. If these incontrovertible *principles* and *facts* be admitted, I can see no reason for your exclaiming so violently, as you do, against the *late* (my italics) revolution in France."

(Letters to EB, p.4)

In the next letter he considers the position of the French king and queen, in the situation obtaining at that early stage in the revolution:

"You make the most tragical representation of the degraded state of the present king of France calling it 'the most horrid, atrocious, and afflicting spectacle that perhaps ever was exhibited to the pity and indignation of mankind'; considering him as a person who received his crown from his ancestors, and who had himself done nothing to deserve the treatment that he met with. Admitting this, if by a succession of incroachments, the power of the *crown itself* had long been enormous, should that be continued, to the terror and distress of the country, for the sake of the innocent head that happens to wear it . . . . If you say that his power is only nominal, I answer that the power of most arbitrary princes is little more. They are, in general, only instruments in the hands of those who are about them. As to doing what a man really wishes to do, the last king of France had very little of it; and in general, the higher any man stands in the order of society, the less power he has of doing what he really likes, and the more of his time he spends in doing what he had rather wish not to do, than other men."

(pp.16–17)

He could have gone much farther back for his example, to Israel's King David in his declining years faced with the revolt of his son, Absolom. *(2 Samuel: 13–19)*

In the third letter he deals with fundamental principles regarding the head of state, telling Burke:

"You strongly reprobate the doctrine of *kings being the choice of the people*, a doctrine advanced, but not first advanced by Dr. Price in his Revolution sermon. This doctrine *(you say, p.14)* as applied to the prince now on the British throne, is either nonsense, and therefore neither true nor false, or it affirms a most unfounded, dangerous, illegal, and unconstitutional position. According to this spiritual doctor of politics, if his majesty does not owe his crown to the choice of his people, he is no lawful king, etc."

"On the same principle you equally reprobate the doctrine of the king being the *servant* of the people, whereas the law, as you say *(p.31)* calls him *our sovereign lord the king*. But since you allow that 'kings are in one sense, undoubtedly, the servants of the people, because their power has no other rational end than that of the general advantage' it is evident that it is only Dr. Price's *words* that you quarrel with. Your *ideas* are, in fact, the very same with his, though you call his doctrine, not only *unconstitutional*, but *seditious;* adding that, 'it is now publickly taught, avowed and printed', whereas it was taught, avowed, and even printed, before either you or Dr. Price were born."

(pp.26–7)

In a footnote Priestley adds:

"This title of *sovereign lord*, derived from the Feudal system, given to a king of England, is by no means agreeable to the nature and spirit of our present constitution, which is a *limited monarchy* and not *unlimited*, as that title implies. Our only proper sovereign is the parliament."

He continues:

"Has not the chief magistrate in every country, as well as the chief officer in every town, a certain *duty* to perform, with certain emoluments, and *privileges*, allowed him in consideration of the proper discharge of that duty? And if the town officer, though having chief authority in his district, yet in consequence of being *appointed* and *paid* for his services by the town, is never considered in any other light than that of the *servant of the town;* is not the chief magistrate in any country, let him be called *sovereign, king* or what you please, (for that is only a name) the servant of the people? What real difference can there be in the two cases? They each discharge a certain duty, and have a certain stipulated reward for it. The office being *hereditary*, makes no real difference. In our laws, and those of other nations, there are precedents enow of men's whole estates being confiscated for crimes; and this of course excludes the heir."

"If as you expressly acknowledge, the only rational end of the power of a king is the *general advantage*, that is the *good of the people*, must not the people be of course the judges, whether they derive advantage from him and his government, or not, that is, whether they be well or ill *served* by him? Though there is no express, there is, you must acknowledge, a virtual, *compact between the king and the people*. This, indeed, is particularly mentioned in the Act which implies the abdication of King James, though you say *(p.29) it is too guarded, and too circumstantial;* and what can this compact be, but a stipulation for protection etc. on the part of the king, and allegiance on the part of the people? If therefore

instead *of protection* they find *oppression,* certainly allegiance is no longer
due. Hence according to common sense, and the principles of the Revolution, the right of a subject to resist a tyrant, and dethrone him; and
what is this, but, in other words, shocking as they may sound to your
ears, *dismissing* or *cashiering* a *bad servant,* as a person who has abused
his trust."

(p.27)

Priestley is at his weakest here at the end of this section in using the example
of the dethronement of James II. Can he honestly state that this was an example
of the people, as a whole, taking action? Was it not, rather, the action of an
aristocratic clique, who promised allegiance to the reigning monarch whilst
conspiring with a foreign prince, then swiftly changing sides when the trap
was sprung. In England it would have seemed no more than a dynastic reshuffle,
such as had occurred on previous occasions in the history of the nation, but
on the Celtic fringe it had more the nature of Civil War, which dragged on
over the next couple of years. However Priestley's general thesis is sound and
back on course he continues:

"So fascinating is the situation in which our kings are placed, that it is of
great importance to remind them of the true relation they bear to *the
people,* or as they are so fond of calling them *their people.* They are too
apt to imagine that their rights are independent of the will of the people,
and consequently that they are not accountable to them for any use they
may make of their power; and their numerous dependants, and especially
the clergy, are too apt to administer this pleasing intoxicating poison. . . .
Your whole book Sir, is little else than a vehicle for the same poison,
inculcating, but inconsistently enough, a *respect for princes,* independently
of their being originally the choice of the people, as if they had some
natural and indefeasible right to reign over us, they being born to command, and we to obey; and then, whether the origin of this power be
divine, or have any other source independent of the people, it makes no
difference to us."

(pp.28–9)

Priestley taunts Burke with his obsequious attitude to royalty when he writes:

"You are proud of what, in my opinion, you ought to be ashamed, the
idolatry of a fellow creature, and the abasement of yourself. It discovers
a disposition from which no 'manly sentiment or heroic enterprize' can
be expected. I submit to a king, or to any other civil magistrate, because
the good order of society requires it, but I feel no *pride* in that *submission;*
and the 'subordination of my heart' I reserve for *character* only, not for
station. As a citizen the object of my respect is *the nation* and *the laws.*
The magistrates, by whatever name they are called, I respect only as the
confidential servants of the nation, and the administrators of the laws.
    These sentiments, just in themselves, and savouring of no superstition,
appear to me to become men, whom nature has made equal, and whose

great object when formed into societies, it should be to promote their common happiness. I am proud of feeling myself *a man among men*, and I leave it to you, Sir, to be 'proud of your *obedience* and to keep alive', as well as you can, 'in servitude itself the spirit of an exalted freedom'. I think it much easier, at least, to be preserved *out* of a state of servitude than *in it*. You take much pains to gild your chains, but they are chains still.

(p.30)

He goes on to mock Burke for his sentimental outburst in regard to the French queen and this at a time before her life was seriously endangered, nor was he the only one to have this view; even the cartoonists did not miss the point. Priestley continues:

"If, Sir, you profess this 'generous loyalty, this proud submission, this dignified obedience, and this subordination of the heart' both to rank and sex, how concentrated and exalted must be the sentiment, where rank and sex are united! What an *exalted freedom* would you have felt, had you had the happiness of being a subject of the Empress of Russia; your sovereign being then a *woman?* Fighting under her auspices, you would, no doubt, have been the most puissant of knights errant, and her redoubted champion, against the whole Turkish empire, the sovereign of which is only a *man.*"

(p.31)

This is Priestley at his most severe and ironical, but he quickly returns to principle:

"It is of no purpose to say, as you do, *(p.16)* that 'the king of Great Britain reigns at this day by a fixed rule of succession, according to the laws of his country, and that he holds his crown in contempt of the choice of the Revolution Society, which has not a single vote for a king among them, either individually or collectively'; when you acknowledge that 'all the kingdoms of Europe were, at a remote period elective', and that 'the present king holds his rank no longer than while the legal conditions of the compact of sovereignty are performed by him'. This, Sir, is granting all that we, seditious as our doctrine is, contend for. Here is according to yourself, a certain *condition* on which kings reign. If therefore, that *condition* be not performed, the obligation of allegiance is discharged."

"Though we do not chuse any particular king, the nation originally chose to be governed by kings, with such limitations, with respect to their duty and prerogatives, as they then chose to prescribe. And whether the departure from the original and proper duty of a king be made at once, or by degrees, which has generally been the case; and though the people may have been restrained by their circumstances from checking the incroachment of their kings, the *right* of doing it must ever remain inherent in them. They must always have a power of resuming what themselves gave, when the condition on which it was given is not performed. They can surely recall a trust that has been abused, and reinstate themselves in their former situation, or in a better, if they can find one."

(*pp.31–2*)

"If there be, what you allow, *a compact of sovereignty*, who are *the parties, but the people* and the *king;* and if the compact be broken on his side, are not the rank and the privileges, which he held upon the condition of observing the terms of the compact forfeited? 'The rule of succession' you say,' is according to the laws of his country'. But what, according to yourself, is the origin of both our common and statute law?"'

(*p.32*)

"'Both these descriptions of law', you say (*p.22*), 'are of the same force, and are derived from an equal authority, emanating from the common agreement, and original compact of the state, and as such are equally binding on king and people too, as long as the terms are observed, and they continue the same body politic'. Laws then, not coming down from heaven, but being *made* by men, may also be *changed* by them; and what is a *constitution of government*, but the *greater laws* of the state? Kings therefore, as well as the people, may violate these laws by which they are equally bound; and if other violators of law be punishable, by degradation or otherwise, why should kings be excepted? Are *their* violations of the law, or the constitution, less injurious to the commonwealth than those of other transgressors? Let the punishment of kings be as *grave* and *decorous* as you please, but let justice, substantial justice, be done."

(*p.33*)

In a later chapter Priestley takes Burke to task on his ideas of continuity and its value based on long established power; Burke has been contending that what has been established is:

". . . the slow growth of ages, and a foundation of *great powers*, which if once destroyed will never rise again. It was, therefore, nothing else than madness, you would say, in the first reformers, to aim at the subversion of these powers, by refuting the opinions on which they were founded. They should have contented themselves with preserving the powers, sacred and inviolable, and have contrived to make a right use of them."

(*p.110*)

Here Priestley is primarily concerned with power which is both sacred and secular, but he returns briefly to the monarchical theme, continuing:

"For the same reason, had you in any country, as in Morocco, found the idea of absolute power in the prince, of the sacredness of his person, and of the happiness of dying by his hand, you would have been careful not to destroy that *power*, which you might not be able to reproduce; but being happily in possession of it, would have made it subservient to the good of the country. I am glad, however, to find that, though all powers are to be *continued*, you allow of some improvement in the application of them, which implies some change for the better."

(*p.111*)

What Priestley is concerned about here is a largely uncritical attitude, amounting to a species of idolatry, which should not be the state of a morally healthy community. Further on he develops this point:

"The generality of governments have hitherto been little else than a combination of *the few*, against *the many*; and to the mean passions, and low cunning of these few, have the great interest of mankind been too long sacrificed. Whole nations have been deluged with blood, and every source of future prosperity drained, to gratify the caprices of some of the most despicable, or the most execrable, of the human species. For what else have been the generality of kings, their ministers of state, or their mistresses, to whose wills whole kingdoms have been subject? What can we say of those who have hitherto taken the lead in conducting the affairs of nations, but that they have commonly been either weak or wicked, and sometimes both? Hence the common reproach of all histories, that they exhibit little more than a view of the vices and miseries of mankind. From this time, therefore, we may expect that it will wear a different, and more pleasing aspect."

(*p.144*)

In his *Essay on a Course of Liberal Education for Civil and Active Life* (1765) he urged the study of Civil History and Civil Policy, believing that history should be used:

". . . to contribute to forming the able statesman, and the intelligent and useful citizen . . . . Many of the political evils under which this and every other country in the world labour, are not owing to any want of love for our country, but to ignorance of its real constitution and interests. . . . History frees the mind from many prejudices, but will confirm the attachment of a Briton to his country. . . . All improvements in the science of government derived from history."

Priestley also condemns, as products of monarchy, imperial expansion abroad, and civil wars at home, saying:

"The very idea of *distant possessions* will be even ridiculed. The East and the West Indies, and everything *without ourselves* will be disregarded, and wholly excluded from all European systems, and only those divisions of men, and of territory, will take place, which the common convenience requires, and not such as the mad and insatiable ambition of princes demands. No part of America, Africa, or Asia, will be held in subjection to any part of Europe, and all the intercourse that will be kept up among them, will be for their mutual advantage."

"The causes of *civil wars*, the most distressing of all others, will likewise cease, as well as those of foreign ones. They are chiefly contentions for *offices*, on account of the power and emoluments annexed to them. But when the *nature* and *uses* of all civil offices shall be well understood, the powers and emoluments annexed to them, will not be an object sufficient to produce war. Is it at all probable that there will ever be a civil war in America about the presidentship of the United States?"

(Letters, p.147)

Priestley could not have known that Britain was on the brink of its greatest imperial expansion; that empire on which the sun never set, until it started to disintegrate again more than a century later. Also that other European nations, notably Germany, France, Belgium and Russia, were to build up empires which in the 20th century would dwindle away again. Meanwhile large portions of Asia and Africa were held in subjection, and as they have been released again many of the emerging nations are proving to be far from healthy as autonomous entities, having acquired bad habits. Priestley's vision was certainly Utopian and not realised in the short term, but prospects are better in many places, although none would be tempted to such a bright vision for the near future; not while we have problems such as Iran and Iraq; Israel and Palestine; Somalia; Rwanda, Haiti, Cuba, Chile, and other South American states, to mention but a few. Civil wars are not wanting and not likely to disappear in this century, nor well into the next. America did not have a civil war about the presidency, but it did have a bloody conflict in the 19th century on an issue not foreseen by Priestley and if the culture being developed under Richard Nixon had gone unchecked, even Priestley's unthinkable might have come to pass.

Priestley has been quoted at considerable length on the subject of monarchy, as well as other constitutional issues, but only because he himself had devoted much thought and study to them. He did not have Burke's legal training, nor his parliamentary experience; what he did have was academic dedication and a sharp disciplined mind. Especially in his time at Warrington Academy, he devoted a great deal of attention to history in general, British history in particular, and above all constitutional law. We have seen that Burke professed to despise philosophers whose attention was concentrated on constitutional and political issues, but at that time and facing the problems that confronted them, Priestley was more than a match for Burke. However, the latter was in harmony with the establishment and so his views prevailed. Burke's *Reflections* were widely read and highly commended; Priestley's readership was much more restricted, and although his writings were not suppressed they were certainly brushed aside. This is why his profound thoughts on basic political theory and practice, together with those of Tom Paine and a handful of other, like-minded but lesser luminaries, need to be revived and studied afresh. They have much to offer Europe and the wider world, as we reach the millennium. They can easily be dismissed on the strength of their particular topical predictions, but the thinking they developed on the problems of their own time, and of the years ahead, are basically sound and could be applied with profit to ours.

Some other thoughts of Burke on this topic should be mentioned, starting with a rather lengthy reflection, justifying the Williamite succession of 1688.

"Unquestionably there was at the Revolution, in the person of King William, a small and a temporary deviation from the strict order of a regular hereditary succession; but it is against all genuine principles of jurisprudence to draw a principle from a law made in a special case, and regarding an individual person. . . . If ever there was a time favourable for establishing the principle that a king of popular choice was the only legal king, without all doubt it was at the Revolution."

(Reflections, p.18)

There is special pleading here: how can Burke sustain his claim that William was 'a king of popular choice'? This rather stretches the meaning of *popular.* It was hardly so in the sense that actions taken in America or France in Burke's time were popular. So, was it then as asserted – 'a small and temporary deviation from the strict order of regular hereditary succession'? The king who was deposed had a legitimate male heir who was never restored to his inheritance; so it certainly was not a temporary deviation, and how was the small size of the deviation judged? We are not told. A little further on Burke continues:

"It would be to repeat a very trite story, to recall to your memory all those circumstances which demonstrated that their accepting King William was not properly a *choice;* but to all those who did not wish, in effect, to recall King James, or to deluge their country in blood, and again to bring their religion, laws, and liberties, into the peril they had just escaped, it was an act of *necessity,* in the strictest moral sense in which necessity can be taken."

"In the very act, in which for a time, and in a single case, parliament departed from the strict order of inheritance, in favour of a prince, who, though not next, was, however, very near in the line of succession, it is curious to observe how Lord Somers, who drew the Bill called the Declaration of Right, had comported himself on that delicate occasion. It is curious to observe with what address this temporary solution of continuity is kept from the eye; whilst all that could be found in this act of necessity to countenance the idea of an hereditary succession is brought forward, and made the most of, by this great man and by the legislature who followed him. Quitting the dry, imperative style of an act of parliament he makes the lords and commons fall to a pious, legislative ejaculation and declare, that they consider it, 'as a marvellous providence, and merciful goodness of God to this nation, to preserve their said majestic *royal* persons, most happily to reign over us *on the throne of their ancestors,* for which, from the bottom of their hearts, they return their humblest thanks and praises."

(p.19)

So, Burke admits that it was necessary to keep 'this temporary solution of continuity' from view, whilst everything considered necessary 'to countenance the idea of an hereditary succession is brought forward'; and this is presented to us gift-wrapped as a virtue. What extraordinary reasoning! Others have made a better attempt to justify the procedures of which Burke is speaking, without resorting to this spurious logic, but on he goes:

"The two Houses, in the act of King William, did not thank God that they had found a fair opportunity to assert a right to choose their own governors, much less to make an election the *only lawful* title to the crown. Their having been in condition to avoid the very appearance of it, as much as possible, was by them considered as a providential escape. *They threw a politic, well wrought veil over every circumstance tending to weaken the rights,* which in the meliorated order of succession they meant to perpetuate; or which might furnish a precedent for any future departure from *what they had then settled forever.* (my italics) Accordingly, that they might not relax the nerves of their monarchy, and that they might preserve a close conformity to the practice of their ancestors, as it appeared in the declaratory statutes of Queen Mary and Queen Elizabeth, in the next clause they vest, by recognition, in their majesties, *all* the legal prerogatives of the crown, declaring, 'that in them they are most *fully*, rightfully, and *entirely* invested, incorporated, united and annexed'. In the clause which follows, for preventing questions, by reason of *any pretended titles* (my italics) to the crown, they declare . . . that on the preserving 'a *certainty* in THE SUCCESSION thereof, the unity, peace, and tranquillity of the nation, doth, under God, wholly depend."

(p.20)

Here we are told that the conspirators in both houses of parliament had found a convenient opportunity to achieve their own ends, without appealing to the populace at large. No referendum here! We are reminded of the attitude of certain political leaders in our own time who are much averse to consulting the nation on any issue no matter how basic. The Williamite parliament had achieved a very neat cover up, and this is to state simply what Burke has dressed up in high sounding prose, which is so impressive until we get down to analysing it. In a previous paragraph we are told that this "temporary solution of continuity (has been) kept from the eye", but now that it has been achieved it becomes "*what they had settled forever*". We shall be considering another view on such an *eternal solution* in a later section, but Burke has something more to add:

"They knew that a doubtful title of succession would but too much resemble an election, and that an election would be utterly destructive of the 'unity, peace, and tranquillity of this nation' which they thought to be considerations of such moment. To provide for these objects, and therefore to exclude forever the Old Jewry doctrine (Dr. Price et al.) of 'a right to choose our own governors' they follow with a clause, containing a most solemn pledge, taken from the preceding act of Queen Elizabeth, as solemn a pledge as was or ever can be given in favour of an hereditary succession, and as solemn a renunciation as could be made of the principles by this society imputed to them. 'The Lords spiritual and temporal and commons, do, in the name of all the people aforesaid, most humbly and faithfully submit *themselves, their heirs and posterities forever;* and do faithfully promise, that they will stand to, maintain, and defend, their said majesties, and also the *limitation of the crown,* herein specified and contained, to the utmost of their powers, etc. etc."

"So far is it from being true, that we acquired a right by the Revolution to elect our kings, that if we had possessed it before, the English nation did at that time, most solemnly renounce, and abdicate it for themselves and for *all their posterity forever."* (my italics)

(pp.20–1)

Does Burke not know whether this right of election existed before? But if it did he is now quite happy that this *danger* has been removed forever. So any of our politicians, or political philosophers, who are today advocating abolition of the monarchy are deluding themselves and wasting their time, having been bound hand and foot at the Revolution of 1688! Going back to his own time we have further assurance from Burke:

"These gentlemen may value themselves as much as they please on their Whig principles, but I never desire to be thought a better Whig than Lord Somers; or to understand the principles of the Revolution better than those by whom it was brought about; or to read in the Declaration of Right any mysteries unknown to those whose penetrating style has engraved in our ordinances, and in our hearts, the words and spirit of *that immortal law."* (my italics)

"It is true that aided with the powers derived from force and opportunity, the nation was at that time, in some sense, free to take what course it pleased for filling the throne; but only free to do so upon the same grounds on which they might have wholly abolished their monarchy, and every other part of their constitution. However they did not think such bold changes within their commission. It is indeed difficult, perhaps impossible to give limits to the mere *abstract* competence of the supreme power, such as was exercised by parliament at that time; but the limits of a *moral* competence, subjecting, even in powers more indisputably sovereign, occasional will to permanent reason, and to the steady maxims of faith, justice, and fixed fundamental policy, are perfectly intelligible, and perfectly binding upon those who exercise any authority under any name, or under any title, in the state. The House of Lords, for instance, is not morally competent to dissolve the House of Commons; no, nor even to dissolve itself, nor to abdicate, if it would, its portion in the legislature of the kingdom. Though a king may abdicate for his own person, he cannot abdicate for the monarchy."

(pp.21–2)

Does Burke not trust his own judgement, that he must hide behind the skirts of Lord Somers, and those by whom the Revolution was brought about? In this long and complex dissertation he has many opinions to air on a wide variety of topics, so why should he be so coy at this stage; is it not that in his heart of hearts he realises he is on a very shaky foundation, and so must revert to *authority?* Again, in appealing to *"that immortal law"*, has he not heard of the *eternally immutable* 'Law of the Medes and the Persians', and does he not know that in the end it was neither eternal nor immutable? But his thesis at this point is needed to gainsay the French in the changes they are making to their constitution, and even more importantly to gainsay their supporters in Britain. However, the thesis runs on:

> "It is far from impossible to reconcile, if we do not suffer ourselves to be entangled in the mazes of metaphisic sophistry, (tut tut!) the use of both a fixed rule and an occasional deviation; the sacredness of an heredi-tary principle of succession in our government, with a power of change in its application in cases of extreme emergency. Even in that extremity (if we take the measure of our rights by our exercise of them at the Revolution) the change is to be confined to the peccant part only; to the part which produced the necessary deviation; and even then it is to be effected without a decomposition of the whole civil and political mass, for the purposes of originating a new civil order out of the first elements of society."
>
> *(pp.22–3)*

Apart from his swipe at the philosophers, metaphysicians, sophisters, or in other words those who think profoundly before they act, all he is saying here is that if an old building is in a state of some disrepair, and unless it is totally derelict, then to refurbish it, it will not be necessary to demolish it completely and start again. This principle does not need profound philosophical thought to understand it, but its application in the circumstances being considered is much more likely to do so. However Burke acknowledges this, he is only anxious to deny the philosophers of his own time, but not the pragmatists of the English Revolution, so he continues:

> "A state without the means of some change is without the means of its conservation. Without such means it might even risk the loss of that part of the constitution which it wished the most religiously to preserve. The two principles of conservation and correction operated strongly at the two critical periods of the Restoration and Revolution, when England found itself without a king. At both those periods the nation had lost the bond of union in their ancient edifice; they did not, however, dissolve the whole fabric. . . . They acted by the ancient organised states in the shape of their old organisation, and not by the organic moleculoe (sic) of a disbanded people. At no time, perhaps, did the sovereign legislature mani-fest a more tender regard to that fundamental principle of British consti-tutional policy, than at the time of the Revolution, when it deviated from the direct line of hereditary succession. The crown was carried somewhat out of the line in which it had before moved; but the new line was derived from the same stock. It was still a line of hereditary descent; still an

hereditary descent in the same blood, though an hereditary descent qualified with Protestantism. When the legislature altered the direction, but
kept the principle, they showed that they held it inviolable."

(p.23)

Burke seems to believe that if he repeats his point often enough, but with
altered phrasing and resorting to paradox, his reader will be lulled into submission, but again his argument should be dissected. "The two critical periods
of the Restoration and the Revolution" should not be bracketed together and
confused. At the Restoration parliament was restoring the legitimate heir who
might well have become king in 1649 on his father's demise; the succession
was merely delayed. At the Revolution the reigning monarch was deposed but
not beheaded, his son and heir went into exile with him, but was never to
succeed. Burke explains that, "King James was a bad king with a good title,
and not an usurper". And had there not been bad kings in the past who were
never deposed because they were firmly entrenched?

In describing the disbanded people of England as *an organic molecule* he is
for a second time showing a consciousness of Priestley looking over his shoul-
der, but Burke is no chemist; a people might be described as a mass of molecules,
whereas he himself would be but one of those molecules. The cobbler should
stick to his last! As for the "hereditary descent qualified with Protestantism"
we must leave it to Priestley and others to tackle that thorny problem in a
later section. Burke goes on to consider the later succession up to his own
time:

> "The princes who succeeded according to the act of parliament which
> settled the crown on the Electress Sophia and on her descendants, being
> Protestants, came in as much by a title of inheritance as King James did.
> He came in according to the law, as it stood at his accession to the crown;
> and the Princes of the House of Brunswick came to the inheritance of
> the crown, not by election, but by law, as it stood at their several acces-
> sions, of Protestant descent and inheritance.
>
> "The law by which this royal family is specifically destined to the
> succession, is the act of the 12th and 13th of King William. The terms of
> this act bind us and our heirs, and *our posterity,* to them their *heirs,* and
> their *posterity,* being Protestants, to the end of time, in the same words
> as the Declaration of Right had bound us to the heirs of King William
> and Queen Mary. It therefore secures both an hereditary crown and an
> hereditary allegiance. On what ground except the constitutional policy of
> forming an establishment to secure that kind of succession which is to
> preclude a choice of the people for ever, could the legislature have
> fastidiously rejected the fair and abundant choice which our own country
> presented to them, and searched in strange lands for a foreign princess,
> from whose womb the line of our future rulers were to derive their title
> to govern millions of men through a series of ages?"

(p.25)

Burke goes on to develop his point at greater length, but the gist of his argument is already expressed above. Although he never practised at the bar his training was in law, and in difficult cases like this, of the succession and the limitations placed upon it, he resorts to complex legal formulae, which tend to blind the average citizen with his science. He is obviously wholly contented that this brilliant legal manoeuvre quite justifies placing upon the British throne a foreign prince who could not even speak the English language and was not really interested in the nation's affairs. The arrangement suited parliament very well indeed, because there was now a monarch they could comfortably ignore. When in time, the third of these Hanoverian Georges had become English enough to start taking a hand in affairs of state, Burke himself was one of those who was sufficiently disturbed by what he saw as backsliding towards absolutism, and felt a need to oppose him. However, come 1790, he became so disturbed by events in France that his tender heart came to rule his lawyer's head, with the results we have just reviewed, and for which he produces further arguments:

"The ceremony of cashiering kings, of which these gentlemen (Price et al.) talk so much at their ease, can rarely, if ever be performed without force. It then becomes a case of war, and not of constitution. . . . The Revolution of 1688 was obtained by a just war, in the only case in which any war, and much more a civil war can be just. . . . The question of dethroning, or, if these gentlemen like the phrase better, 'cashiering kings', will always be, as it has always been, an extraordinary question of state, and wholly out of the law; a question (like all other questions of state) of dispositions, and of means, and of probable consequences, rather than of positive rights. As it was not made for common abuses, so it is not to be agitated by common minds. The speculative line of demarcation, where obedience ought to end, and resistance must begin, is faint, obscure, and not easily definable. It is not a single act, or a single event, which determines it. Governments must be abused and deranged indeed, before it can be thought to; and the prospect of the future must be as bad as the experience of the past. When things are in that lamentable condition, the nature of the disease is to indicate the remedy to those whom nature has qualified to administer in extremities this critical, ambiguous, bitter potion to a distempered state. Times, and occasions and provocations, will teach their own lessons. The wise will determine from the gravity of the case; the irritable from sensibility to oppression; the high minded from disdain and indignation at abusive power in unworthy hands; the brave and bold from the love of honourable danger in a generous cause; but, with or without right, a revolution will be the very last resource of the thinking and the good."

(pp.32–3)

This long passage is quoted in full, not so much for anything it adds to the argument for or against dethroning a monarch, as to display and give opportunity to explore the mind of Burke at its most fanciful. There is a flavour of

Cartoon of Burke. "Don Dismalo" After an absence of 16 years Embracing his beautiful vision

romance here, but the language is ill suited to a romantic novel. Perhaps the best way to categorise it is as being the polished performance of an expert, and experienced lawyer, attempting to defend an extremely poor brief. In the real world and throughout history kings have been removed in a variety of ways, and for a variety of motives, some of which we might approve and others we might abhor. Edmund Burke as an experienced man of affairs, well versed in history, knows this, but has undertaken a well nigh impossible task, and is determined to shine through as the 'Parfait knight' and man of honour whatever the odds. This passage is excelled only by his more famous "Age of Chivalry" performance"

"I thought ten thousand swords must have leaped from their scabbards to avenge even a look that threatened her (Queen Marie Antoinette) with insult. But the age of chivalry is gone. That of sophisters, economists and calculators, has succeeded; and the glory of Europe is extinguished forever. Never, never more, shall we behold that generous loyalty to rank and sex, that proud submission, that dignified obedience, that subordination of the heart, which kept alive, even in servitude itself, the spirit of an exalted freedom. The unbought grace of life, the chief defence of nations, the nurse of manly sentiment and heroic enterprise is gone! It is gone, that sensibility of principle, that chastity of honour, which felt a stain like a wound, which inspired courage whilst it mitigated ferocity, which ennobled whatever it touched, and under which vice itself lost half its evil, by losing all its grossness."

(p.83)

What splendid sentiments! This unfortunate queen was a sad victim of circumstances, right back to childhood, and most people who have studied her history have a deep sympathy; she was a prisoner long before she ever saw the inside of a prison, which she had still not done when Burke was writing. One wonders if he ever reflected on the part which his own actions played in the genesis of this tragedy; a diplomatic rather than such an excessively emotional approach could have ensured a much happier outcome. And a more topical reflection on his age of "sophisters, economists and calculators"; were he with us today, experiencing the management culture which pervades Britain approaching the millennium, he would realise that *his* economists and calculators were mere novices and that we have a greater need than ever for dedicated sophisters to bring ours to heel. His next reflection is on constitutional alternatives:

"Have these gentlemen (of the revolution) never heard, in the whole circle of the worlds of theory and practice, of anything between the despotism of the monarch and the despotism of the multitude? Have they never heard of a monarchy directed by laws, controlled and balanced by the great hereditary wealth and hereditary dignity of a nation; and both again controlled by a judicious check from the reason and feeling of the people at large, acting by a suitable and permanent organ?"

(p.136)

But surely, what Burke has in mind is monarchy backed by the multitude of aristocrats who have great 'hereditary wealth', but many of whom had long since lost any 'hereditary dignity' in the eyes of the 'people at large'. And what is this suitable and permanent organ in the hands of the people at large? In a further reflection he contemplates what may follow if the republic fails and monarchy is restored without any adequate check:

"So far from this able disposition of some of the old republican legislators, which follows with a solicitous accuracy the moral conditions and propensities of men, they have levelled and crushed together all the orders which they have found, even under the coarse unartificial arrangement of the monarchy, in which mode of government the classing of the citizens is not of so much importance as in a republic. It is true however, that every such classification, if properly ordered, is good in all forms of government; and composes a strong barrier against the excesses of despotism, as well as it is the necessary means of giving effect and permanence to a republic. For want of something of this kind, if the present project of a republic should fail, all securities of a moderated freedom fail along with it; all the indirect restraints which mitigate despotism are removed; in so much that if monarchy should ever again obtain an entire ascendancy in France, under this or any other dynasty, it will probably be, if not voluntarily tempered, at setting out, by the wise and virtuous counsels of the prince, the most completely arbitrary power that has ever appeared on earth. This is to play a most desperate game."

(pp.205–6)

It is difficult much of the time to fathom the mind of Burke and to follow his argument, but in this instance he seems blinded by his abiding faith in British constitutionalism, and his utter conviction that the French are quite incompetent, not to be trusted to handle, without disaster, whatever transitions are facing them in the years ahead. Is he forgetting the experience of recent British history and the several transitions which had been weathered? The issue of competence in all of this is not necessarily relevant, in the terms in which he is posing the problem.

Did not parliament in 1649 bring its Civil War to a conclusion when it beheaded Charles I? And did not Cromwell's republic fail after his death? Then parliament restored the monarchy in 1660; in less than 30 years, when the reigning monarch was adjudged to be unsuited because of his religious allegiance, he too was deposed and replaced by another more compatible with the ruling clique. Through all of this, parliament, though it changed complexion more than once kept itself and the nation on a relatively even keel. Burke could not know how democracy in France might evolve, but he was quite sure that it could not survive to anything like the extent that it had done in Britain.

The Reign of Terror owed at least as much to the enemies of France, including Burke, as it did to its own terrorists. Even with this disastrous upheaval France was restored to normal, and ultimately in a way that Burke had predicted:

"In the weakness of one kind of authority, and in the fluctuation of all, the officers of an army will remain for some time mutinous and full of faction, until some popular general, who understands the art of conciliating the soldiery, and who possesses the true spirit of command, shall draw the eyes of all men upon himself. Armies will obey him on his personal account."

(p.243)

Prophetic words; the general was, of course, to be Napoleon, but what would Burke have made of his imperial pretensions, and could he have predicted the restoration of monarchy after Waterloo, even if that was not to last, and a republic was the enduring entity. No matter how great the upheaval, any community must return to stability in the long run and France was a good example. Having achieved a constitutional monarchy France could have followed Britain's example and retained that form of government but who is to say that it would have been better off for such a restoration. Paine or Priestley would have said not. Burke certainly had no confidence in the status of the French king as he was placed in 1790:

"Let us turn our eyes to what they have done towards the formation of an executive power. For this they have chosen a degraded king. . . . To consider the French scheme for an executive officer, in its two natural divisions of civil and political – in the first it must be observed that, according to the new constitution, the higher parts of judicature, in either of its lines, are not in the king. The King of France is not the fountain of justice. The judges, neither the original, nor the appellate, are of his nomination. He neither proposes the candidates, nor has a negative on the choice. He is not even the public prosecutor. He serves only as a notary to authenticate the choice made of the judges in the several districts. By his officer he is to execute their sentence. When we look into the true nature of his authority, he appears to be nothing more than a chief of bum bailiffs, serjeants-at-mace, catchpoles, jailers and hangmen. It is impossible to place anything called royalty in a more degrading point of view. . . . Everything in justice that is vile and odious is thrown upon him. . . ."

"View this new executive officer on the side of his political capacity, as he acts under the orders of the National Assembly. To execute laws is a royal office; to execute orders is not to be a king. However a political executive magistracy . . . is a great trust. . . . The office of execution is an office of exertion. It is not from Impotence we are to expect the tasks of power. What sort of person is a king to command executory service, who has no means whatever to reward it? Not in a permanent office, not in a grant of land; no, not in a pension of fifty pounds a year; not in the vainest and most trivial title. In France the king is no more the fountain of honour than he is the fountain of justice. All rewards, all distinctions are in other hands. Those who serve the king can be actuated by no natural motive but fear; by a fear of everything except their master. . . . He has no negative: yet his name and authority is used to enforce every harsh decree."

(pp.220–2)

Burke belabours the French, that they have degraded their king. Is he implying that monarchy with absolute power is the ideal? Surely his own record would deny this; he had struggled against any such pretensions on the part of George III, especially during the American revolt; and was there not a tradition of degrading British kings? What of Charles II, James II, William of Orange, George I, George II, and onwards? Could there be a more cynical example of degradation than that of the first Hanoverian monarch, who was quite stymied by his own disabilities, especially in the matter of language, and his lack of any real interest in the nation other than as real estate?

The French king "has no negative", or in other words no veto. How much of this power did any British king possess from the Civil War onward? "To execute laws is a royal office; to execute orders is not to be a king." Burke is appalled; but was not John Wilkes MP, persecuted by king, government, and parliament for pointing out in his periodical *The North Briton* (No.45) that in the King's speech from the throne he was advocating what was being imposed upon him; something in which he did not really believe? And, who prescribes what is included in the Queen's speech in our own day? Do we not know well in advance from politicians and from the media what it will contain, or certainly the most significant items? And, if the day should come when a party in power decides on abolition of the monarchy, the monarch at that time must include this item in the speech. Admittedly the only remaining veto could be exercised, which is abdication. This might cause some popular unrest, but ultimately it would indirectly achieve parliament's aim by leaving a vacant throne. The only power at present remaining, apart from a residuum of patronage, is the monarch's ability to maintain a constitutional balance between political parties to ensure that they shall not sacrifice national to self- interest.

The last of Burke's anxieties, in the passage just quoted, is that the French king is no longer "the fountain of honour"; royal bounty is thwarted, honours, distinctions and rewards are in other hands, and so it would be in Britain eventually. We have annually the Queen's Birthday Honours, but what role does the monarch play other than that of a rubber stamp; she may be humoured in a very small proportion of cases in so far as these accord with the will of the government. And was not Burke himself concerned about any extra-- parliamentary cabal which the king in his own circumstances might be employing for doubtful or even dangerous purposes? The French king should not have his powers limited by evil minded revolutionaries, but the British monarch should be tightly controlled by an all wise parliament.

The word *cabal* itself is highly significant. It is of sufficient age for most people no longer to realise that it is an early acronym; it derives from the kitchen cabinet which Charles II gathered around him following the restoration: Clifford, Arlington, Buckingham, Ashley Cooper, and Lauderdale. To quote G M Trevelyan's *History of England:*

"The Cabal contained not one sound Anglican and scarcely one true patriot. Clifford was an ardent Romanist and Arlington more a Romanist than anything else; Lauderdale and Buckingham were unprincipled adventurers, and Anthony Ashley Cooper, Earl of Shaftesbury, was the man destined first to found the Whig party and then to ruin it by furious driving. Released by these mercurial companions from Clarendon's control, Charles, his own master at last, entered upon strange courses."

(Book IV Chapter VI)

In spite of all that has been said, Burke has one further and dramatic reflection on the British monarchy in *A Letter to a Member of the National Assembly* . . . 1791:

"I believe, Sir, that many on the Continent altogether mistake the condition of a king of Great Britain. He is a real king and not an executive officer. If he will not trouble himself with contemptible details, nor wish to degrade himself by becoming a party in little squabbles, I am far from sure that a king of Great Britain, in whatever concerns him as a king, or indeed as a rational man, who combines his public interest with his personal satisfaction, does not possess a more real, solid, extensive power, than the King of France was possessed of before this miserable revolution. The direct power of the King of England is considerable. His indirect, and far more certain power, is great indeed. He stands in need of nothing towards dignity, of nothing towards spleandour; of nothing towards authority, of nothing at all towards consideration abroad. When was it that a King of England wanted wherewithal to make him respected, courted, or perhaps even feared in every state of Europe?"

(Letter to a Member . . . 1791, p.318)

Probably the last king to have been feared throughout Europe up to Burke's time was Louis XIV; surely not any English monarch later than Elizabeth? And what of this "indirect, and far more certain power"; was it so great? And was it not that very species of power operating through a *cabal* which Burke himself had been at such great pains to curb? A few further reflections on this topic came in December 1791 in his Essay *Thoughts on French Affairs*, which came after the ill fated flight of the French royal family to Varennes, but before the Reign of Terror erupted with the September massacres in '92. He starts:

"In all our transactions with France, and at all periods, we have treated with that state on the footing of a monarchy. Monarchy was considered in all the external relations of that kingdom with every power in Europe as its legal and constitutional government, and that alone in which its federal capacity was vested."

"It is not yet a year since M. de Montmorin formally, and with as little respect as can be imagined to the king, and to all crowned heads, announced a total revolution in that country. He has informed the British ministry that its frame of government is wholly altered; that he is one of the ministers of the new system; and in effect that the king is no longer his master . . . but the *first of the ministers* in the new system."

"The second notification was that of the king's acceptance of the new constitution; accompanied with fanfaronades in the modern style of the French bureaus; things which have much more the air and character of the saucy declamations of their clubs, than the tone of regular office."

(Thoughts, p.325)

In this passage Burke's attitude is reminiscent of nothing so much as that of King Canute of ancient British fame, who commanded the tide to desist in its onshore flow. France had always been a monarchy; Burke and the British administration wished it so to remain, and it was very tiresome that the people of France should wish otherwise. A different attitude with encouragement from Britain, once the French king had accepted the new constitution and his changed status, could have made all the difference facilitating a smooth transition, instead of provoking a hostile reaction which escalated as external opposition grew, and slid into a warlike mode as surrounding kingdoms coalesced.

Why should the French nation not designate its monarch as 'the first of the ministers of the new system' especially if the man himself was willing to accept that status? The reason, of course, is that other monarchs felt immediately threatened by this alteration in the French constitution, but their nations were not called upon to follow suit, and if those monarchs had reflected calmly, taking sound advice, they too might have moved to some variety of constitutional monarchy suited to their own particular circumstances. Europe as a whole stood to gain, but this was to expect too much, as we can observe from the slow progress of European Union two centuries later, and following two disastrous World Wars.

Following through the idea that the French disease may be, or may become, infectious, Burke has another thought:

". . . A system of French conspiracy is gaining ground in every country. . . . A predominant inclination towards it appears in all those who have no religion, when otherwise their disposition leads them to be advocates even for despotism. Hence Hume, though I cannot say that he does not throw out some expressions of disapprobation on the proceedings of the levellers in the reign of Richard II, yet affirms that the doctrines of John Ball were 'conformable to the ideas of primitive equality, which are engraven in the hearts of all men'."

(Thoughts, p.357)[*]

It is strange that at this late stage in his writings Burke should bring forth this example from England's history to use against the French. It is one of the darker episodes in this history, an early example of a *'rights of man revolt'* and perchance precipitated by popular reaction to a *Poll Tax.* Mrs Thatcher and her ministers should have studied this episode closely,

---

[*] G M Trevelyan's *History of England*, Book II, chapter VII gives a simple and lucid account of this complicated uprising.

because if they had done so they might have saved themselves and the nation a great deal of distress, misery, and eventual grave embarrassment. They did however at least avoid the fatal confrontation which resulted in the foul assassination of Wat Tyler by the Mayor of London in the presence of the young and immature King Richard II, who was still a minor, but who was used as a symbol of sovereign authority.

The English, four centuries earlier, were just as capable of manipulating a weak monarch as Burke believed the French were doing during the Revolution. But the difference was that the young and inexperienced Richard was probably quite bemused by the events taking place in his kingdom, whereas Louis XVI, although adjudged weak, naive and malleable, was no fool. He knew full well what the majority of people wanted, and for the most part was in agreement with them, even if he was not a strong enough personality to lead and guide in the manner called for at that time. Burke could see this, up to a point, and in a late passage from *Thoughts . . .*, he comments:

> "It is with persons of condition that sovereigns chiefly come into contact. It is from them that they generally experience opposition to their will. . . . But of the common people, in pure monarchical governments, kings know little or nothing; and therefore being unacquainted with their faults . . . kings generally regard them with tenderness and favour, and turn their eyes towards that description of their subjects, particularly when hurt by opposition from higher orders. It was thus that the King of France (a perpetual example to all sovereigns) was ruined."
>
> "I have it from very sure information that the king's counsellors had filled him with a strong dislike to his nobility, his clergy, and the corps of his magistracy. They represented to him that he had tried them all severally, in several ways, and found them all intractable. That he had twice called an assembly (the notables) composed of the first men of the clergy, the nobility and the magistrates; that he had himself named every one member in those assemblies, and that, though so picked out, he had not, in this their collective state, found them more disposed to a compliance with his will than they had been separately. That there remained for him, with the least prospect of advantage to his authority in the states-general, which were to be composed of the same sort of men, but not chosen by him, only the *tiers état*. In this alone he could repose any hope of extricating himself from his difficulties, and of settling him in a clear and permanent authority."
>
> "This unfortunate king (not without a large share of blame to himself) was deluded to his ruin by a desire to humble and reduce his nobility, clergy, and his corporate magistracy; not that I suppose he meant wholly to eradicate these bodies; in the manner since effected by the democratic power. . . . With his own hand, however, Louis XVI pulled down the pillars which upheld his throne. . . ."
>
> *(Thoughts, pp.362–3)*

Here we have Burke telling us that the king was 'deluded to his ruin by a desire to humble and reduce his nobility, clergy, and the corps of his magistracy'. But he has just told us that these same people had been intractable, and not disposed to compliance with the royal will; in other words the nobility, the higher clergy and the magistrates had been given their chance to support the king but had failed him. The rot was at the very heart of the old establishment, and it took little more than the fall of the Bastille to bring panic which destroyed its cohesion and its morale.

If Burke was besotted with monarchy, this is certainly not so of **Tom Paine** who was one of the fiercest critics ever of this form of rule. He first addresses himself to the problem in his short pamphlet entitled *Common Sense*, written for Americans, and published in Philadelphia, at the outbreak of the revolt from British rule in 1776. King George III did not want to lose his empire, and led a fierce opposition to this revolt, making him a prime target for opponents in America, as well as for those in Britain itself who sympathised with their cause, prominent among whom was Edmund Burke; this in spite of the stance he later took during the French Revolution.

After some introductory remarks on the English constitution, Paine plunges straight into the problem of monarchy which he says is:

". . . something exceedingly ridiculous. . . . It first excludes a man from the means of information, yet empowers him to act in cases where the highest judgement is required. The state of a king shuts him from the world, yet the business of a king requires him to know it thoroughly; wherefore the different parts, unnaturally opposing and destroying each other, prove the whole character to be absurd and useless."

(CS, p.69)

This is a profound observation which gets straight to the heart of the matter, but it is a problem which, to a greater or lesser extent bears upon any individual operating in an exalted position which tends to block communication with people in the lower orders of society. Quickly Paine gets right *back to basics* with an appeal to the Jewish Old Testament citing the occasion when the people of Israel first demand to be given a king, so that they may be led in the same way as other nations around them; they have obviously been seduced by the pomp and circumstance surrounding these monarchs, and feel themselves degraded.

It is interesting and significant that Paine should enter the fray at this point because it reflects his origins as an Anglican with a Quaker father and schooled in the Bible. His *Rights of Man* is an enlargement and development of the thesis which he first sets forth in this earlier and simpler essay, but in 1791 he would no longer use this argument from scripture in spite of its powerful impact. The point is that 15 years on his Christianity has atrophied, and been replaced by an agnostic Deism; he is now much closer to his *Age of Reason* of 1793–4. Like Priestley he had become a creature of the Enlightenment, except that Priestley did not abandon his Christian roots and philosophy, but balked at the Divinity of Christ and the consequent doctrine of the Trinity.

Paine tells us that, "monarchy is ranked in scripture as one of the sins of the Jews, for which a curse in reserve is denounced against them". *(CS, p.73)* Their first attempt was in the days of Gideon, their successful general whom they expected to tempt, saying to him: "Rule thou over us, thou and thy son and thy son's son", a sore temptation indeed, not only the kingship, but hereditary monarchy in its fullness. But Gideon, a pious man, would have none of it saying, "I will not over you, neither shall my son rule over you, THE LORD SHALL RULE OVER YOU". *(Judges 8:22,23)*

The Jews backed down in the face of this Godly response, but the idea did not go away; it went on the back burner for one hundred and thirty years until the days of Samuel, the last of the Judges, when it surfaced again with the proposition: "Make us a king to judge us like all the other nations". Samuel, remembering Gideon, was not pleased and resorted to God in prayer, only to be told to let the people have their way, but with dire warnings of the consequence. So Samuel told them:

> "This shall be the manner of the king that shall reign over you; he will take your sons and appoint them for himself for his chariots, and to be his horsemen, and some shall run before his chariots . . . *('This description agrees with the present in mode of impressing men' comments Paine, in parentheses.)* . . . and he will appoint him captains over thousands and captains over fifties, and will set them to ear his ground, and reap his harvest, and to make his instruments of war . . . and he will take your daughters to be confectionaires and to be cooks and to be bakers . . . *(This describes the expense and luxury as well as the oppression of kings. TP)*. . . and he will take your fields and your olive yards, even the best of them and give them to his servants; and he will take the tenth of your seed, and of your vineyards and give them to his officers and to his servants . . . *(By which we see that bribery, corruption, and favouritism are the standing vices of kings. TP)* . . . and he will take the tenth of your men servants, and your goodliest young men and your asses, and put them to his work, . . . and ye shall be his servants, and ye shall cry out in that day because of your king which ye shall have chosen, and the Lord will not hear you in that day."
>
> *(I Samuel 8:5–18)*

Paine continues:

> "This accounts for the continuation of monarchy; neither do the characters of the few good kings which have lived since, either sanctify the title, or blot out the sinfulness of the origin. . . ."
>
> *(pp.74–5)*

Paine's judgement here is sound and significant, his logic ruthless, and he has much more to add in his *Rights of Man*. His style is discursive, and it is a measure of his obsession with this particular topic that he is so repetitive. It will be necessary therefore to deal with the matter under subheadings in order to achieve a clear focus, starting with:

Basic Problems and Faults of Monarchy as an Institution

"What is monarchy more than the management of the affairs of a Nation? It is not, and from its very nature cannot be, the property of any particular man or family, but of the whole community, at whose expense it is supported; and though by force or contrivance it has been usurped into an inheritance, the usurpation cannot alter the right of things. Sovereignty, as a matter of right, appertains to the Nation only, and not to any individual; and a Nation has at all times an inherent indefeasible right to abolish any form of Government it finds inconvenient, and establish such as accords with its interest, disposition, and happiness. The romantic and barbarous distinction into Kings and subjects, though it may Suit the condition of courtiers, cannot that of citizens and is exploded by the principle upon which Governments are now founded. Every citizen is a member of the Sovereignty, and as such can acknowledge no personal subjection; and his obedience can be only to the laws."

(Rights, p.165)

"It could have been no difficult thing in the early and solitary ages of the world, while the chief employment of men was that of attending flocks and herds, for a banditti of ruffians to overrun a country, and lay it under contributions. Their power being thus established, the chief of the band contrived to lose the name of robber in that of Monarch; and hence the origin of Monarchy and Kings."

"The origin of the government of England, so far as it relates to what is called its line of monarchy, being one of the latest, is perhaps the best recorded. The hatred which the Norman invasion and tyrant begat, must have been deeply rooted in the nation, to have outlived the contrivance to obliterate it. Though not a courtier will talk of the curfew-bell, not a village in England has forgotten it."

(p.190)

The reader will be impressed as we proceed with Paine's particular detestation of the Norman conquest and of William the Conqueror in particular. He certainly ignores the degree of continuity which existed between the last Anglo-Saxon king, Edward the Confessor, who was himself part Norman and William. There is more than a hint here of residual Anglo-Saxon resentment, which may perhaps stem from Paine's origins in Norfolk, close to the fen country where Hereward the Wake's final resistance was fought out. Was the curfew-bell a particularly vivid folk memory in Thetford where he was born and reared?

"Kings succeed each other, not as rationals, but as animals. It signifies not what their mental or moral characters are. Can we then be surprised at the abject state of the human mind in monarchical countries, when the government itself is formed on such an abject levelling system? – It has no fixed character. Today it is one thing; tomorrow it is something else.

It changes with the temper of every succeeding individual, and is subject to all the varieties of each. It is government through the medium of passions and accidents."

(pp.194–5)

Now for a Contrast in Style of Government

"What is called a *republic,* is not any *particular form* of government. . . . RES-PUBLICA, the public affairs, or the public good; or, literally translated, the *public thing.* It is a word of a good original, referring to what ought to be the character and business of government; and in this sense it is naturally opposed to the word *monarchy,* which has a base, original signification. It means arbitrary power in an individual person; in the exercise of which, *himself* and not the *res-publica,* is the object."

(p.200)

There is here some overstatement of the case, because any reasonable historian will show that monarchy does not inevitably exclude the best interests of the nation at all levels. There have been kings who were good and strong leaders, well disposed towards all their people and Paine does occasionally show that he understands this. But now he presents a further basic problem:

Is Monarchy the Executive Power?

"What is the best form of government for conducting the RES-PUBLICA, or the PUBLIC BUSINESS of a nation, after it becomes too extensive and populous for the simple democratical form? . . . It is possible . . . to lay down a system on principles . . . but the practice requires a knowledge of a different kind. . . . It is an assemblage of practical knowledge, which no one individual can possess; and therefore the monarchical form is as much limited in useful practice, from the incompetency of knowledge, as was the democratical form, from the multiplicity of population. The one degenerates, by extension, into confusion; the other, into ignorance and incapacity, of which all the great monarchies are an evidence."

(p.201)

"I leave to courtiers to explain what is meant by calling monarchy the executive power. It is merely a name in which acts of government are done; and any other, or none at all would answer the same purpose. Laws have neither more nor less authority on this account. It must be from the justness of their principles, and the interest which a nation feels therein; if they require any other than this, it is a sign that something in the system of government is imperfect."

(p.221)

"Were a government so constructed, that it could not go on unless a goose or a gander were present in the senate, the difficulties would be just as great and as real on the flight or sickness of the goose or the gander, as if it were called a King. We laugh at individuals for the silly difficulties they make to themselves, without perceiving that the greatest of all ridiculous things are acted in governments."

(p.224)

Here, many people would be tempted to ridicule Paine himself for this silly analogy, were it not that he is able to cite a case in point, which he gives in a footnote relating how the people of Berne in Switzerland had, from time immemorial, kept a bear, at public expense, believing that if they had not a bear they should have all been undone. Then, in the recent past, the reigning bear had died suddenly, before a replacement could be provided. In the interim there were no dire consequences, and so the people decided they had no further need for a bear, saying: "A bear is a very voracious, expensive animal, and we were obliged to pull out its claws, lest he should hurt the citizens." The point is well taken, and it is just surprising that Paine, with his remarkable sense of irony, did not go on to suggest that kings should also be shorn of their claws! Individuals are often gullible, but it is useful to reflect that whole communities can also be affected, many accepting the myth unquestioningly, while the wiser, and the agnostics, will use the situation for their own ends. A gullible community is a malleable people.

Monarchy the Master Fraud

"When extraordinary power and extraordinary pay are allotted to any individual, in a government, he becomes the centre, round which every kind of corruption generates and forms. Give to any man a million a year, and add thereto the power of creating and disposing of places, at the expense of a country, and the liberties of that country are no longer secure. What is called the spleandour of a throne is no other than the corruption of the state. It is made up of a band of parasites, living in luxurious indolence, out of the public taxes."

"When once a vicious system becomes established it becomes the guard and protection of all inferior abuses. The man who is in receipt of a million a year is the last person to promote a spirit of reform, lest, in the event, it should reach to himself. It is always his interest to defend inferior abuses, as so many outworks to protect the citadel; and in this species of political fortification, all the parts have such a common dependence that it is never to be expected they will attack each other."

"Monarchy would not have continued so many ages in the world, had it not been for the abuses it protects. It is the master-fraud which shelters all others. By admitting a participation of the spoil, it makes itself friends; and when it ceases to do this, it will cease to be the idol of courtiers."

(pp.225–6)

Monarchy has continued for many ages in the world and throughout the Judaeo-Christian tradition, in spite of Samuel's warning to the rebellious Jews, quoted by Paine in his *Common Sense.* If Christian monarchs and their spiritual advisers had taken more note of scripture we should never have heard the expression "Most Christian Majesty" which in Samuel's book is a contradiction in terms. Now Paine has a further lesson to teach on:

The Social Evils of Monarchical Government

"When in countries that are called civilised, we see age going to the workhouse and youth to the gallows, something must be wrong in the system of government. It would seem, by the exterior appearances of such countries, that all was happiness; but there lies hidden from the eye of common observation, a mass of wretchedness that has scarcely any other chance, than to expire in poverty and infamy. Its entrance into life is marked with the presage of its fate; and until this is remedied it is in vain to punish."

"Civil government does not consist in executions; but in making that provision for the instruction of youth, and the support of age, as to exclude, as much as possible, profligacy from one and despair from the other. Instead of this the resources of a country are lavished upon kings, upon courts, upon hirelings, imposters, and prostitutes; and even the poor themselves, with all their wants upon them, are compelled to support the fraud that oppresses them."

"Why is it that scarcely any are executed but the poor? The fact is a proof, among other things, of a wretchedness in their condition. Bred up without morals, and cast upon the world without a prospect they are the exposed sacrifice of vice and legal barbarity. The millions that are superfluously wasted upon governments, are more than sufficient to reform those evils, and to benefit the condition of every man in a nation, not included within the purlieus of a court."

(p.240)

As monarchy appeared to be flourishing, but was in fact failing, during the 19th century, these evils which Paine presents so starkly, were further stressed by novelists like Charles Dickens, Elizabeth Gaskell, Victor Hugo, and others. It is easy to be cynical, to say that nothing much has changed, and point to the autocratic tyrants that have reared up in parts of Africa, South East Asia, South America, and other Third World countries, but there have been major improvements as well, many of which would gladden the hearts of Tom Paine and his friends. The great need now is to ensure that these improvements will be maintained and spread to those nations which are at present greatly deprived. A new Paine is needed today to add further chapters to his *Rights of Man*, to deal with the large supranational corporations, and their ruthless barons, especially those engaged directly, or indirectly in the arms trade. Small nations are extremely vulnerable to these giants, and even large powerful nations can be overawed. While they dominate we shall never exorcise the ghosts of monarchy, Roman Empire, Holy Roman Empire, or the many other tyrannies of ages past. Paine takes up again his theme of:

The Overpaid Monarch

"It signifies a nominal office of a million sterling a year, the business of which consists in receiving the money. Whether the person be wise or foolish, sane or insane, a native or a foreigner, matters not. Every ministry acts upon the same idea that Mr Burke writes, namely, that the people must be hoodwinked, and held in superstitious ignorance by some bugbear or other; and what is called the crown answers this purpose, and therefore it answers all the purposes to be expected from it. . . . The hazard to which this office is exposed in all countries, is not from anything that can happen to the man, but from what may happen to the nation – the danger of its coming to its senses!"

(p.251)

We might wonder what Paine would make of the knowledge that the British crown has survived two centuries on, when others have expired; and also what he would make of the dramatic changes following the great fire at Windsor: a Queen paying taxes, a palace opened to paying visitors, the scrapping of a royal yacht, and what next? He would certainly have some pithy comments. He had some harsh comments on *war* as a direct consequence of monarchy, though we well know that going to war is not the exclusive prerogative of kings. Europe experienced 'a war to end all wars' at the beginning of this present century, but as the century closes and a new millennium is upon us there appear to be more wars, all at once, than the world has ever before experienced, for a variety of reasons and generated by a variety of different agencies, the universal arms trade probably having more to answer for than any other. Paine's comments on **Warmongers** were as follows:

"It will perhaps be said that though the power of *declaring war* descends in the heritage of the conquest, it is held in check by the right of parliament to withhold the supplies. It will always happen, when a thing is originally wrong, that amendments do not make it right; and it often happens, that they do as much mischief one way as good the other. . . ."

"On this question of *war*, three things are to be considered. First, the *right* of declaring it: Secondly, the *expense* of supporting it: Thirdly, the mode of conducting it after it is declared. The French constitution places the right where the *expense* must fall, and this union can be only in the nation. The mode of conducting it after it is declared, it consigns to the executive department. – Were this the case in all countries we should hear but little more of wars."

(pp.100-1)

This fine theory does not really hold up in view of experience since that time, but the argument continues further on at another level.

"Whatever is the cause of taxes to a Nation, becomes also the means of revenue to a government. Every war terminates with an addition of taxes, and consequently with an addition of revenue; and in any event of war, in the manner they are now commenced and concluded, the power and interest of governments are increased. War, therefore, from its productiveness, as it easily furnishes the pretence of necessity for taxes and appointments to places and offices, becomes a principal part of the system of old Governments; and to establish any mode to abolish war, however advantageous it might be to Nations, would be to take from such government the most lucrative of its branches. The frivolous matters upon which war is made, show the disposition and avidity of Governments to uphold the system of war, and betray the motives on which they act."

"As war is the system of Government on the old construction, the animosity which Nations reciprocally entertain is nothing more than what the policy of their Governments excites, to keep up the spirit of the system. Each Government accuses the other of perfidy, intrigue, and ambition, as a means of heating the imagination of their respective Nations, and incensing them to hostilities. Man is not the enemy of man, but through the medium of a false system of Government. Instead therefore of exclaiming against the ambition of Kings, the exclamation should be directed against the principle of such Governments; and instead of seeking to reform the individual, the wisdom of a Nation should apply itself to reform the system."

(pp.167–8)

At first glance this may appear to be letting Monarchy off the hook, but in fact what Paine is discussing here is what he refers to elsewhere as *Mixed Government* or, in other words, **Constitutional Monarchy**. Having contrasted true representative government with government by hereditary succession he goes on to comment:

"As . . . each of these forms acts on a different base, the one moving freely by the aid of reason, the other by ignorance, we have next to consider, what it is that gives motion to that species of Government which is called a mixed Government . . . (and which) is an imperfect everything, cementing and soldering the discordant parts together by corruption, to act as a whole."

(p.162)

And now again the Utopian vision shines through when he suggests:

"From what we now see, nothing of reform in the political world ought to be held improbable. It is an age of Revolutions, in which everything may be looked for. The intrigue of Courts, by which the system of war is kept up, may provoke a confederation of Nations to abolish it: and an European Congress, to patronise the progress of free Government, and promote the civilisation of Nations with each other, is an event nearer in probability, than once were the Revolutions and Alliance of France and America."

(pp.168–9)

Statue of Paine at Morristown.

Prophetic words, but how much longer it has all taken than Paine might have predicted and how imperfect is the achievement so far. Nevertheless, reflecting on his sentiments, we must be grateful that the *League of Nations* was a sequel to the First World War, and though it failed dismally when the Second followed so soon, in its turn this was succeeded by the more powerful *United Nations Organisation* which, though far from perfect, has had many positive achievements to its credit. It is remarkable that Paine predicted not only this global organisation but also a European Union as well, which, having since arrived, is struggling hard to perfect itself, whilst steadily enlarging its territory and has some worthy achievements to its credit also. He is also right in his appreciation that the great upheavals in America and France, to which he himself was a party, would sooner or later lead on to these greater things. But he had not finished with the topic of **War spawned by Kings;** he returns to it again in Part 2 of his *Rights of Man*.

"All the monarchical governments are military. War is their trade, plunder and revenue their objects. While such governments continue, peace has not the absolute security of a day. What is the history of monarchical governments, but a disgustful picture of human wretchedness, and the accidental respite of a few years repose? Wearied with war, and tired with human butchery, they sat down to rest, and called it peace. This certainly is not the condition that Heaven intended for man; and if *this be monarchy*, well might monarchy be reckoned among the sins of the Jews."

"The revolutions which formerly took place in the world, had nothing in them that interested the bulk of mankind. They extended only to a change of persons and measures, but not of principles, and rose or fell among the common transactions of the moment."

(p.183)

Paine has one final reflection on monarchy and this comes in the contrast he has observed with the American Presidency.

"As to Mr Burke, he is a stickler for monarchy . . . (but) with respect to America, he has been very complimentary. He has always contended, at least in my hearing, that the people of America, were more enlightened than those of England, or of any country in Europe; and that therefore the imposition of show was not necessary in their governments."

(p.196)

"The President of the United States of America is elected only for four years. He is not only responsible in the general sense of the word, but a particular mode is laid down in the constitution for trying him. He cannot be elected under 35 years of age; and he must be a native of the country."

(p.226)

Then a personal tribute to Paine himself, in a letter from George Washington, the first president:

Rocky-Hill,
September 10th, 1783,

I have learned since I have been at this place that you are at Borden-Town. Whether for the sake of retirement or economy, I know not. Be it for either, for both, or whatever it may, if you will come to this place and partake with me, I shall be exceedingly happy to see you at it. Your presence may remind Congress of your past services to this country; and if it is in my power to impress them, command my best exertions with freedom, as they will be rendered cheerfully by one, who entertains a lively sense of the importance of your works, and who, with much pleasure, subscribes himself,

your sincere friend,
G. Washington.
(p.243)

America's republic has not, nor does not always, cover itself with glory, but its constitution has, at least, protected it from the worst excesses of monarchy. Heredity is another matter, and dynasties do arise even in republics, though they are less likely to be for long continued in power.

CHAPTER VIII

The Hereditary Element

A ruffian like Henry VIII talked as gravely about the divine powers vested in him, as if he had been an inspired prophet. A wretch like James I not only believed that there was in himself a particular sanctity but other people believed him.

Thackeray's 'Book of Snobs'

HEREDITY HAS BEEN TOUCHED ON MANY TIMES ALREADY IN PASSAGES QUOTED, but there are others even more specific which should be grouped together for continuity:

Civil Wars provoked by Kings

"The civil wars which have originated from contested hereditary claims, are more numerous, and have been more dreadful, and of longer continuance, than those which have been occasioned by election. All the civil wars in France arose from the hereditary system; they were either produced by hereditary claims, or by the imperfection of the hereditary form, which admits of regencies, or monarchy at nurse. With respect to England, its history is full of the same misfortunes. The contest for the succession between the houses of York and Lancaster, lasted a whole century; and others of a similar nature, have renewed themselves since that period. Those of 1715 and 1745 were of the same kind. The succession war for the crown of Spain, embroiled almost half Europe. . . . A government calling itself free, with an hereditary office, is like a thorn in the flesh that produces a fermentation which endeavours to discharge it.'

(Rights of Man, pp.196–7)

"Admitting that Government is a contrivance of human *wisdom*, it must necessarily follow, that hereditary succession and hereditary rights (as they are called), can make no part of it, because it is impossible to make wisdom hereditary; and on the other hand, that cannot be a wise contrivance, which in its operation may commit the government of a nation to the wisdom of an idiot." . . .

"Who is the wisest man? (Mr Burke) must now show that everyone in the line of hereditary succession was a Solomon, or his title is not good to be a king. – What a stroke has Mr Burke now made! To use a sailor's phrase, he has *swabbed the deck*, and scarcely left a name legible in the list of Kings; and he has mowed down and thinned the House of Peers, with a scythe as formidable as Death and Time."

"But Mr Burke appears to have been aware of this retort; and he has taken care to guard against it, by making government to be not only a *contrivance* of human wisdom, but a *monopoly* of wisdom. He puts the nation as fools on one side, and places his government of wisdom, all wise men of Gotham, on the other side; and then proclaims, and says, that *Men have a RIGHT that their WANTS should be provided for by this wisdom'*. Having thus made proclamation, he next proceeds to explain to them what their *wants* are, and also what their *rights* are. In this he succeeds dexterously, for he makes their *wants* to be a *want* of wisdom; but as this is but cold comfort, he then informs them that they have a *right* (not to any of the wisdom) but to be governed by it and in order to impress them with a solemn reverence for this monopoly – government of wisdom, and of its vast capacity for all purposes, possible or impossible, right or wrong, he proceeds with astrological mysterious importance, to tell them of its powers, in these words – 'The Rights of men in government are their advantages, and these are often in balances between differences of good; and in compromises sometimes between *good* and *evil*, and sometimes between *evil* and *evil*."

(pp.138–9)

Then, bringing forward the way in which Burke appears to have changed his stance within a short time, Paine declares:

"Hard as Mr Burke laboured the Regency Bill and Hereditary Succession two years ago, and much as he dived for precedents, he still had not boldness to bring up William of Normandy, and say,'There is the head of the list! There is the fountain of honour! The son of a prostitute, and the plunderer of the English nation."

(p.140)

"Mr Burke talks about what he calls an hereditary crown, as if it were some production of Nature; or as if, like Time, it had a power to operate, not only independently, but in spite of man; or as if it were a thing or a subject universally consented to. Alas! it has none of those properties, but is the reverse of them all. It is a thing in imagination, the propriety of which is more than doubted, and the legality of which in a few years will be denied."

"But, to arrange this matter in a clearer view than what general expressions can convey, it will be necessary to state the distinct head under which (what is called) an hereditary crown, or more properly speaking, an hereditary succession to the government of a Nation, can be considered; which are,

"First, The Right of a particular Family to establish itself.

Secondly. The Right of a Nation to establish a particular Family.

With respect to the *first* of these heads, . . . all men will concur in calling it despotism; and it would be trespassing on their understanding to attempt to prove it.

But the *second* head, that of a Nation establishing a particular Family with *hereditary powers,* does not present itself as despotism on the first reflection; but if men will permit a second reflection to take place, and carry that reflection forward but one remove out of their own persons to that of their offspring, they will then see that hereditary succession becomes in its consequences the same despotism to others, which they reprobated for themselves. It operates to preclude the consent of the succeeding generation; and the preclusion of consent is despotism. When the person, who at any time shall be in possession of a Government, or those who stand in succession to him shall say to a Nation, I hold this power in 'contempt' of you, it signifies not on what authority he pretends to say it. It is no relief, but an aggravation, to a person in slavery, to reflect that he was sold by his parent; and as that which heightens the criminality of an act cannot be produced to prove the legality of it, hereditary succession cannot be established as a legal thing."

". . . Hereditary succession is out of the question with respect to the *first* generation, (so) we have now to consider the character in which *that* generation acts with respect to the commencing generation, and to all succeeding ones."

"It assumes a character, to which it had neither right nor title. It changes itself from a legislator to a testator, and affects to make its Will, which is to have operation after the demise of the makers, to bequeath the Government; and it not only attempts to bequeath, but to establish on the succeeding generation, a new and different form of government under which itself lived. . . . It now attempts, by virtue of a will and testament, . . . to take from the commencing generation, and all future ones, the rights and free agency by which itself acted.

(pp.144–5)

Paine's style is very different from that of Burke, but when he moves into the legal mode, he is as verbose as any of that craft. However, this theme of heredity is the one which most excites him and so he must be allowed some free rein. Nevertheless, it will be observed that a modicum of pruning has been employed; but he is not yet spent:

"All hereditary government is in its nature tyranny. An heritable crown, or . . . throne, or by whatever fancy name such things maybe called, have no other significant explanation than that mankind are heritable property. To inherit a government is to inherit the people, as if they were flocks and herds."

"Government ought to be a thing always in full maturity. It ought to be so constructed as to be superior to all the accidents to which individual man is subject; and therefore, hereditary succession, by being *subject to them all*, is the most irregular and imperfect of all systems of government."

(p.194)

"Would we make any office hereditary that required wisdom and abilities to fill it? And where wisdom and abilities are not necessary, such an office, whatever it may be, is superfluous or insignificant. Hereditary succession is a burlesque upon monarchy. It puts it in the most ridiculous light, by presenting it as an office which any child or idiot may fill. It requires some talents to be a common mechanic; but to be a king requires only the animal figure of man – a sort of breathing automaton. This sort of superstition may last a few years more, but it cannot long resist the awakened reason and interest of man."!

(p.196)

"Experience, in all ages, and in all countries has demonstrated that it is impossible to control Nature in her distribution of mental powers. . . . Whatever is the rule by which she . . . scatters them among mankind, that rule remains a secret to man. It would be as ridiculous to attempt to fix the hereditaryship of human beauty as of wisdom. Whatever wisdom constituently is, it is like a seedless plant; it may be reared when it appears, but it cannot be produced. There is always a sufficiency somewhere in the general mass of society for all purposes; but with respect to the parts of society, it is continually changing its place. . . . The hereditary system is, therefore, as repugnant to human wisdom as to human right; and is as absurd as it is unjust. . . ."

"How irrational the hereditary system which establishes channels of power, in company with which wisdom refuses to flow! By continuing this absurdity, man is perpetually in contradiction with himself; he accepts for a king, or a chief magistrate, or a legislator, a person whom he would not elect for a constable.

"It appears to general observation that revolutions create genius and talents; but those events do no more than bring them forward. There is existing in man, a mass of sense lying in a dormant state, and which, unless something excites it to action, will descend with him, in that condition, to the grave."

(pp.197–8)

It might be objected that Paine did not have the scientific knowledge of heredity which we now possess and which is still growing, but this would not greatly affect his case. We all know that the same parents will regularly produce children who are quite differently endowed, and even if one or more is outstandingly clever, it will not necessarily be the eldest, or the eldest male, and so Paine would tell us that the system which he is criticising is still hamstrung by primogeniture. His point about hidden talent recalls the lines from Gray's *Elegy in a Country Churchyard:* "Some mute inglorious Milton here may rest". Nature is profligate of talent: "Full many a flower is born to blush unseen and waste its sweetness on the desert air". Regarding the opposite side of the coin again, Paine has some points to make on failings which arise in individuals who inherit monarchy:

> "When we see that nature acts as if she disowned and sported with the hereditary system; that the mental character of successors, in all countries, are below the average of human understanding; that one is a tyrant, another an idiot, a third insane, and some all three together, it is impossible to attach confidence to it, when reason in man has power to act."
>
> *(p.195)*

> "That which is called government, or rather that which we ought to conceive government to be, is no more than some common centre in which all the parts of society unite. This cannot be accomplished by any method so conducive to the various interests of the community, as by the representative system. It concentrates the knowledge necessary to the interest of the parts, and of the whole. It places government in a state of constant maturity. It is, as has been already observed, never young, never old. It is subject neither to nonage, or dotage. It is never in the cradle, nor on crutches. It admits not of separation between knowledge and power, and is superior, as government always ought to be, to all the accidents of individual man, and is therefore superior to what is called monarchy."
>
> *(p.203)*

Here he points up the usual human defects and deficiencies, to which all flesh is heir, and which as he argues, frequently make a nonsense of inherited monarchy. History is full of examples and, in fact, there are more poorly endowed, weak or positively vicious kings than there are any outstandingly good. We need go no farther than the Old Testament which Paine has cited earlier, to the two Books of Kings and the Chronicles; it is all there. His next problem is the under-age monarch, together with regency for this or any other cause:

> "The question of Regency was a question of a million a year, which is appropriated to the executive department: and Mr Pitt could not possess himself of any management of this sum, without setting up the supremacy of parliament; and when this was accomplished it was indifferent who should be Regent, as he must be Regent at his own cost. Among the curiosities which this contentious debate afforded, was that of making the Great Seal into a King; the affixing of which to an act, was to be royal authority. If, therefore, Royal Authority is a Great Seal, it consequently is in itself nothing; and a good Constitution would be of infinitely more

value to the Nation, than what the three Nominal Powers, as they now stand, are worth."

(pp.152–3)

This, of course, concerns the crisis precipitated by the mental illness of George III, which caused a considerable stir in parliament, fortunately relieved, when the king unexpectedly recovered, but what Paine was saying underlined the fragile and false nature of things in Britain, lacking a clear and logical constitution such as America acquired for itself when it broke away. But there were other potential risks and Paine addresses these also:

". . . The only system to which the word *levelling* is truly applicable is the hereditary monarchical system. It is a system of *mental levelling*. It indiscriminately admits every species of character to the same authority. Vice and virtue, ignorance and wisdom, in short, every quality, good or bad, is put on the same level. Kings succeeding each other, not as rational, but as animals. It signifies not what their mental or moral characters are. Can we then be surprised at the abject state of the human mind in monarchical countries, when the government itself is formed on such an abject levelling system? – It has no fixed character. Today it is one thing; tomorrow it is something else. It changes with the temper of every succeeding individual, and is subject to all the varieties of each. It is government through the medium of passions and accidents. It appears under all the various characters of childhood, decrepitude, dotage, a thing at nurse, in leading-strings, or in crutches. It reverses the wholesome order of nature. It occasionally puts children over men, and the conceits of nonage over wisdom and experience."

(pp.194–5)

In this last sentence, it would seem that Paine is overstating his case; surely the danger arises, not from a child being put in charge, but from those who gain control of that child, during a regency. There is always a temptation, when absolute power is acquired temporarily, to abuse it. It is not the conceits of the child that will over-ride wisdom and experience, but those of the regent; but however expressed, Paine is stressing a problem which is well known to have led to trouble throughout history; he uses mockery and irony to make his point:

"A regency is a mock species of republic, and the whole of monarchy deserves no better description. . . . It has none of the stable character that government ought to possess. Every succession is a revolution, and every regency a counter-revolution. . . . To render monarchy consistent with government the next in succession should not be born a child, but a man at once, and that man a Solomon. It is ridiculous that nations are to wait, and government be interrupted, till boys grow to be men."

(p.204)

Next, Paine contrasts the American Presidency with Monarchy in regard to age limit and basic qualifications:

"In the American federal government, more power is delegated to the President of the United States, than to any other individual member of Congress. He cannot, therefore, be elected to this office under the age of 35 years. By this time the judgement of man becomes matured, and he has lived long enough to be acquainted with men and things, and the country with him. – But on the monarchical plan . . . the next in succession, whatever he may be, is put at the head of a nation, and a government at 18 years. Does this appear like an act of wisdom? Is it consistent with the proper dignity and manly character of a nation? Where is the propriety of calling such a lad the father of the people? In all other cases, a person is a minor until the age of 21 years. Before this period, he is not trusted with the management of an acre of land, or with the heritable property of a flock of sheep, or an herd of swine; but, wonderful to tell! he may, at the age of 18 years, be trusted with a nation."

(p.205)

Turning next to particular application in the case of British monarchy, Paine's own special bête noir is William the Conqueror and he is not prepared to give him or his administration any credit, not allowing that England was far from being an Anglo-Saxon kingdom, weak and waiting to be conquered; much of it was or had been in the recent past under Scandinavian domination, and the Normans had been peacefully infiltrating the land before the Conquest; King Edward himself having a Norman mother and a Norman upbringing.* England was not truly a nation, but an assortment of smaller kingdoms with varied rulers, like many other parts of Europe, destined in time to become nation states. This was a process of evolution bound to proceed; in England it was facilitated and brought forward by the Normans, albeit in a ruthless and often oppressive manner. Perhaps this phase in evolution could best be achieved under a monarch, but Tom Paine would not be convinced; his basic reaction has already been noted above *(Rights, p.190)* and he develops the point later:

"If we begin with William of Normandy, we find that the government of England was originally a tyranny, founded on an invasion and conquest of the country. This being admitted, it will then appear, that the exertion of the nation, at different periods, to abate that tyranny, and render it less intolerable, has been credited for a constitution."

"Magna Carta . . . was not more than compelling the government to renounce a part of its assumptions. It did not create and give powers to a government in the manner a constitution does; but was, as far as it went, of the nature of re-conquest, and not of a constitution; for could the

---

* G. M. Trevelyan, *History of England*, Book I, Chap. VII.

nation have totally expelled the usurpation, as France has done its despotism, it would then have had a constitution to form."

"The history of the Edwards and the Henries, and up to the commencement of the Stuarts, exhibits as many instances of tyranny as could be acted within the limits to which the nation had restricted it. The Stuarts endeavoured to pass those limits and their fate is well known. In all those instances we see nothing of a constitution, but only of restrictions on assumed power."

(pp.214–5)

These points are well taken, especially in the first paragraph where he highlights the exertion of the nation, at different periods, to abate royal tyranny, this being credited for a constitution. Here he is explaining the evolution of constitutional monarchy, as it was successively pruned back by parliament during the Stuart period, followed by the Dutch and then the Hanoverian. But Paine has further comments which reflect more directly on William himself and the style of his administration:

". . . A race of conquerors arose, whose government, like that of William the Conqueror, was founded in power, and the sword assumed the name of a sceptre. Governments, thus established, last as long as the power to support them lasts; but that they might avail themselves of every engine in their favour, they united fraud to force and set up an idol which they called *Divine Right*, and which, in imitation of the Pope, who affects to be spiritual and temporal, and in contradiction to the founder of the Christian religion, twisted itself afterwards into an idol of another shape, called *Church and State*. The key of St. Peter and the key of the Treasury, became quarted on one another, and the wondering cheated multitude worshipped the invention."!

(p.92)

Paine's images are powerfully drawn, and any literary being, whether agreeing with him or not, must envy him that concluding phrase. He follows on:

"The English government is one of those which arose out of a conquest, and not out of society, and consequently it arose over the people; and though it has been much modified from the opportunity of circumstances, from the time of William the Conqueror, the country has never yet regenerated itself, and is therefore without a constitution."

(p.94)

We must keep it clearly in our minds that Paine is harking back to his recent experience in America, an experience in which he himself played no small part. He is also focusing on developments in France, which lead on to his next comment:

"When the question on the right of war and peace was agitating in the National Assembly, the people of England appeared to be much interested in the event, and highly to applaud the decision. – As a principle, it applied as much to one country as to another. William the Conqueror, as a *conqueror,* held this power of war and peace in himself, and his descendants have ever since claimed it under him as a right."

(p.100)

Turning now to the so-called *Great and Glorious Revolution* of 1688, we get some of Paine's thoughts on its deficiencies, beginning with Edmund Burke's comment on Dr. Price's sermon at the Old Jewry:

"Mr Burke, speaking of this sermon, says,'The political Divine proceeds dogmatically to assert, that by the principles of the Revolution, the people of England have acquired three fundamental rights:

1.To choose our own governors;
2.To cashier them for misconduct;
3.To frame a a government for ourselves'

Dr. Price does not say that the right to do these things exists in this or in that person, or in this or in that description of persons, but that it exists in the *whole;* that it is a right resident in the nation. – Mr Burke, on the contrary, denies that such a right exists in the nation, either in whole or in part, or that it exists anywhere; and, what is still more strange and marvellous, he says, 'that the people of England utterly disclaim such a right, and that they will resist the practical assertion of it with their lives and fortunes'. That men should take up arms, and spend their lives and fortunes, *not* to maintain their rights, but to maintain that they have *not* rights, is an entirely new species of discovery, and suited to the paradoxical genius of Mr Burke."

(p.62)

Paine goes on to tell us that Burke bases his argument on the notion that the persons, or generation of persons, in whom they did exist, are dead and with them the right is dead also. Burke is basing this, not entirely without logic, on a declaration made by parliament to William and Mary, binding the people together with: "Our heirs, and our posterity, to them, their heirs, and their posterity, to the end of time". The question is not whether such a contract was made, but whether either side ever had the right to make it, either in law, or in common sense? He goes on to remind us that Burke has further said: "That if the people of England possessed such a right before the Revolution," (which he acknowledges to have been the case, not only in England, but throughout Europe, at an earlier period) "yet that the *English Nation* did, at the time of the *Revolution,* most solemnly renounce and abdicate it, for themselves, and for *all their posterity, for ever'.* Paine concludes:

"There never did, there never will, and there never can exist a parliament, or any description of men, or any generation of men, in any country, possessed of the right or the power of binding and controlling posterity to the end of time."

(p.63)

"In the address of the English Parliaments to their Kings, we see neither the intrepid spirit of the old Parliaments of France, nor the serene dignity of the present National Assembly; neither do we see in them anything of the style of English manners, which border somewhat on bluntness. Since then they are neither of foreign extraction, nor naturally of English production, their origin must be sought for elsewhere, and that origin is the Norman Conquest. They are evidently of the vassalage class of manners, and emphatically mark the prostrate distance that exists in no other condition of men than between the conqueror and the conquered. That this vassalage idea and style of speaking was not got rid of even at the Revolution of 1688, is evident from the declaration of parliament to him and Mary in these words: 'We do most humbly and faithfully submit ourselves, our heirs and posterities for ever'. Submission is wholly a vassalage term, repugnant to the dignity of freedom, an echo of the language used at the Conquest."

(pp.112–3)

It is interesting that Paine, who was an eye witness, should refer to "the serene dignity" of the French National Assembly, since this is not the kind of image we get from most commentators, who were not themselves present. Again it is necessary to remind ourselves that this was the early and best phase of the Revolution, albeit the phase that provoked Burke's *Reflections*, and to ponder again the problem of why the movement went sour: was it basically due to internal causes, or to what extent did external forces help to bring it about?

"When Mr Burke attempts to maintain that the *English Nation did at the Revolution of 1688, most solemnly renounce and abdicate their right for themselves, and for all their posterity forever*, he speaks a language that merits not reply, and which can only excite contempt for his prostitute principles, or pity for his ignorance."

(p.146)

Paine was voted a member of the French Legislative Assembly, in which he took some part, but had Britain had a truly representative parliament, instead of the weakly constituted body which was the House of Commons at that time, there can be little doubt that he would have been voted a member thereof and that a number of constituencies would have been vying to elect him. Chief among these would have been the growing towns where the Industrial Revolution was beginning to blossom, but which in spite of their size were still disenfranchised at that time, among them would have been Manchester, Birmingham and Sheffield. Had this been the position, Tom Paine would have been able to argue his views in parliament; but the establishment of that period would have been greatly embarrassed and irritated. The outcome would have been most interesting; they could scarcely have sidelined him in the way they did John Wilkes before him and William Cobbett right up to 1832.

When Part II of *Rights of Man* was published in February 1792, the establishment was outraged; in May the government began proceedings against the publisher; then, a week later, a Royal Proclamation was issued against 'wicked sedition writings printed, published, and industriously dispersed'. On the same day a summons was served on Paine at his lodgings; Free Speech was in shackles and the concept of 'seditious libel' reigned. This was a mighty instrument used to great effect on other liberal thinkers, but Paine's trial instead of taking place in June was postponed until December. Was the establishment running scared? The man had his own agenda and a busy life to live; he was invited to Paris and was there at the year's end when he was declared an outlaw; he never again returned to England. But we are not finished with his musings; there are still Britain's other foreign kings that come after the Conqueror. Still on the Revolution of 1688 he had this to say:

> "Mankind will scarcely believe that a country calling itself free, would send to Holland for a man, and clothe him with power, on purpose to put themselves in fear of him, and give him almost a million sterling a year for leave to submit themselves and their posterity, like bond-men and bond-women forever."
>
> *(p.113)*

Edmund Burke has been railing against the English Revolution Society, saying that the King holds his crown in contempt of their choice, since they do not have 'a single vote for a King among them either individually or collectively'. Paine retorts:

> "It is not the Revolution Society that Mr Burke means; it is the Nation, as well in its *original*, as in its representative character. . . . The Society is composed of citizens of all denominations, and of members of both Houses of Parliament; and consequently, if there is not a right to vote in any of the characters, there can be no right to any, either in the nation, or in its parliament. This ought to be a caution to every country, how it imports foreign families to be kings. It is somewhat curious to observe, that although the people of England have been in the habit of talking about kings, it is always a Foreign House of Kings, hating foreigners, yet governed by them. – It is now the House of Brunswick, one of the petty tribes of Germany."
>
> *(pp.141 –2)*

> "Government with insolence is despotism; but when contempt is added it is worse; and to pay for contempt is the excess of slavery. This species of government comes from Germany; and reminds me of what one of the Brunswick soldiers told me, who was taken prisoner by the Americans in the late war: 'Ah!' said he, 'America is a fine free country, it is worth the people's fighting for; I know the difference by knowing my own: in my country, if the Prince says: Eat straw, we eat straw.' God help that country, thought I, be it England or elsewhere, whose liberties are to be protected by German principles of government, and Princes of Brunswick."
>
> *(p.143)*

"The wisdom of every country, when properly exerted, is sufficient for all its purposes; and there could exist no more real occasion in England to have sent for a Dutch Stadtholder, or a German Elector, than there was in America to have done a similar thing. If a country does not understand its own affairs, how is a foreigner to understand them, who knows neither its language, its laws, nor its manners? . . . If I ask a man in America, if he wants a King he retorts, and asks me if I take him for an idiot?"

(p.147)

"When the people of England sent for George the First . . . they ought at least to have conditioned for the abandonment of Hanover. Besides the endless German intrigues that must follow from a German Elector being King of England, there is a natural impossibility of uniting in the same person the principles of Freedom and the principles of Despotism, or as it is usually called in England Arbitrary Power. A German Elector is in his electorate a despot: How then could it be expected that he should be attached to principles of liberty in our country, while his interest in another was to be supported by despotism? The union cannot exist; and it might easily have been foreseen, that German Electors would make German Kings, or in Mr Burke's words, would assume government with 'contempt'. The English have been in the habit of considering a King of England only in the character in which he appears to them: whereas the same person, while the connexion lasts, has a home seat in another country, the interest of which is different to their own, and the principles of the governments in opposition to each other – To such a person England will appear as a town-residence, and the Electorate as the estate. The English may wish, as I believe they do, success to the principles of Liberty in France, or in Germany; but a German Elector trembles for the fate of despotism in his electorate: and the Duchy of Mecklenburg, where the present Queen's family governs, is under the same wretched state of arbitrary power, and the people in slavish vassalage."

"There never was a time when it became the English to watch continental intrigues more circumspectly than at the present moment, and to distinguish the politics of the Electorate, from the politics of the Nation. The Revolution of France has entirely changed the ground with respect to England and France as nations: but the German despots with Prussia at their head, are combining against Liberty; and the fondness of Mr Pitt for office, and the interest which all his family connexions have obtained, do not give sufficient security against this intrigue."

(pp.148–9)

This is strong talk, and Paine, who was usually well informed must have been confident of his facts to be so outspoken. After all, he was risking his own reputation, and if he had come to trial, a lot more besides. He was too shrewd an operator to take such risks, unless he was sure of himself; the state could have brought him to trial in June, and held him in custody pending trial. The very fact that they did not choose to do so, suggests that they did not wish to explore in court many of the issues which he had brought forward in his writings. Even at almost eighty years on from its accession, the Hanoverian establishment and its English supporters would not have welcomed close scrutiny in public against such a forthright and capable adversary, as we may judge from the above rather extensive extracts.

But Paine has more the say of foreign monarchs in Part II of his *Rights of Man* which was not published until February 1792, about a year after the first part and when further significant events had taken place both in France and in England. This was not just an academic debate about issues long since concluded, it was dialogue conducted against a fast moving current activity between men with rival views and a stake in the outcome. He returns to the dynastic upheavals of 1688 and 1714.

"The act, called the Bill of Rights comes here into view. What is it but a bargain, which the parts of government made with each other to divide powers, profits and privileges? You shall have so much, and I will have the rest; and with respect to the nation, it is said, for *your share*, you *shall have the right of petitioning*. This being the case, the bill of rights is more properly a bill of wrongs, and of insult. As to what is called the convention parliament, it was a thing that made itself, and then made the authority by which it acted. A few persons got together and called themselves by that name. Several of them had never been elected and none of them for that purpose."

(p.215)

"In England the person who exercises prerogative is often a foreigner; always half a foreigner, and always married to a foreigner. He is never in full natural or political connexion with the country, is not responsible for anything, and comes of age at 18 years; yet such a person is allowed to form foreign alliances, without even the knowledge of the nation, and to make war and peace without its consent."

"But this is not all. Though such a person cannot dispose of the government, in the manner of a testator, he dictates the marriage connections, which in effect, accomplishes a great part of the same end. He cannot directly bequeath half the government to Prussia, but he can form a marriage partnership that will produce almost the same thing . . ."

"The presidency of America . . . is the only office from which a foreigner is excluded, and in England it is the only one to which he is admitted. A foreigner cannot be a member of parliament, but he may be what is called a king. If there is any reason for excluding foreigners, it ought to be from those offices where mischief can most be acted."

(p.227)

"With the revolution of 1688, and more since the Hanover succession, came the destructive system of continental intrigues, and the rage for foreign wars, and foreign dominion; systems of such secure mystery that the expenses admit of no accounts; a single line standing for millions. To what excess taxation might have extended had not the French Revolution contributed to break up the system, and put an end to pretences, is impossible to say."

(pp.253–4)

Paine writes as if he believes that most of these evils he is describing are already consigned to the past, or shortly so to be. How surprised he would have been, had he known that, more than a century later, in fact right up to the 1st World War, Europe's leading monarchs, such as the Kaiser, the Czar, the King of Great Britain (all blood relatives) would hold private and secret meetings, without reference to any parliament (by Divine Right?) and make decisions with far reaching consequences for their own and other nations. He is concerned at the cost of monarchy to the nation, in simple monetary terms:

"It has cost England almost seventy millions sterling, to maintain a family imported from abroad, of very inferior capacity to thousands in the nation; and scarcely a year has passed that has not produced some new mercenary application. Even the physicians bills have been sent to the public to be paid. No wonder the jails have been crowded, and taxes and poor rates increased. Under such systems nothing is to be looked for, but what has already happened; and as to the reformation whenever it come, it must be from the nation, and not from the government."

(p.259)

Paine intones a final farewell for monarchy; it combines irony with mockery; it is prophetic, but again, it would have amazed him to know how long it would take for this prophecy to come fully to pass. Recent crises for that institution have given rise to renewed public awareness, and certainly to a growing interest in the media of communication, which may presage fundamental changes in the not too distant future. Here comes the dismissal:

"The fraud, hypocrisy, and imposition of governments, are now beginning to be too well understood to promise them any long career. The farce of monarchy and aristocracy, in all countries, is following that of chivalry, and Mr Burke is dressing for the funeral. Let it pass then quietly to the tomb of all other follies, and the mourners be comforted."

"The time is not very distant when England will laugh at itself for sending to Holland, Hanover, Zell, or Brunswick for men, at the expense of a million a year, who understood neither her laws, her language, not her interests, and whose capacities would scarcely have fitted them for the office of a parish constable. If government could be trusted to such hands, it must be some easy and simple thing indeed, and material fit for all the purposes may be found in every town and village in England."

(p.286)

Winston Churchill, whilst he did not totally ignore Tom Paine, can hardly be regarded as one of his particular admirers; yet in this matter of the Hanoverian accession their minds are much in tune. Churchill has a lengthy and scathing paragraph starting his chapter on the House of Hanover:

"During the late Summer of 1714 all England awaited the coming of King George I. On September 18 he landed at Greenwich. This fortunate German prince, who could not speak English, viewed his new realm without enthusiasm. In accepting the throne of the United Kingdom he was conferring, as it seemed to him, a favour upon his new subjects. He was meeting the convenience of English politicians. In return he expected that British power and wealth would be made serviceable to his domains in Hanover and to his larger interests on the European scene. His royal duties would entail exile from home in an island he had only once previously visited and which he did not like. For years past, as heir presumptive, he had attentively watched the factious course of English politics. He had followed distastefully the manoeuvres of the party leaders, without understanding the stresses that gave rise to them or the principles that were at stake. Now on the banks of the Thames he looked about upon the nobles and Ministers who had come to greet him with suspicion and wariness, not unmingled with contempt. Here on English soil stood an unprepossessing figure, an obstinate and humdrum German martinet with dull brains and coarse tastes. As a commander in the late wars he had been sluggish and incompetent, and as a ruler of men he had shown no quickening ability or generosity of spirit. Yet the rigidity of his mind was relieved by a slow shrewdness and a brooding common sense. The British throne was no easy inheritance, especially for a foreign prince. King George took it up grudgingly, and it was ungraciously that he played his allotted part. He owed his crown to the luck of circumstance, but he never let it slip from his grasp."

(W S C, Age of Revolution, p.87)

Churchill has no better opinion of the successor, George II:

". . . Only since the installation of the Hanoverian dynasty had the royal influence been largely exercised by the Whig Ministers in Parliament. Walpole and Newcastle had been much more than Ministers; they were almost Regents. There had been many reasons why they and their supporters had achieved and held such power for nearly half a century. Both George I and George II were aliens in language, outlook, upbringing, and sympathy; the court was predominantly German; their interest and ambitions had centred on Hanover and on the continent of Europe, and they owed their throne to the Whigs. Now all was changed. George III was, or thought he was, an Englishman born and bred. At any rate he tried to be. He had received a careful education in England from his mother, and from the Earl of Bute, who was a Scotsman and in his opponents' eyes a Tory. George's earliest literary achievement is a boyhood essay on Alfred the Great. 'George, be King', his mother had said, according to tradition and George did his best to obey. That he failed in the central problems of his reign may, in the long run of events, have been fortunate for the ultimate liberty of England."

(p.135)

Both Paine and Burke would each, from his own point of view have agreed with this summary. Between George II and George III came Frederick, Prince of Wales, who predeceased his father, leaving the throne to his son; he is notable only for his malign political influence, again according to Churchill: "In 1735 . . . Those Whigs who were out of office grouped themselves around Frederick, the new Prince of Wales. He, in his turn, became the hope of the opposition, but all they could produce was an increased Civil List for this ungifted creature." *(p.99)* "In 1741 . . . under the Septennial Act elections were due. The Prince of Wales spent lavishly in buying up seats, and his campaign . . . brought 27 Cornish seats over to the opposition." *(p.103)* A sad reflection on incipient democracy. "In 1751 Frederick, Prince of Wales, the nominal head of the Opposition, died. Pitt and other young politicians had once entertained great hopes of achieving power when this nonentity should succeed to the throne." *(p.113)* Readers must decide for themselves whether Paine or Churchill had the better assessment of the Hanoverian phenomenon.

Paine was sidelined as rapidly as the establishment could achieve that end; but certainly before the agitation which preceded the Reform Act of 1832, his ideas and ideals were to the fore in the minds of the 'common people'. His views on monarchy were embarrassing, despite the fact that many politicians, in private at least, would have agreed with him. It was other more fundamental issues which they were really anxious to push out of view, such as fair and just representation, together with a thorough overhaul of parliament, and the radical social measures for amelioration of the lot of those citizens less able to fend for themselves. This brought on an acute anxiety state in the minds of legislators and administrators, whose education and thinking had not prepared them for anything of the kind, but who were terrified at what they saw happening in France, while misunderstanding and misinterpreting all the lessons that were there to learn. And who would expect them to learn anything from an ignorant East Anglian staymaker, jumped up to become a tax gatherer. Oh yes, he had emigrated for a time to America, where he had meddled in affairs of state, at quite a high level, in difficult times, but when peace returned the rulers there soon discovered his failings, or for what other reason had he returned again to Europe, except to stir up trouble? It can be only too easy to denigrate an individual with undesired views, once those in power have their target in focus. A ruling clique can be brought to heel by a united and determined opposition, but this was the very element missing at the vital time, because Edmund Burke had split the Whig party, thus making it so much easier for Pitt and his followers, no longer embarrassed by a monarch, now disabled by mental disorder.

Paine has had much to say about imported monarchs, concentrating on the two Williams and the Hanoverian Georges, but is there not a missing link in this story? The Stuarts were uneasy rulers at their best, and orthodox historians would be slow to portray them as foreigners, but they were never truly English.

Scotland was, and still is, in many ways another country, with traditions, customs, laws and a religious affiliation peculiarly unEnglish. Mary Queen of Scots, with her French upbringing and connections, was kept at arms' length and eventually beheaded. Yet her son was soon after imported to occupy Elizabeth's vacant throne. He did his best to adapt himself, but he was no Englishman, and who should know better than that historian from the border lands, G. M. Trevelyan who tells us that: "Not only did England remain *terra incognita* to James, but he never became aware of his ignorance." *(p.383)* His dynasty never really settled down. When trouble brewed the Stuarts instinctively resorted to France and allied themselves with powerful French monarchs, who were far from being England's friends. Not particularly religious themselves, they had a leaning towards Catholicism and again, this tendency was fostered by the French link, although being Scottish they also had Presbyterian sympathies.

A modern historian has encapsulated this Stuart, Scottish-French phenomenon in a particularly interesting and lucid way when he posed the question recently in a lecture at St. James', Piccadilly. (March 1995):

"... In search of explanations more satisfying than certifiable madness in whole populations, where do we start? To get at the tap root of our prejudice we must go back at least to those flames in Smithfield and to their brilliant exploitation in John Foxe's *Book of Martyrs*. Behind that on the far side of the Reformation divide we shall find a deep root in an English xenophobia much commented on by foreigners in the later Middle Ages and either a piece of indigenous and timeless insularity or a particular cultural construct coming out of the Hundred Years' War with France: a xenophobia which expressed itself in forceful derogation and to a lesser extent, of what an Elizabethan bishop called 'the piddling Scots'."

(Prof P. Collinson, Cambridge)

This distrust of the Scots, as clients of France, should never be under-estimated, and do we not have here as well an indication of the virus responsible for our current epidemic of Euroscepticism, together with a powerful rejection of Scottish nationalism?

G.K. Chesterton was another who expressed himself potently on this theme of Scottish identity:

"The Stuarts ... brought from Scotland a more medieval and therefore more logical view of their own function; for the note of their nation was logic. It is a proverb that James I was a Scot and a pedant; it is hardly sufficiently noted that Charles I also was not a little of a pedant, being very much of a Scot. He had also the virtues of a Scot, courage, and a quite natural dignity and an appetite for the things of the mind. Being somewhat Scottish he was very un-English, and could not manage a compromise: he tried instead to split hairs, and seemed merely to break promises."

(Short History, p.171)

Elizabeth's England did not favour continental Protestantism, especially the Genevan variety, but avoided any direct confrontation; they had enough trouble with residual Catholicism, or recusancy, as it was known, and they did not wish to resurrect the problems of Mary's reign. However, as King Canute had realised, so many centuries before, the tide cannot be gainsaid, and Calvin's disciples were gradually infiltrating; reaction centred first on the Earl of Strafford who was beheaded and then on Archbishop Laud who was a doughty Defender of the Faith; stubborn enough to bring about his own downfall and execution. It was probably this, more than any other single factor, which exposed the vulnerability of Charles I, bringing him in turn to the headsman's block.

Like George II, a century later, both of them second generation, in their respective dynasties, neither was as yet truly English, although Charles was more recognisably British. But, now, after the Civil War, it was the Cromwellians who had discovered the weakness of a less than English monarch, who did not have a close relationship with the native aristocracy, let along the squirearchy. During the interregnum of the 1650s, the next generation of Stuarts again became foreigners, residing in France, learning French ways, making alliance with the French monarchy, and being drawn back towards Catholicism, albeit through a weak and corrupt French model.

Parliament had existed for generations in muted form. James I ('the wisest fool in christendom') highlighted his own conception of sovereignty when he observed that: "The state of monarchy is the supremest thing on earth. For kings are not only God's Lieutenants upon earth, and sit upon God's throne, but even by God himself they are called Gods."! (*Political Writings of King James VI and I, p.181*) Later, in a letter to the Speaker of the Commons, he rebuked "some fiery and popular spirits" who had dared "to debate and argue publickly, *in matters far beyond their reach or capacity . . . trenching upon our Prerogative Royal.*" (*p.252*) This was the phenomenon of 'Divine Right' at its most ludicrous, and so it is no surprise that, in the next reign, transition from courtly to parliamentary government was an acute event, achieved in one generation, accompanied by a bloody Civil War, and although there would be attempts by some monarchs, egged on by a faction in court, to claw back power, right up to George III, the situation was never reversed.

The reactionary Restoration parliament crushed Cromwellian Nonconformity and purged these elements from the Church of England, but it had learned one lesson from its erstwhile foes, and learned it well: a monarch at odds with most of the aristocracy and a majority in the Commons, was a weak monarch and could be held in check. This worked well enough with Charles II, who learned to adapt; but when his brother succeeded him, he was a different and more intransigent character, who failed in state-craft, was hoodwinked by his apparent, if lukewarm, supporters, until the trap was sprung, when they deserted him, and brought an even more foreign claimant to the throne.

James II, after a protracted Civil War, most of which was fought out in Ireland, returned to France, where he and his successors, the Old and Young

Pretenders, lived out most of their lives in close harmony with a powerful French monarchy which was hostile to Britain and therefore diminished even further any possible chance of staging a come-back. With the demise of Queen Anne, Britain's rulers had perfected their technique, and brought on the latest in foreign monarchy, which we have seen Tom Paine castigate so roundly. He professes to be concerned that these Hanoverians were introducing Germanic despotism into the British system, but he himself overthrows that suggestion when he points to the real weakness of this new dynasty, founded by a king of Great Britain 'who understood neither her laws, her language, nor her interest'. Parliament was now in complete control and knew it. The English Revolution had been a slow process, from the accession of James I to that of George I; now it was complete. George III would attempt to claw back something of absolute monarchy, but parliament had learned its craft well, and strong minded members, among whom one of the most determined was Edmund Burke, gradually broke the attempt. Significant failure for the king, came with defeat in America, and his subsequent mental illness ensured that he would henceforth be compliant, as would his successors.

The one remaining threat was from collusion, within a royal tribe, spread across Europe, and assuming, from time to time, a species of supranational power, which could, and did, undermine legitimate governments. But this was a phenomenon that did not develop in the lifetime of Paine or Burke, so we do not know the thoughts of either, although we can surmise from what they did write on abuse of monarchy; neither would have approved.

Paine has written extensively on the British monarchy but he does have comments on some French kings as well, the earliest being the noble Henri Quatre, distinguished for his understanding and leniency, at a crucial period in his country's post-Reformation struggles, and author of the *Edict of Nantes* which gave succour to hard pressed Huguenots, feeling threatened after the Massacre of St. Bartholomew.

> "It is attributable to Henry the Fourth of France, a man of a large and benevolent heart, that he proposed, about the year 1610, a plan for abolishing war in Europe. The plan consisted in constituting an European Congress, or as the French authors style it a Pacific Republic; by appointing delegates from the several Nations, who were to act as a Court of arbitration in any disputes that might arise between nation and nation."
>
> "Had such a plan been adopted at the time it was proposed, the taxes of England and France, as two of the parties, would have been at least ten millions sterling annually to each Nation less than they were at the commencement of the French Revolution."
>
> *(Rights of Man, pp.166–7)*

Then following on this enlightened reign which might well have given us a European Union several centuries ago (?would Britain then have joined, and been by now well established at the heart of Europe!) Paine comments on the great change which occurred in French monarchy between then and the Revolution.

"I will here, as concisely as I can, trace out the growth of the French Revolution, and mark the circumstances that have contributed to produce it. The despotism of Louis XIV united with the gaiety of his Court, and the gaudy ostentation of his character, had so humbled, and at the same time so fascinated the mind of France, that the people appeared to have lost all sense of their own dignity, in contemplating that of the Grand Monarch: and the whole reign of Louis XV, remarkable only for weakness and effeminacy, made no other alteration than that of spreading a sort of lethargy over the nation, from which it showed no disposition to rise."

(p.115)

The English revolutionary, John Milton, said it beautifully in his *Samson Agonistes:*

"But what more oft in nations grown corrupt
And by their vices brought to servitude,
Than to love bondage more than liberty,
Bondage with ease than strenuous liberty."

Or, as the Israelites during their Exodus from Egypt moaned to Moses:

"If only we had died at the Lord's hand in Egypt, where we sat by the fleshpots, and had plenty of bread!"

(Exodus 16:3)

"The only signs which appeared of the spirit of Liberty during those periods, are to be found in the writings of the French philosophers. Montesquieu, president of the parliament of Bordeaux, went as far as a writer under a despotic government could well proceed: and being obliged to divide himself between principle and prudence, his mind often appears under a veil, and we ought to give him credit for more than he has expressed."

"Voltaire, who was both the flatterer and the satirist of despotism took another line. His forte lay in exposing and ridiculing the superstitions which priestcraft united with statecraft had interwoven with governments. It was not from the purity of his principles, or his love of mankind, (for satire and philanthropy are not naturally concordant), but from his strong capacity of seeing folly in its true shape, and his irresistible propensity to expose it, that he made those attacks. They were however as formidable as if the motives had been virtuous; and he merits the thanks rather than the esteem of mankind."

"On the contrary, we find in the writings of Rousseau, and the Abbé Raynal, a loveliness of sentiment in favour of liberty, that excites respect, and elevates the human faculties; but having raised this animation, they do not direct its operations, and leave the mind in love with an object, without describing the means of possessing it."

"The writings of Quesnay, Turgot, and the friends of those authors, are of the serious kind; but they laboured under the same disadvantage

with Montesquieu: their writings abound with moral maxims of government, but are rather directed to economise and reform the administration
of the government, than the government itself."

"But all those writings and many others had their weight; and by the
different manner in which they treated the subject of government, Montesquieu by his judgement and knowledge of laws, Voltaire by his wit,
Rousseau and Raynal by their animation, and Quesnay and Turgot by
their moral maxims and systems of economy, readers of every class met
with something to their taste, and a spirit of political enquiry began to
diffuse itself through the nation at the time the dispute between England
and the then colonies of America broke out."

(pp.115–6)

After these reflections on the period of decadence with its superficial splendour,
its monarchy and its philosophers, we need to consider Paine's view of the
current French king, Louis XVI.

"'We have seen (says Mr Burke) the French rebel against a mild and lawful
Monarch, with more fury, outrage, and insult than any people has been
known to rise against the most illegal usurper, or the most sanguinary
tyrant.' – This is one amongst a thousand other instances, in which Mr
Burke shows that he is ignorant of the springs and principles of the French
Revolution."

"It was not against Louis XVI, but against the despotic principles of
the government, that the nation revolted. These principles had not their
origin in him, but in the original establishment, many centuries back; and
they were become too deeply rooted to be removed, and the augean stable
of parasites and plunderers, too abominably filthy to be cleansed, by
anything short of a complete and universal revolution. When it becomes
necessary to do a thing, the whole heart and soul should go into the
measure, or not attempt it. The crisis was then arrived, and there remained
no choice but to act with determined vigour, or not to act at all. The king
was known to be the friend of the nation, and this circumstance was
favourable to the enterprise. Perhaps no man bred up in the style of an
absolute King, ever possessed a heart so little disposed to the exercise of
that species of power as the present King of France. But the principles
of the government itself still remained the same. The Monarch and the
Monarchy were distinct and separate things; and it was against the established despotism of the latter, and not against the person or principles of
the former, that the revolt commenced, and the revolution has been
carried."

"Mr Burke does not attend to the distinction between *men* and *principles*; and therefore he does not see that a revolt may take place against
the despotism of the latter, while there lies no charge of despotism against
the former."

"The natural moderation of Louis XVI contributed nothing to alter
the hereditary despotism of the monarchy. All the tyrannies of former

reigns, acted under that hereditary despotism, were still liable to be revived in the hands of a successor. It was not the respite of a reign that would satisfy France, enlightened as she was then become. A casual discontinuance of the *practice* of despotism, is not a discontinuance of its *principles;* the former depends on the virtue of the individual who is in immediate possession of the power; the latter, on the virtue and fortitude of the nation. In the case of Charles I, and James II of England, the revolt was against the personal despotism of the men; whereas in France it was against the hereditary despotism of the established government. But men who can consign over the rights of posterity forever on the authority of a mouldy parchment, like Mr Burke are not qualified to judge of this revolution. It takes in a field too vast for their views to explore, and proceeds with a mightiness of reason they cannot keep pace with."

"When a man reflects on the condition which France was in from the nature of her government, he will see other causes for revolt than those which immediately connect themselves with the person or character of Louis XVI. There were . . . a thousand despotisms to be reformed in France, which had grown up under the hereditary despotism of the monarchy, and became so rooted as to be in a great measure independent of it. Between the monarch, the parliament, and the church, there was a *rivalship* of despotism besides the feudal despotism operating locally, and the ministerial despotism operating everywhere. But, Mr Burke, by considering the King as the only object of a revolt, speaks as if France was a village, in which everything that passed must be known to its commanding officer, and no oppression could be acted, but what he could immediately control. Mr Burke might have been in the Bastille his whole life, as well under Louis XVI, as Louis XIV and neither one nor the other have known that such a man as Mr Burke existed. The despotic principles of the government were the same in both reigns, though the dispositions of the men were as remote as tyranny and benevolence."

(pp.68–70)

Paine is certainly convinced that what is happening in France is in no way to be blamed on the reigning monarch, and that, in fact, this man is really well disposed towards his people and their aspirations. It is the establishment which needs to be reformed and not the individual replaced. This was borne out later, in a very practical fashion when Tom Paine risked his own life in voting against taking the king's life. It is also significant, in the passage just quoted, that he refers to the Revolution as a *fait accompli* – past history. In a later passage detailing the proceedings of the States-General, at the outset of the Revolution, he describes the blocking tactics of the secular aristocracy together with the aristocratical higher clergy, but again excluding the king who was of a quite different disposition:

"The King, who very different from the general class called by that name, is a man of good heart, showed himself disposed to recommend an union of the three chambers, on the ground the National Assembly had taken;

but the malcontents exerted themselves to prevent it, and began to have another project in view."

(p.128)

He goes on to describe how the king was outmanoeuvred at first, as the reactionaries schemed to block progress and precipitated the crisis at Versailles when the members of the National Assembly were locked out from the premises in which they had been meeting, and retired instead to a neighbouring tennis ground where they took an oath never to separate from each other until they had achieved a new constitution. This is the event known to history as the *Tennis Court Oath*, which brought the Revolution fully into being three weeks before the Bastille was captured. But secret machinations continued, and the Assembly was surrounded by troops, with thousands more arriving daily:

> "On this a very strong declaration was made by the National Assembly to the King, remonstrating on the impropriety of the measure, and demanding the reason. The King, who was not in the secret of this business, as himself afterwards declared, gave substantially for answer, that he had no other object in view than to preserve the public tranquillity, which appeared to be much disturbed."

(p.130)

The court was in session at Versailles, and the National Assembly meeting only a short distance away, but there was no real communication between them. The malcontents, as Paine dubs them, continued their scheming; orders went out to assemble 30,000 troops under the command of the Duc de Broglie, one of the new-intended Ministry. Troops arrived, but as the plot was becoming obvious at Versailles, things were also coming to a head in Paris and the Bastille was taken. The conspirators took fright and fled; de Broglie's foreign troops dispersed and the counter-revolution collapsed. It is remarkable that the leaders were not pursued, nor did the Assembly attempt any retaliation. Had the king been party to these intrigues, there is little doubt that he and all members of the royal family would have been spirited away smartly and would almost certainly have made good their escape while conditions were so favourable, instead of facing the sorry debacle at Varennes much later. This in itself confirms the fact that the king was innocent of the plot being hatched; he himself was being duped just as much as members of the National Assembly. As Paine tells it: "The hopes of those opposed to the revolution, rested in making the King of their party, and getting him from Versailles to Metz, where they expected to collect a force and set up a standard." (p.83)

But the king was minded differently, his heart was with his people and he wanted the best for them, even if this meant some loss of status for himself; the pity is that the new leaders coming on could not appreciate this fact and capitalise upon it for the good of the nation as a whole. That he, later on, became concerned, not only for his own safety and welfare, but also for his family as well, is hardly surprising, when we consider how the revolution was turning sour and getting out of hand. So he and his family fled and almost escaped, but having been captured and brought back to face trial and eventually the guillotine, he conducted himself with commendable dignity, deserving an honoured place in the minds of Frenchmen to this day, a place which he does not seem to have with most of them, even residual royalists.

It is fitting that we should follow this king through to the end, even though this comes just after the period we are considering, because he was an exceptionally good man contrasted with his immediate predecessors. If the leading revolutionaries, at the more advanced stage, had the good sense to continue co-operation with him, or even to use him sensibly, the worst excesses of the Reign of Terror might have been avoided, but the September massacres of 1792 having already taken place it was then too late.

Not all commentators share Paine's benign view of Louis XVI, although it is difficult to gainsay his assessment, based on the events unfolding in 1789, when in October the counter-revolutionaries would have spirited the king away from Versailles to Metz had he co-operated. One of those who saw it differently was Winston Churchill who, although his view of the French Revolution is far from hostile on the whole, has a rather cynical attitude to the king's behaviour, even in the early stages:

"... *émigrés* ... took refuge in Germany and Italy ... From beyond the frontiers they busily intrigued against the new order in France. With them the King, the Queen, and the Court were in clandestine correspondence. The National Assembly and the mobs of Paris stood in constant fear that their newly made constitutional King would betray them by joining with the *émigrés*, and supported by foreign aid, reimpose the Old Regime. Nor were their fears groundless. Like Charles I of England, the King counted duplicity as a royal prerogative. He saw nothing wrong in accepting many distasteful reforms while secretly, at the instigation of the Queen, working for their overturn."
(WSC, Age of Revolution, p.226)

These views of Paine and Churchill are extreme, opposed, and representative of two irreconcilable groups, which will persist as long as history is written, but we do have the evidence of the king's actions from his accession in 1774.

"(He) had not waited for the gathering of the revolutionary storm in order to redress the evils from which the people suffered; in the very first year of his reign he had embarked on the work of reform with the co-operation of Turgot and Malesherbes. In 1775 he had attempted to introduce the free circulation of grain, – thereby enraging the monopolisers ... in 1779 he had abolished all forms of servitude in his domains inviting 'all seigneurs of fiefs and communities to follow his example'; in 1780 he had abolished torture; in 1784 he had accorded liberty of conscience to the Protestants; ... in 1787 and 1788 he had proposed reforms in the administration of justice, ... the abolition of *lettres de cachets*, and greater liberty of the press. Meanwhile he had continued to reduce the expenses of his household and had reformed the prisons and hospitals."
(NH Webster, p.6)

Edmund Burke does not set out these steps in details, but he expresses the same process in summary, referring to the king's predicament.

"A misfortune it has indeed turned out for him, that he was born king of France. But misfortune is not a crime, nor is indiscretion always the greatest guilt. I shall never think that a prince, the acts of whose whole reign were a series of concessions to his subjects, who was willing to relax his authority, to remit his prerogatives, to call his people to a share of freedom, not known, perhaps not desired by their ancestors; . . . I shall be led with great difficulty to think he deserves the cruel and insulting triumph of Paris."

(Reflections, p.90)

There is also the evidence of this king's remarkable calmness and fortitude when facing an agitated mob on several crucial occasions; when he was menaced at Versailles, together with his queen; when he was brought back from Varennes; and again twelve months later when the mob invaded the Tuileries:

"That day he wrote to his confessor, asking him to come to him: 'I have never had so great need of your consolations; I have done with men, it is towards Heaven that I turn my eyes. Great disasters are announced for tomorrow; I shall have courage'. And as he looked out that summer evening across the great gardens of the Tuileries to the sun sinking behind the Champs Elysees, to good old Malesherbes standing by him, 'Who knows whether I shall see the sun set tomorrow'?"

(Webster p.220)

On the morrow, he was as good as his word; his courage and calm demeanour once again saved the day: but by then the end was not much longer to be delayed. At his trial in January following, the death sentence was only achieved by menacing and threatening his supporters and sympathisers.

"Malesherbes has related that when he went to the Temple to break the news to Louis XVI, he found him seated in the semi-darkness, his back turned to the lamp, his elbows resting on a little table, and his face buried in his hands. As the old man entered the King rose and looking him in the eyes, said solemnly: 'Monsieur de Malesherbes, for two hours I have been trying to discover whether in the course of my reign I have deserved the least reproach from my subjects. Well, I swear to you in all truth as a man about to appear before God that I have always wished for the happiness of my people, that I have never formed a wish opposed to them'

'Ah, Sire', answered Malesherbes with tears,'I still have hope; the people know the purity of your intentions, they love you and they feel for you. I found myself, on going out from the debate, surrounded by a number of people who assured me that you would not perish, or at least not until they and their friends had perished themselves. . .

'Do you know these people?' Louis XVI interposed hastily, 'Go back to the Assembly, try to find some of them, tell them that I should never forgive them if a drop of blood were shed for me; I refused to shed it when it might have saved me my throne and my life . . . and I do not repent . . .'

"The cause of this unrepentance is not far to seek. Louis XVI realised that his trust in the people had not been misplaced, for it was not by the people he had been condemned – an appeal to the people must inevitably have saved him. He knew no doubt, the intrigues that had brought about the fatal sentence."

(Webster, pp.273–4)

The king would have known very well who his real enemies were; not only the most prominent republicans, but even his own kith and kin; the Duc d'Orleans, Phillipe Egalité, was one of those most determined to see him out of the way. But in England also there were the warmongers whose Francophobia had helped to raise the temperature by spraying petrol on the revolutionary flames. Once the king had been despatched, they achieved their aim, when war was declared within weeks. Heredity had been no boon to this unfortunate man, instead it had brought about his downfall.

CHAPTER IX

Paine and Lafayette

America and France

Men are born, and always continue, free and equal, in
respect of their rights. Civil distinctions therefore, can be
founded only on public utility.
Declaration of the Rights of Man and of
Citizens, by the National Assembly of France

BEFORE MOVING ON FROM MONARCHY and secular government as a whole it behoves us to consider one more outstanding character, both in his own right and as a close friend of Paine. They were involved together both in America and France. In a footnote to Part I of his Rights of Man (p.84) Paine refers to "M. de Lafayette, with whom I have lived in habits of friendship for 14 years". They first made acquaintance in America during the War of Independence. Like his king, Lafayette has been sidelined in history, regarded by royalists as a traitor and by the revolutionaries as a renegade. The sad fate of certain great men throughout time is to have been survivors, without managing to become either martyrs or significant heroes, they are quickly written out of any popular script.

Marie Jean Gilbert, Marquis de Lafayette, was born in 1757, and lost his father early in life, a fact to which one writer at least *(Cronin)* attributes his liberal and somewhat rebellious nature, because authority was missing in his early family life. This writer goes on to compare him to Danton and St. Just, who also lost their fathers in their early years. As a very young man he acquired an army commission, more or less automatically, as any nobleman could. But as events were shaping up in France, following the Seven Years War, financial stringency was beginning to bite, so in 1776 two French army companies were disbanded and young Captain Lafayette was turned loose. Many Frenchmen were eager to strike at England to avenge defeats in the late war. America was erupting in revolt, so here was their opportunity, Lafayette was one of the few who joined the American rebels and saw it through.

After landing in America he had a poor reception, but insisted on being seen personally by Congress; he made a favourable impression and had soon won the friendship of George Washington, becoming a Major General on his staff. Like Paine, whose friend he became almost immediately, they survived the first disastrous campaign winter when men were dying all round them from privation and disease. Come the Spring, he was in command of a unit of 2,000 men, as he reached the age of twenty. He had distinguished service throughout the war, and by the time it ended at Yorktown in 1781 he commanded a Light Infantry Division in that decisive encounter, when the English under Cornwallis were defeated and America became truly free. For this stage, again we have Paine's testimony:

"As I have introduced M de Lafayette, I will take the liberty of adding an anecdote respecting his farewell address to the Congress of America in 1783, and which occurred fresh to my mind when I saw Mr Burke's thundering attack on the French Revolution: M. de Lafayette went to America at an early period of the war, and continued a volunteer in her service to the end. His conduct through the whole of the enterprise is one of the most extraordinary that is to be found in the history of a young man, scarcely then 20 years of age. Situated in a country that was like the lap of sensual pleasure and with the means of enjoying it, how few are there to be found who would exchange such a scene for the woods and wildernesses of America, and pass the flowery years of youth in unprofitable danger and hardship! But such is the fact. When the war ended and he was on the point of taking his final departure, he presented himself to Congress, and contemplating in his affectionate farewell, the revolution he had seen, expressed himself in these words: '**May this great monument raised to Liberty, serve as a lesson to the oppressor, and an example to the oppressed!**' When this address came to the hands of Dr. Franklin, who was then in France, he applied to Count Vergennes to have it inserted in the French Gazette, but never could obtain his consent. The fact was, that Count Vergennes was an aristocratical despot at home, and dreaded the example of the American Revolution in France, as certain other persons now dread the example of the French Revolution in England; and Mr Burke's tribute of fear . . . runs parallel with Count Vergenne's refusal."

(Rights, p.68)

Marie-Antoinette became an admirer of Lafayette and gave him several audiences, while he was back home in France for a time in 1779; she also made and kept a copy of some verses written in his honour, one of which translates:

"He knows how to defend a camp and capture walls; like a young soldier he loves battles, like a veteran general he knows how to avoid them: I find him a joy to follow, and even to imitate".

Then back in France permanently, which he had left as a teenage lad, and now still in his mid-twenties, Lafayette had matured rapidly; with his intense military experience and having followed political progress in the new republic in its early formative stage, he was a man of much greater knowledge and deeper perception than most of his contemporaries at home, especially among the erstwhile ruling classes.

In dedicating Part II of his *Rights of Man* to this friend, Paine tells him:

"After an acquaintance of nearly 15 years, in difficult situations in America, and various consultations in Europe, I feel a pleasure in presenting to you this small treatise, in gratitude for your services to my beloved America, and as a testimony of my esteem for the virtues, public and private, which I know you to possess."

"When the American revolution was established, I felt a disposition to sit serenely down and enjoy the calm. It did not appear to me that any object could afterwards arise great enough to make me quit tranquillity and feel as I had felt before. But when principle, and not place, is the energetic cause of actions, a man, I find is everywhere the same."

"I am now once more in the public world; and as I have not a right to contemplate on so many years of remaining life as you have, I am resolved to labour as fast as I can; and as I am anxious for your aid and your company, I wish you to hasten your principles, and overtake me."

(p.173)

But this was in February 1792 and much water had flowed down the Seine in the intervening years, also Lafayette had been much involved in affairs of state. When the States General were called in 1789 he was still a noble, but very much a liberal, and immediately became involved.

"Count Vergennes (the leading minister in the French government) resisted for a considerable time the publication in France of the American constitutions, translated into the French language; but even in this he was obliged to give way to public opinion, and a sort of propriety in admitting to appear what he had undertaken to defend. The American constitutions were to liberty, what a grammar is to language; they define its parts of speech, and practically construct them into syntax."

"The peculiar situation of the then Marquis de Lafayette is another link in the great chain. He served in America as an American officer under a commission of Congress, and by the universality of his acquaintance, was in close touch with the government of America, as well as with the military line. He spoke the language of the country, entered into the discussions on the principles of government, and was always a welcome friend at any election."

"When the war was closed, a vast reinforcement to the cause of Liberty spread itself over France, by the return of the French officers and soldiers. A knowledge of the practice was then joined to the theory; and all that was wanting to give it real existence, was opportunity. Man cannot, properly speaking, make circumstances for his purpose, but he always has it in his power to improve them when they occur; and this was the case in France."

(pp.117–8)

An Assembly of Notables was called together in 1787; this was a body whose members were nominated by the King, or perhaps it is more correct to say that most of them were nominated to him, and endorsed by him. M. Calonne, the Finance minister dominated this body and manipulated its constitution in such a way that he believed he could always command a majority; it was a species of gerrymandering, achieved primarily by dividing the Assembly into seven committees.

"But all his plans deceived him, and in the event became overthrown. The then Marquis de Lafayette was placed in the second committee, of whom Count D' Artois (the King's brother) was president: and as money-matters was the object, it naturally brought into view every circumstance connected with it. M. de Lafayette made a verbal charge against Calonne, for selling crown-lands to the amount of two millions of livres, in a manner that appeared to be unknown to the King. The Count D'Artois (as if to intimidate, for the Bastille was then in being) asked the Marquis if he would render the charge in writing? He replied that he would. The Count D' Artois did not demand it, but brought a message from the King to that purport. M. de Lafayette then delivered his charge in writing, to be given to the King, undertaking to support it. No farther proceedings were had upon this affair; but M. Calonne was soon after dismissed by the King, and set off to England."

"As M. de Lafayette, from the experience of what he had seen in America, was better acquainted with the science of civil government than the generality of the members who composed the Assembly of the Notables could then be, the brunt of the business fell considerably to his share. The plan of those who had a constitution in view, was to contend with the Court on the ground of taxes, and some of them openly professed their object. Disputes frequently arose between the Count D' Artois and M. de Lafayette, upon various subjects. With respect to the areas already incurred, the latter proposed to remedy them by accommodating the expenses; and as objects of reform, he proposed to abolish the Bastille, and all the State-prisons throughout the nation (the keeping of which was attended with great expense) and to suppress *Lettres de Cachets.*

"But those matters were not then much attended to; and with respect to *Lettres de Cachets*, a majority of the Nobles appeared to be in favour of them."

(*pp.119–20*)

Lettres de Cachets were sealed instructions by which the King could order the imprisonment of any of his subjects without charge or trial. Churchill explains:

"Louis XVI, the most benevolent of the Bourbons, had hitherto issued no fewer than 14,000 *lettres de cachet*, consigning his subjects to prison often with good reason, but always without trial. The fall of the Bastille marked the end of such royal absolutism."

(*W S C vol. III, p.225*)

This is all very interesting and shows the evolution already taking place prior to the fully fledged revolution itself. The royal brother was attempting to intimidate Lafayette in a fashion that would have terrified and completely disarmed many a man in the past; he could have been put away by persuading the king to sign a Lettre de Cachet, but the time was past. This man with his international record and reputation was not one to be treated thus, nor would the king be disposed to cooperate. The game was up, the old system was collapsing, and its protégés knew this in their heart of hearts, even if they could not bring themselves to acknowledge it. And so events moved on.

"On the subject of supplying the Treasury by new taxes, the Assembly declined taking the matter on themselves, concurring in the opinion that they had not authority. In a debate on the subject, M. de Lafayette said, that raising money by taxes could only be done by a National Assembly, freely elected by the people, and acting as their representatives. Do you mean, said the Count D'Artois, the *States General*? M. de Lafayette replied that he did. Will you, said the Count D'Artois, sign what you say, to be given to the King? The other replied, that he would not only do this, but that he would go farther, and say, that the effectual mode would be, for the King to agree to the establishment of a Constitution."

(p.120)

Various devices were tried to force the parliaments and especially the Parlèment de Paris to approve new taxes, but show and parade were losing their traditional power, as well as intimidation was doing. The Count D'Artois attempted to overawe the Parisian assembly but without success. On this occasion Paine himself was an eye-witness and he reports:

"On alighting from his carriage to ascend the steps of the Parliament House, the crowd threw out trite expressions saying 'This is M. D'Artois, who wants more of our money to spend.' The marked disapprobation which he saw impressed him with apprehensions; and the words *Aux Armes! (to Arms!)* was given out by the officer of the guard who attended him,' It was so loudly vociferated, that it echoed through the avenues of the House, and produced a temporary confusion: I was then standing in one of the apartments through which he had to pass, and could not avoid reflecting how wretched was the condition of a disrespected man."

(p.122)

The call to have a States General summoned was strongly resisted at first by the hard liners, but gradually it became clear that the nation would not settle for anything less. Having got its will, events moved rapidly, and on from evolution to revolution. Hear Paine again:

"While I am writing this, there are accidentally before me some proposals for a declaration of rights by the Marquis de Lafayette . . . to the National Assembly on the 11th of July 1789, three days before the taking of the Bastille; and I cannot remark but with astonishment how opposite the sources are from which that Gentleman and Mr Burke drew their principles. Instead of referring to musty records and mouldy parchments to prove that the rights of the living are lost, 'renounced and abdicated for ever', by those who are now no more, as Mr Burke has done, M. de Lafayette applies to the living world, and emphatically says, 'Call to mind the sentiments which Nature has engraved in the heart of every citizen, and which take a new force when they are solemnly recognised by all: 'For a nation to love liberty, it is sufficient that she knows it; and to be free, it is sufficient that she wills it.' How dry, barren, and obscure, is the source from which Mr Burke labours! And how ineffectual, though gay with flowers, are all his declamations and his arguments, compared with these clear, concise, and soul-animating sentiments!"

(pp.67–8)

Soon after the revolution was established Lafayette was back again in a military role, and so acted until he finally removed himself towards the end of the Reign of Terror. During these years, the king and the royal family owed him much for the protection he afforded them, even when he appeared to be with the National Assembly and its successor against them. This role commenced quite early on, when the 'women of Paris' at the beginning of October 1789, marched to Versailles to avenge an insult by the *Garde du Corps* (the Royal bodyguard) who had dishonoured the National cockade, which they sported under duress. Paine gives a very different account to what Burke professed to believe:

".... Considerable uneasiness was at this time excited at Paris, by the delay of the King in not sanctioning and forwarding the decrees of the National Assembly, particularly that of the *Declaration of the Rights of Man*, and the decrees of the *fourth of August.* (abolishing Feudal privileges) . . . enemies of the revolution derived hope from the delay, and friends . . . uneasiness."

"During this state of suspense, the *Garde du Corps,* which was composed . . . of persons much connected with the court, gave an entertainment at Versailles (October 1st) to some foreign regiments then arrived; and . . . on a given signal they tore the national cockade from their hats, trampled it underfoot, and replaced it with a counter cockade prepared for the purpose. An indignity of this kind amounted to defiance. It was like declaring war; and if men will give challenges, they must expect consequences. But all of this Mr Burke has kept out of sight. .... By keeping the Garde du Corps out of sight, Mr Burke has afforded himself the dramatic licence of putting the King and Queen in their places, as if the object of the expedition was against them . . ."

"This conduct of the *Garde du Corps,* . . . alarmed and enraged the Parisians . . . (who) were determined to call the *Garde* . . . to account. There was certainly nothing of the cowardice of assassination in marching in the face of day to demand satisfaction, . . . of a body of armed men who had voluntarily given defiance . . . We have . . . two different objects presenting themselves at the same time . . . the one, to chastise the *Garde,* . . . which was the object of the Parisians; the other, to render the confusion of such a scene an inducement to the King to set off for the Metz. (where they expected to collect a force, and set up a standard)"

"On the 5th of October, a very numerous body of women, and men in the disguise of women, collected . . . at Paris, and set off for Versailles. Their professed object was the *Garde du Corps;* but prudent men readily recollect that mischief is more easily begun than ended; . . . As soon, therefore as a sufficient force could be collected M. de Lafayette, by orders from the civil authority of Paris, set off after them at the head of twenty thousand of the Paris militia . . . to prevent . . . the consequences that might ensue between the *Garde* . . . and this phalanx of women and men, he forwarded expresses to the King, that he was on his march to Versailles . . . for the purpose of peace and protection, expressing . . . the necessity of restraining the *Garde* . . . from firing upon the people." *(Paine adds in a footnote that he had this information personally from Lafayette.)*

"He arrived at night. *The Garde* . . . was drawn up, and the people had arrived some time before, . . . Lafayette became the mediator between the enraged parties; and the King, to remove the uneasiness that had arisen from the delay already stated, sent for the President of the National Assembly, and signed the *Declaration of the Rights of Man,* and such other parts of the constitution as were in readiness."

(The people settled down for the night, as well as those in the palace.)

"In this state matters passed till the break of day, when a fresh disturbance arose from the censurable conduct of some of both parties . . . One of the *Garde* . . . appeared at one of the windows of the palace, and the people who had remained during the night in the streets accosted him with reviling and provocative language. Instead of retiring . . . he presented his musket, fired and killed one of the Paris militia. The peace . . . broken, the people rushed into the palace in quest of the offender. They attacked the quarters of the *Garde* . . . within the palace, and pursued them throughout the avenues of it, and to the apartments of the King. On this tumult, not the Queen only, as Mr Burke represented it, but every person in the palace, was awakened and alarmed; M. de Lafayette . . . had a second time to interpose between the parties, the event which was that the Garde . . . put on the national cockade, and the matter ended . . . after the loss of two or three lives."

"During the latter part of the time in which this confusion was acting, the King and Queen were in public at the balcony, and neither . . . concealed for safety's sake, as Mr Burke insinuates. *(See also Priestley's Letters to EB, pp.17–18)* Matters being thus appeased, and tranquillity restored, a general acclamation broke forth, of Le Roi a Paris . . . the King to Paris. It was the shout of peace, and immediately accepted on the part of the King. By this measure, all future projects of . . . setting up the standard of opposition to the constitution, were prevented and the suspicions extinguished. The King and his family reached Paris in the evening, and were congratulated on their arrival by M. Bailley, the Mayor of Paris, in the name of the citizens. . . . Not less than 300,000 persons arranged themselves in the procession from Versailles to Paris, and not an act of molestation was committed during the whole march."

(pp.82–5)

It is well known that the King and his family had a tiring and thoroughly unpleasant journey from Versailles to Paris on that day, during which they were menaced, but never actually assaulted. Burke's sympathy and anxiety was not entirely misplaced, but he seems to have missed the most important features of the event and what might have been learned from them: large numbers were involved, the situation was explosive throughout, and yet, apart from the one incident at Versailles, it was contained, and largely due to the brave and level-headed management of Lafayette. The king acted with commendable calm and defused the situation by providing his signature at the crucial moment, convincing the people, once again, of his good will. If all at home had kept their heads and foreign governments had refrained from making mischief, the signs augured well at this point and the revolution could have proceeded peacefully.

In his recent biography of Tom Paine, John Keane paints a less flattering portrait of Lafayette, referring to him as a "swashbuckling political figure", which scarcely reflects Paine's own sentiments, and appears to be based on a single major controversy. He tells us that the first years of the revolution have been called "The years of Lafayette", and identifies his supporters as the Patriot Party or Fayettistes. This party favoured a constitutional monarchy, which others would have approved at that time. Controversy arose when Lafayette's party carried measures in the National Assembly, limiting the vote to citizens who paid direct taxes worth at least three days labour, and eligibility for national political office to men who paid annual direct taxes equivalent to a *marc d'argent*, a silver mark worth about 54 days labour.

Robespierre and Paris as a whole attacked this legislation and Lafayette obviously over-reached himself when in January 1790 he took 3,000 troops into the Cordeliers district, the heart of democratic liberalism, to arrest the incandescent and inflammatory journialist Marat. Danton was the district president and refused to surrender Marat. From then on Lafayette's power was waning. *(Keane, pp.285–6)*

He continued to be involved, and had custody of the king with his family, on yet another and less auspicious occasion; this was after the ill-fated flight to Varennes, when the royal party was apprehended just short of the border. Arrived back at the Tuileries, Lafayette, having placed his guards, was about to withdraw, and asked his majesty's orders. The king replied bitterly: "I seem to be more at your order, than you are at mine." We can understand the king's bitterness and frustration, but it is also remarkable that his captor should still find it appropriate to show respect, acting his accustomed part as an officer and a gentleman, albeit a revolutionary. He was denounced as a traitor by the National Assembly in 1792, shortly after the king was suspended; he defected to the Austrians, but was to spend the next five years in German and Austrian gaols. Returning to France in 1802 he spent some time in retirement, after which he was elected a deputy up until 1824. In the Revolution of 1830 again he commanded the National Guard. He died in 1834. Both Louis and Lafayette merit respect from historians, much more than they normally receive.

CHAPTER X

Ecclesiastical Affairs
and Church Establishment

*The key of St. Peter, and the key of the Treasury, became
quartered on one another, and the wondering cheated multitude worshipped the invention.*

Paine, Rights of Man

THIS IS THE LAST OF THE MAJOR TOPICS AT ISSUE BETWEEN EDMUND
BURKE AND HIS CRITICS, but whereas Tom Paine was his major adversary
on Monarchy, Aristocracy and Constitutional matters, Dr. Priestley is the one
who engages him on Church Establishment, and who puts the arguments for
Disestablishment. Priestley and his friends were licking their wounds, because,
having had great hopes of seeing the harsh Penal Laws, the Test and Corporation Acts, revoked, in the wake of the First Catholic Relief Act of 1778, they
had suffered a severe reverse at the last fence, and Burke was one of those who
had deserted their cause. Let us first hear Burke on the *Majesty of the Church*,
and the necessity for a *Protestant succession:*

"As the mass of any description of men are but men, and their poverty
cannot be voluntary, that disrespect which attends on all lay property,
will not depart from the ecclesiastical. Our provident constitution has
therefore taken care that those who are to instruct presumptuous ignorance, those who are to be censors over insolent vice, should neither incur
their contempt, nor live upon their alms; nor will it tempt the rich to a
neglect of the true medicine of their minds. For these reasons, while we
provide first for the poor, and with a parental solicitude, we have not
relegated religion (like something we are ashamed to show) to obscure
municipalities or rustic villages. No! we will have her to exalt her mitered
front in courts and parliaments. The people of England will show to the
haughty potentates of the world, and to their talking sophisters that a
free, a generous, an informed nation honours the high magistrates of its
church; that it will not suffer the insolence of wealth and titles or any
other species of proud presentation to look down with scorn on what
they look up to with reverence; nor presume to trample on that acquired
personal nobility, which they intend always to be, and often is, the fruit,
not the reward . . . of learning, piety and virtue. They can see without
pain or grudging an archbishop precede a duke. They can see a Bishop
of Durham, or a Bishop of Winchester, in possession of ten thousand

pounds a year; and cannot conceive why it is in worse hands than estates to the like amount in the hands of this Earl or that Squire; although it may be true that so many dogs and horses are not kept by the former, and fed with the victuals which ought to nourish the children of the people"

(Reflections, p.113)

"When once the commonwealth has established the estates of the church as property, it can consistently hear nothing of the more or the less . . . In England most of us conceive that it is envy and malignity towards those who are often the beginners of their own fortune, and not a love of the self-denial and mortification of the ancient church that make some look askance at the disunities and the honours, and revenues, which taken from no person are set apart for virtue. The ears of the people of England are distinguishing. They hear these men speak broad. Their tongue betrays them. Their language is in the *patois* of fraud; and in the cant of gibberish and hypocrisy. The people of England must think so, when these praters affect to carry back the clergy to that primitive, evangelical poverty, which, in the spirit, ought always to exist in them, but in the thing must always be varied."

(p.114)

"This oblation of the state itself, as a worthy offering on the high altar of universal praise, should be performed as all public solemn acts are performed, in buildings, in music, in decoration in speech, in the dignity of persons, according to the customs of mankind, taught by their nature; that is with modest splendour, with unassuming state, with mild majesty and sober pomp."

". . . The majority of the people of England, far from thinking a religious national establishment unlawful, hardly think it lawful to be without one. In France you are wholly mistaken if you do not believe us above all other things attached to it, and beyond all other nations; and when this people has acted unwisely and unjustifiably in its favour (as in some instances they have done most certainly) in their very errors you will discover their zeal."

"This principle runs through the whole system of their polity. They do not consider their church establishment as convenient, but as essential to their state . . . They consider it as the foundation of the whole constitution, with which, and with every part of which, it holds an indissoluble union. Church and state are ideas inseparable in their minds and scarcely is the one ever mentioned without mentioning the other."

(pp.108–9)

What a splendid presentation! Pure poetry or, as Priestley expressed it *(p.29)*, what a "great pomp of words", and what dazzling use of paradox. An Oxford Union meeting or some other learned body, might spend an evening debating these passages, and in the light of present controversy the conclusions would be fascinating. But the last sentence quoted here has its own strange irony; and again we must get into clear focus the sequence of events at that time. Burke's *Reflections* came at the end of 1790, followed closely by Priestley's *Letters* and Paine's *Rights of Man*, early in '91. Then in mid-July came the Birmingham Riots in which Priestley and a number of his friends lost their homes, and much of their property; some of them and in particular Joseph Priestley, were fortunate to escape with their lives. The body which was responsible for these outrages was popularly known as the 'Church and King Mob', a title freely acknowledged and no attempt made to gloss it over; Church and State inseparable indeed; deploring wicked French savages! And not only these, but the home-grown variety as well, whose "tongue betrays them, speaking broad in the patois of fraud; in the cant of gibberish and hypocrisy"! *(above)* So, Burke wants *no change:*

"Thanks to our sullen resistance to innovation, thanks to the cold sluggishness of our national character, we still bear the stamp of our forefathers. We have not lost the generosity and dignity of thinking, of the fourteenth century; nor as yet have we subtilized ourselves into savages. We are not the converts of Rousseau, we are not the disciple of Voltaire; Helvetius has made no progress amongst us. Atheists are not our preachers; madmen are not our lawgivers."

(Reflections, p.94)

"If our religious tenets should ever want a further elucidation, we shall not call on atheism to explain them. We shall not light up our temple from that unhallowed fire. It will be illuminated with other lights. It will be perfumed with other incense, than the infectious stuff which is imported by the smugglers of adulterated metaphysics . . . Violently condemning neither Greek, nor the Armenian, nor, since heats are subsided, the Roman system of religion, we prefer the Protestant; not because we think it has less of the Christians religion in it, but because, in our judgement, it has more. We are Protestants, not from indifference, but from zeal."

". . . If, in the moment of riot, and in drunken delirium, from the hot spirit drawn out of the alembic of hell, which in France is now so furiously boiling, we should uncover our nakedness, by throwing off that Christian religion, which has hitherto been our boast and comfort, and one great source of civilisation amongst us, and among many other nations we are apprehensive . . . that some uncouth pernicious and degrading superstition might take place of it."

"For that reason, before we take from our establishment the *natural human means of estimation*, and give it up to contempt, as you have done (and in doing so have incurred the penalties you well deserve to suffer), we desire that some other may be presented to us in place of it. We shall then form our judgement."

"On these ideas, instead of quarrelling with establishments, as some do, who have made a philosophy and a religion of their hostility to such

institutions we cleave closely to them. We are resolved to keep an established church, and established monarchy, and established aristocracy, and an established democracy, each in the degree it exists, and no greater"
(pp.99–100)

". . . I beg leave to speak of our church establishment, which is the first of our prejudices, not a prejudice destitute of reason, but involving it in profound and extensive wisdom . . . it is first, and last, and midst in our minds. For, taking ground on that religious system, of which we are now in possession, we continue to act on the early received, and uniformly continued sense of mankind. That sense not only, like a wise architect, hath built up the august fabric of states, but like a provident proprietor, to preserve the structure from profanation and ruin, as a sacred temple, purged from all the impurities of fraud, and violence, and injustice, and tyranny, hath solemnly and forever consecrated the commonwealth, and all that officiate in it."

"The consecration of the state, by a state religious establishment, is necessary also to operate with a wholesome awe upon free citizens; because in order to secure their freedom, they must enjoy some determinate proportion of power. To them therefore, a religion connected with the state, and with their duty towards it, becomes ever more necessary than in such societies, where the people, by the terms of their subjection, are confined to private sentiment, and the management of their own family concerns. All persons possessing any portion of power ought to be strongly and awfully impressed with an idea that they act in trust to the one great Master, Author, and Founder of Society."
(pp.100–2)

It will be obvious from the fragmentation of text that there is more besides; so what is the author concealing that may put a different gloss upon certain passages. Be assured that selection has only been used to give the gist of Burke's argument, but the reader can easily resort to the original text; unlike some of the others in use here, it is accessible in or through any public library, and many others as well. The quoted passages may be found lengthy, but the remainder is even lengthier. However, Burke's resistance to change is not exhausted:

"The people of England think that they have constitutional motives, as well as religious, against any project of turning their independent clergy into ecclesiastical pensioners of state. They tremble for their liberty, from the influence of a clergy dependent upon the crown; they tremble for the public tranquillity from the disorders of a factious clergy, if it were made to depend upon any other than the crown. They therefore made their church, like their king and their nobility, independent."

"From the united consideration of religion and constitutional policy, from their opinion of a duty to make a sure provision for the consolation of the feeble and the instruction of the ignorant, they have incorporated and identified the estate of the church with the mass of *private property*, of which the state is not the proprietor, either for use or dominion, but the guardian only and the regulator. They have ordained that the provision of this extra establishment might be as stable as the earth on which it stands, and should not fluctuate with the Euripus of funds and actions."

(pp.110–1)

There is some strange logic here; the people tremble if they find the clergy dependent upon the crown, but they also tremble at clergy dependent upon any other than the crown. So, which is it to be? And was it "the people" who made the monarchy, the aristocracy and the church independent? We have already seen a considerable variety of views upon these constitutional issues; by no means a closed book! As to church property, it is only necessary to hark back to the reign of Henry VIII to realise how little security church property has when secular rulers have large needs, a situation recurring in France at that very moment and against which Burke was vehemently railing. But with the English settlement, the real estate: cathedrals, abbeys, churches, rectories, vicarages and land, together with endowments, constitute a vast property vested in a powerful corporation which is the church, beholden to the state and scarcely to be accurately described as *private property*. Another serious concern must be considered:

"The Christian statesmen of this land would indeed first provide for the *multitude*; because it is the *multitude*; and is therefore, as such, the first object in the ecclesiastical institution, and in all institutions. They have been taught that the circumstance of the Gospel's being preached to the poor was one of the great tests of its true mission. They think, therefore, those do not believe it, who do not take care it should be preached to the poor. But as they know that charity is not confined to any one description, but ought to apply itself to all men who have wants, they are not deprived of a due and anxious sensation of pity to the distresses of the miserable great. They are not repelled through a fastidious delicacy, at the stench of their arrogances and presumption, from a medicinal attention to their mental blotches and running sores.. They are sensible that religious instruction is of more consequence to them than to others; from the greatness of the temptation to which they are exposed; from the important consequences that attend their faults; from the contagion of their ill example; from the necessity of bowing down the stubborn neck of their pride and ambition to the yoke of moderation and virtue; from a consideration of the fat stupidity and gross ignorance concerning what imports men most to know, which prevails at courts, and at the head of armies, and in senates, as much as at the loom and in the field."

"The English people are satisfied, that to the great the consolations of religion are as necessary as its instructions. They too are among the unhappy. They feel personal pain and domestic sorrow . . . Some charitable dole is wanting to these, our often very unhappy brethren, to fill the gloomy void that reigns in minds which have nothing to do, something to excite an appetite to existence in the palled society which attends on all pleasures which may be bought, where nature is not left to her own process, where even desire is anticipated, and therefore fruition defeated by meditated schemes and contrivances of delight; and no interval, no obstacle is interposed between the wish and accomplishment."

(pp.111–2)

This is a stirring eulogy addressed to the great and powerful, and brings back Burke at his best, the Burke who led in the impeachment of Warren Hastings and who condemned the government for its short-sightedness in its handling of the American revolt. But if we accept that the great Wesleyan revival of that century was such a notable success with the *multitude,* then what does it tell us of the ecclesiastical establishment and those Christian statesmen who were expected to have this concern for the masses at heart. If churchmen and statesmen of the establishment were performing in the manner described by Burke would Methodism ever have featured so prominently in the life of the nation? It is scarcely necessary to pose the question; history provides the answer. But harken to Burke on the originator of the English Church and state establishment, the great defender of the faith himself:

"The tyrant Harry VIII of England, as he was not better enlightened than the Roman Marius's and Syllas, and had not studied in your new schools, did not know what an effectual instrument of despotism was to be found in that great magazine of offensive weapons, the rights of men. When he resolved to rob the abbeys, as the club of Jacobins have robbed all the ecclesiastics, he began by setting on foot a commission to examine into the crimes and abuses which prevailed in those communities. As it might be expected, his commission reported truths, exaggerations, and false-hoods. But truly or falsely it reported abuses and offences. However, as abuses might be corrected, as every crime of persons does not infer a forfeiture with regard to communities, and as property, in that dark age, was not discovered to be a creature of prejudice, all those abuses were hardly thought sufficient ground for such a confiscation as it was for his purpose to make. He therefore procured the formal surrender of these estates. All these operose proceedings were adopted by one of the most decided tyrants in the rolls of history, as necessary preliminaries, before he could venture, by bribing the members of his two servile Houses with a share of the spoil, and holding out to them an eternal immunity from taxation, to demand a confirmation of his iniquitous proceedings by an act of parliament.

(p.127)

What a damning indictment of the founder of that very establishment which Burke so reveres, precisely because it is old and has the blessing of tradition; and never mind how that tradition has come about. But all that comes in a different context, and we are not meant to detect the inconsistency.

Priestley on the Established Church

Priestley's beliefs and attitudes are entirely different from those of Burke, and his starting point is with Christianity before it was patronised by the state:

> "Did our Saviour give his apostles any instructions about connecting his religion with civil power, . . . or did the apostles, more fully instructed after his death and ascension, give any intimation of this kind? On the contrary, our Saviour declared that *his kingdom was not of this world*, which must mean that it did not resemble other kingdoms, in being supported by public taxes, and having its laws guarded by civil penalties. The apostles, and all Christian ministers, for many centuries, lived on the voluntary contribution of their respective churches, and they had no means of enforcing their censures besides exclusion from their societies; and can you say that Christianity wanted any proper *estimation*, or *respectability*, in that period? Did it not abundantly recommend itself to every candid observer, and to every partial enquirer, and did it not, by this means, continually gain ground, notwithstanding it was opposed both by all the temporal powers of the world, and by whatever was most splendid and fascinating in the established systems of heathenism? It was the *virtue*, it was the well known piety, and extensive benevolence, of the primitive Christians, and not wealth or power, that procured respect to themselves and to their cause. Read only the letters of the Emperor Julian, and you cannot but be sensible of this."
>
> *(Letters to EB, pp.67–8)*

This is the familiar argument that the primitive church, prior to the interference and patronage of the Emperor Constantine, was a healthier and more vibrant organism, and it has been the experience of history ever since that the church has been strongest and most virile when resisting persecution.

> "Admitting that religion must be *established*, or supported by civil power, in order to its efficiency, will *any* species of religion answer the purpose; the heathen or the Mahometan, as well as the Christian, and one species of christianity as well as another? Must we have no *discussion* concerning the nature and influence, of the different kinds of religion, in order that, if we happen to have got a worse, we may relieve ourselves by substituting a better in its place? Must everything once established be for that reason only, forever maintained? . . . You condemn the French National Assembly, for innovating in *their* religion, which is Catholic, as much as you could blame the English parliament, for innovating in *ours* which is Protestant. You condemn them for lowering the state of archbishops, bishops and abbots, though they have improved that of the lower orders of the clergy; and therefore you would, no doubt, be equally offended at any diminution of the power of cardinals, or of the pope. We may therefore presume that had you lived in Turkey, you would have been a mahometan, or in Thibet, a devout worshipper of the grand lama."

"Your mind has been so dazzled with the fascinating idea of the *majesty of the church* (a phrase I believe peculiar to yourself) that you have not been able to see anything distinctly on the subject. . . . You have not even been able to distinguish whether it was St. Paul's at London, St. Peter's at Rome, or the church of Sancta Sophia at Constantinople. For your description applies equally to them all. It seems to have been sufficient for you that it was *not a conventicle.*"

"As to everything under *this* denomination*, it has been your maxim, without any examination, to turn your back upon it. You would, no doubt, have done the same with respect to any place, in which Peter, or Paul, was permitted to preach; the christian religion being in their time, unfortunately, nothing more than a *sect*, taught in *conventicles*, and nowhere *authorised by law*. Had you lived at that time, you would, according to your general maxim, have 'cherished your old' heathen 'prejudices, because they were old' and have lived and died a humble worshipper of the Gods, and especially the *Goddesses,* of ancient Greece and Rome."

(pp.60–1)

Priestley was harshly treated by various adversaries and critics around this period. Burke, however, pretended to ignore him, except when he spoke from his privileged and protected eminence in parliament. Priestley wrote feelingly of this disadvantage shortly before he emigrated in 1794, referring to:

"Mr Burke, who (without any provocation except that of answering his book on the French Revolution) has taken several opportunities of inveighing against me, in a place where he knows I cannot reply to him, and from which he also knows that his accusation will reach every corner of the country, and consequently thousands of persons, who will never read any writings of mine. They have another, and still more effective vehicle of their abuse in what are called the treasury newspapers, and other popular publications."

He then added in a footnote:

"Mr Burke having said in the House of Commons that 'I was made a citizen of France on account of my declared hostility to the constitiution of this country,' I, in the public papers, denied the charge and called upon him for the proofs of it. As he made no reply, in the preface to my Fast Sermon of last year, (1793) I said, p.9, that "it sufficiently appeared that he had neither ability to maintain his charge, nor virtue to retract it." A year more of silence on his part having now elapsed, this is become more evident than before."

(Gravel Pit Sermon, 1794. Preface, pp.xii, xiii)

---

* beneath in status, in dignity, the Church of England

Priestley himself could be hard hitting in turn, and quite personal in his invective especially in the case of Burke. He concentrates on the latter's exaggerated reverence for Marie-Antoinette, on more than one occasion, in his oblique references to queens, empresses, and goddesses. A mild man in his domestic and private life, he could lash out in public controversy. He has more to say to Burke:

> "You cannot be so little read in the history of England, as not to know that the *church* and the *state* were as much connected before the Reformation as they have been since, and while the establishment was presbyterian, as well as now that it is episcopalian. You must know also that the inhabitants of this country, were at one time as zealous papists as they now are protestants, and yet they were brought to make a change in their established religion, and this was done without making any material change in the system of civil government. You must know that the presbyterians in Scotland, and the episcopalians in England, have at this very time the same king and the same parliament. But how do these facts agree with your favourite idea of the inseparable union of church and state? What, then, is the foundation of the dread you have entertained of any *future* change in the religion of our country, when no harm, but, as all protestants think, much advantage, has been derived from *past* changes in it?"
>
> *(pp.63–4)*

Priestley has strong views on the respect that is paid to established religion, a false respect he believes, and again he taunts Burke:

> "That you make no difference between christianity and the civil establishment of it, is evident from many parts of your performance, and that you consider the *respect* which it commends, as intirely derived from the circumstances of its establishment, is equally evident. After representing the importance of christianity, as opposed to infidelity, you say in a peculiar strain of eloquence. . . ."

[Then follows a lengthy paragraph already quoted from *Reflections*. (pp.99–100)]

> "It is evident from this passage (the whole of which is so sublimely rhetorical, that I could not help transcribing it, though not absolutely necessary for my purpose) that you consider the christian religion as having no *respectability*, or *effect*, without being *established*, and that the *natural human means of the estimation* in which it is held, is the splendour and riches of such an establishment. . . ."
>
> *(pp.65–66)*

> "If you suppose, as you really seem to do, that christianity is now destitute of these proper *means of estimation*, you know little of its nature or power. The *truths* and the *promises* of the gospel are the same now that they ever were, nor is the *evidence* at all diminished, and *human nature*,

on which it operates, . . . is also the same. And if you could look at anything out of an establishment, you might see that christianity, even now produces as interested and heroic virtue as ever it did. It forms men alike for the most active usefulness, or the most patient suffering. But amusing yourself with the *shadow*, you wholly neglect the *substance*. Looking at *religion*, you see nothing but the civil establishment of it."

. *(p.68)*

In this instance Priestley appears to be misjudging Burke; having taken the moral high ground, he comes across as unfair and unjust. Burke has never set out to write on theology or worship; he is concerned solely with the relationship between church and state; on the merits or otherwise of these organisms being closely bonded, and may only be judged accordingly. Priestley is not without ample ammunition to address that theme.

"According to your maxims, a rich establishment should make its clergy more respected than a poor one. But does this appear to be the case, on the comparison of the state of the clergy in Scotland, with that of those in this country? Dr. Adam Smith, who well knew them both, was of a very different opinion; and the most superficial observer must be sensible that he is in the right. Nay, so unfortunate is the situation of the clergy in this country . . . that, by the confession of many persons in the establishment itself, there are no clergy in christendom more negligent of their proper duty, less strict in their morals, and consequently *more despised* than they are."

(pp.69–70)

"The manner in which your imagination is struck with a splendid church establishment, makes you even exceed yourself in *eloquence;* and, as I always admire you in this field, though not in that of sober *reasoning,* I cannot forbear quoting a pretty long paragraph to this purpose, as it is particularly excellent of its kind."

(Some of this is quoted above from Reflections pp.107–8)

Priestley goes on to attack Burke on his faulty knowledge as to how the early Christian church organised itself, quite apart from the establishment issue. In this field he certainly had the edge, as church history was a constant study with him from early in his career, which it was not for Burke:

"Your idea of the state of things in the primitive church is altogether founded on mistake, It was not from the first, materially different from what it is, or at least ought to be, at this day, and therefore did not require any great difference in the condition of its ordinary ministers. There never was any obligation on christians, as you seem to suppose, to *throw their goods into common.* Whatever was done of this kind, appears from the history of Ananias and Sapphira *(Acts 5: 1–10)*, to have been perfectly voluntary, and could not have been universal; and we read of no such thing in any of the gentile churches. These, from the first, consisted of *rich* and *poor*, and the rich among them made repeated contributions to relieve the poor christians at Jerusalem, which could not have been wanted, if all the rich, even there, had give their *all*. As to the discipline of the primitive church, it was such as I should have no objection to, but have strongly recommended in my *Essay on Church Discipline;* nor was it more strict than is actually exercised in several christian churches, though not in that of England, at this day. But of these things you, sir, seem to speak altogether at random, without any particular knowledge of the subject."

(pp.77–8)

Priestley then goes on to consider whether a civil Establishment is essential to christianity with further reflections on Burke's lack of knowledge on ecclesiastical history:

"If a civil establishment be so essential as you represent it, to the estimation and effect of christianity, you must, no doubt, imagine that it never existed without one, that it has *grown with its growth,* and *strengthened with its strength.* . . . (But), You have not been pleased to give us the definition of an *established church,* . . . In its full extent, it is a church defended, and even regulated, by the state, which either proscribes, tolerates, or barely connives at, other religions. Now, what was the situation of the christian church with respect to the State in primitive times? You must know that so far from being supported by the civil powers (. . . Jewish or Heathen) it was frowned upon by them, and violently persecuted; itself being at that time nothing more than a *sect,* or a *heresy,* sometimes connived at, but never openly tolerated; and yet in these circumstances it existed, and flourished, gradually gaining ground by its own evidence, till it triumphed over all opposition, and the Roman empire itself became christian."

(pp.79–80)

As we have seen, Burke did not deign to reply to Priestley' s *Letters,* but other critics at that time and since have challenged his own heretical leanings. If he was so well grounded in the basic evidence of christianity, why did he revert to the ancient Arian heresy, which faded out gradually from the time of Emperor Constantine, but surfaced again as Unitarianism in the 18th century. He wrote extensively on the subject, and those writings have to be consulted by anyone who wishes to understand where he stood. He was a prominent leader in that movement, together with his friends Dr. Price, Rev. Theophilus Lindsay, Dr. John Jebb, and others. For a time and well into the 19th century these people imagined that their more rational Christianity would inevitably supplant the traditional varieties, but history tells us otherwise.

In Priestley's case the answer may be fairly simple; his secular reputation is based on his standing as a scientist; he was experiencing and contributing to, a great and sudden growth of new knowledge and insights which were transforming physics and chemistry from the mumbo-jumbo of medieval alchemy into a rational and readily understandable natural philosophy. Having experienced this transformation, the mystical element in Christianity suddenly became a challenge; the mystery had to go, but in efforts to achieve this he and his associates were failing to allow that the supernatural could not be reduced by making it conform to nature's laws. But, having challenged our guide on his own standing, let him return to the relationship between church and state:

> "Infinite . . . have been the evils that have resulted to mankind, and especially to the christian world, from the interference of civil power in matters of religion. Hence all persecution in every age, and almost all the hatred and animosity that has arisen among the different sects and parties of christians, for which there would have been very little food, or exercise if civil magistrates had not interfered in the disputes of theologians . . . . As nothing is found more difficult to balance than *two powers*, the one necessarily gaining what the other loses, the struggle between these two was incessant, and productive of the worst effects, for many centuries, in all parts of christendom. At the reformation the power of the church was very much broken, but still too much of it remains in all countries, and more of it in this, than in any Protestant state whatever. For in no other of them have ecclesiastics a seat in the supreme legislature of the nation."
>
> *(p.138)*

Priestley's point about the interference of civil magistrates is borne out in the case of his own deviation; although certain leading churchmen were gravely exercised in facing down Unitarianism, the civil authority did not intervene and so the problem proceeded along its own natural course without any outright civic disturbance; the movement peaked in the 19th century together with humanism, but whereas the latter is still a force to be reckoned with, Unitarianism itself has to a large extent lost ground. Priestley had strong views about personal choice in the matter of allegiance, denominational or otherwise; quoting Burke's dictum that, "whatever each man can separately do, without trespassing upon others, he has a right to do for himself," *(p.64)* he goes on:

> "Since then, I can *eat* and *drink* whatever suits my appetite, without trespassing upon anybody, you will allow that the state has no business to prescribe what I shall eat or drink. . . . You will allow that my neighbours have no right to complain of me, if, when I am indisposed, I treat myself as I think proper, taking whatever advice, or whatever medicines, I please. . . . What right, on this plain and obvious principle, advanced by yourself, has any man to complain of me if I *worship* God in what manner I please, or I do not chuse to worship God at all? Does my conduct in this respect injure them? What then has the state, or my neighbour, to do in this business, any more than with my food or my medicine? . . . In this, and many other things, government has taken a great deal too much upon it, and has by this means brought itself into great and needless embarrassment."
>
> *(pp.54–55)*

"It is time that we no longer *halt between two opinions*, so very important and opposite to each other, as whether religion should be left to every man's free choice, like philosophy, or medicine, or whether it should be imposed upon men, whether they chuse it or not; whether any man, or body of men, have a right to prescribe articles of faith to others, or whether every man should be left to think and act for himself in this respect, accountable only to God, and his own conscience. Let us come to a serious *issue* in this business, and if christian states have gone upon wrong and erroneous principles, neither agreeable to truth, nor favourable to the interests of society, let them by all means be reformed, and as speedily and with as little inconvenience as possible."

(p.140)

All of these writers we are considering could be ascerbic at times and often drew fire upon themselves in consequence; Priestley was no exception, *on Establishment* he has this:

"Every article, within the compass of the civil establishment of christianity, is evidently an *innovation*; and as systems are reformed by reverting to their first principles, christianity can never be restored to its pristine state, and recover its real dignity and efficiency, till it be disengaged from all connexion with civil power. This establishment, therefore, may be compared to a *fungus*, or a *parasitical plant*, which is so far from being coeval with the tree on which it has fastened itself, that it seized upon it in its weak and languid state, and if it be not cut off in time, will exhaust all of its juices and destroy it."

(p.83)

This gave rise to a rather vicious squib in the form of a memorial tablet to Joseph Fungus LLD, FRS, but an earlier gaffe had more serious and long term repercussions. In a pamphlet, *On the importance and Extent of Free Enquiry*, he had suggested that he and associates would use gunpowder to undermine the establishment edifice; it was quite obvious that this was used metaphorically. He consulted his friend and confident, Josiah Wedgwood, who advised against using such language and warned of the almost inevitable consequences. But Priestley chose to go ahead nevertheless. Wedgwood was right, adversaries pretended to take the threat literally; Priestley was lampooned and caricatured as *Gunpowder Joe; the Priestley Politician or the Political Priest*. He tried in vain to repair the damage in his *Letter to William Pitt, on Toleration and Church Establishments* in 1787, when he wrote:

"But to quiet their apprehensions from the dangerous attempts of such furious sectaries as myself and my friends, and the terror they have conceived from our gunpowder plots, etc., I shall inform them that the means we propose to employ are not *force*, but *persuasion*. The *gunpowder* which we are so assiduously laying *grain by grain under the old building of error and superstition*, in the highest regions of which they inhabit, is not composed of saltpeter, charcoal and sulphur, but consists of *arguments*; and

Cartoon of Priestley "Dr Phlogiston" "The Priestley Politician or The Political Priest"

if we lay mines with such materials as these, let them countermine us in the same way, or in any way they please and more congenial to their nature."

(Letter to Pitt, pp.17–18)

Paul in his time seems to have faced similar criticism and replied: "We live in the flesh, of course, but the muscles that we fight with are not flesh. Our war is not fought with weapons of flesh, yet they are strong enough, in God's cause, to demolish fortresses". *(2 Corinithians, 10:3,4)*

All that Priestley had achieved, however, and continuing the metaphor, was to lay a very effective time-bomb for himself, which the 'Church and King Mob' exploded for him on Bastille Day in 1791, a day on which he barely escaped with his life.

Priestley points to the inconsistency in Burke's support for the strange dichotomy in church establishment, as between England and Scotland, going on to stress that the same principle is not applied when Ireland is considered. This must have been gall indeed for Burke, because in his inmost heart he could only agree, and Priestley who knew him, with a degree of intimacy, would almost certainly have known this to be so.

". . . Of late it has been maintained by our high church divines, and by yourself, who must be classed with them, that the civil magistrate has nothing to do with the *truth* of religion, being obliged to provide for that which is professed by the *majority* of the subjects, though he himself should be of a different persuasion. Thus they say the king of Great Britain, must maintain episcopacy in England, and presbyterianism in Scotland, whether he be a presbyterian as King William, a Lutheran as George I or a true churchmen as his present majesty."

"You, sir, appear to defend church establishments on the latter of these principles. 'The christian statesman', you say, *(p.111)* 'must first provide for the multitude, because it is the multitude, and is therefore, as such, the first object in the ecclesiastical institution, and in all institutions' But how does this apply to *your country* of Ireland. For the same reason that episcopacy ought to be established in England, and presbyterianism in Scotland, the Roman Catholic ought to be the established religion of Ireland, because, as I apprehend, it is unquestionably the religion of a very great majority of the inhabitants. As to the great mass of the oppressed Irish if they be asked whether it be *their* religion, or that which they really approve, that they are obliged to maintain, they will say it is *a foreign* one, one that they disbelieve and detest, and yet are compelled to support, whilst from genuine zeal, they think it their duty to maintain their own. It is not supposed that more than one in ten of the inhabitants of Ireland are of the Church of England, and yet the iron hand of power compels them to maintain it. Is this, think you, the way to recommend your religion? Judge by the effect, what converts have been made to it in the last two centuries? The zealous members of your church, in the reign of the two Charles's of blessed memory, imposed episcopacy also upon

Scotland, when not more than one in a hundred of the Scots would attend the service; but the generous spirit of that nation at length threw off the oppressive yoke. The Irish also have the will, but, alas, not the power."

(pp.57–9)

Priestley is contemptuous of this secular interference in matters of faith and worship, condemning it as follows:

"The civil establishment of religion is so far from making it respectable, that it is the very thing that makes it contemptible; because it naturally tends to debase the minds of those who officiate in it, those to whom men will commonly look for examples of its proper spirit and tendency, and by whose principles and conduct they are too apt to form their opinion of it."

(p.96)

Tom Paine has even stronger views to express on this theme, views based on certain historical facts and tendencies, but which he urges with well marked prejudice:

"The natural right which (man) retains, are all those in which the *power* to execute is as perfect in the individual as the right itself. Among this class, as is before mentioned, are all the intellectual rights, or rights of the mind: consequently, religion is one of those rights."

". . . In casting our eyes over the world, it is extremely easy to distinguish the governments which have arisen out of society, or out of the social compact from those which have not: but to place this in a clearer light than what a single glance may afford, it will be proper to take a review of the several sources from which governments have arisen, and on which they have been founded."

"They may all be comprehended under three heads. First, Superstition. Secondly, Power. Thirdly, The common interest of society, and the common rights of man. The first was a government of priestcraft, the second of conquerors, and the third of reason."

"When a set of artful men pretended, through the medium of oracles, to hold intercourse with the Deity, as familiarly as they now march up the back stairs in European courts, the world was completely under the government of superstition. The oracles were consulted and government lasted as long as this sort of superstition lasted."

(Rights, pp.90–2)

Next let us consider the protestant succession, a topic which Burke addresses with great enthusiasm and eloquence and which is coming under much closer scrutiny again as we come to the end of the 20th century.

"The Princess Sophia was named in the act of settlement . . . for a *stock* and root of *inheritance* to our kings, and not for her merits as a temporary administratrix of a power, which she might not, and in fact did not, herself ever exercise. She was adopted for one reason, and for one only, because, says the act, 'the most excellent Princess Sophia, Electress and Duchess Dowager of Hanover, is *daughter* to the most excellent Princess Elizabeth, late Queen of Bohemia, *daughter* of our late *sovereign* lord, King James the First of happy memory, and is hereby declared to be the next *in succession* in the Protestant line', etc. etc.; 'and the crown shall continue to the heirs of her body, being Protestants' . . . Was it that the legislature wanted . . . a due sense of the inconveniences of having two, or three, or possibly more foreigners in succession to the British throne? No! They had a due sense of the evils which might happen from such foreign rule," etc.

(Reflections, p.26)

Priestley, for one, is not impressed by this strange and tortuous reasoning; he sees in this and similar passages "more of the *rhetorician* than the *reasoner*, even supposing you not to mean what you evidently do, the civil establishment of religion, but religion itself." *(Letters, p.86)* Further on he adds:

"If the governors of any country in which religion is established, have no motives to stand in awe of the ministers of religion, which they evidently have not (as they always see the ministers of religion standing in awe of *them*, and courting them) it is of no use to them that it is established at all. If it be of any use, it is simply as *religion*, as a principle acting upon conscience, and influencing individuals, independently of any civil establishment of it."

"Indeed, Sir, you see this whole business in a very wrong point of light. The civil establishment of religion is so far from making it respectable, that it is the very thing which makes it contemptible; because it naturally tends to debase the minds of those who officiate in it. . . ."

(Letters to EB, p.96)

Tom Paine, also, is scathing in his opinion of Burke's arguments when he states:

"All religions are in their nature kind and benign, and united with principles of morality. They could not have made proselytes at first, by professing anything that was vicious, cruel, persecuting, or immoral. Like everything else, they had their beginning; and they proceeded by persuasion, exhortation and example. How is it then that they lose their native mildness, and become morose and intolerant?"

"It proceeds from the connexion which Mr Burke recommends. By engendering the church with the state, a sort of mule-animal, * capable only of destroying, and not of breeding up, is produced, called *The Church established by Law*. It is a stranger, even from its birth, to any parent mother on which it is begotten, and whom, in time, it kicks out and destroys."

---

* *A mule is an infertile hybrid from the union of a he-ass and an equine mare.*

"The inquisition in Spain does not proceed from the religion originally professed, but from this mule-animal engendered between the church and the state. The burnings in Smithfield proceeded from the same heterogeneous production; and it was the regeneration of this strange animal in England afterwards, that renewed rancour and irreligion among the inhabitants, and that drove the people called Quakers and Dissenters to America. Persecution is not an original feature in *any* religion; but it is always the strongly marked feature of all law-religions, or religions established by law. Take away the law-establishment and every religion reassumes its original benignity. In America a Catholic Priest is a good citizen, a good character, and a good neighbour; an Episcopalian Minister is of the same description: and this proceeds independently of the men, from there being no law-establishment in America."

"If also we view this matter in a temporal sense, we shall see the ill-effects it has had on the prosperity of nations. The union of church and state has impoverished Spain. The revoking of the Edict of Nantes drove the silk manufacture from France into England; and church and state are now driving the cotton manufacturer from England to America and France. Let then Mr Burke continue to preach his anti-political doctrine of Church and State. It will do some good. The National Assembly will not follow his advice, but will benefit by his folly. It was by observing the ill effects of it in England, that America has been warned against it, and it is by experiencing them in France, that the National Assembly have abolished it, and like America, have established UNIVERSAL RIGHT OF CONSCIENCE, AND UNIVERSAL RIGHT OF CITIZENSHIP."

(Rights, pp.109–10)

Burke has a great deal to say about *Bishops* as functionaries in a state religion, and their particular virtue; he is concerned for their fate should England follow France at that time; he asks:

"Is the House of Lords to be voted useless? Is episcopacy to be abolished? . . . Are the curates to be seduced from their bishops, by holding out to them the delusive hope of a dole out of the spoils of their own order?"

(Reflections, p.59)

". . . When I took one circumstance into my consideration, *(regarding France)* I was obliged to confess, that much allowance ought to be made for the society, and that the temptation was too strong for common discretion; I mean the circumstance of the . . . triumph, the animating cry which called for '*all* the BISHOPS to be hanged on the lampposts', might well have brought forth a burst of enthusiasm on the foreseen consequences of this happy day."

(p.79)

"Send us your popish archbishop of Paris, and we will send you our protestant Rabbin. We shall treat the person you send us in exchange, like a gentleman, and an honest man, as he is; but pray let him bring with him the fund of his hospitality, bounty and charity; and depend upon it, we shall never confiscate a shilling of that honourable and pious fund, nor think of enriching the treasury with the spoils of the poor-box."

(p.92)

". . . We have not relegated religion (like something we were ashamed to show) to obscure municipalities, or rustic villages. No! We will have her to exalt her mitred front in courts and parliaments."

(p.113)

"Who, that had not lost every trace of humanity, could think of casting down men of exalted rank and sacred function, some of them of an age to call at once for reverence and compassion, of casting them down from the highest situation in the commonwealth, wherein they were maintained by their own landed property, to a state of indigence, depression and contempt."

(p.115)

A historian is bound to ask, how can Burke in these *Reflections,* write thus without *reflecting* on the lessons that France had so well learned from England's Henry VIII; exalted rank, sacred function, advancing years, or the security of *their own* landed property were of as little consequence to England's monarch as they later proved to be for the French revolutionaries. But, Burke has not exhausted this topic; he goes on to consider church affairs in France as the new state evolves:

"Those officers, whom they still call bishops, are to be elected to a provision comparatively mean, through the same arts (that is, election-eering arts,) by men of all religious tenets that are known or can be invented. The new lawgivers have not ascertained anything whatsoever concerning their qualifications, relative either to doctrine or to morals; no more than they have done with regard to subordinate clergy; nor does it appear but that both the higher and the lower may, at their discretion, practice or preach any mode of religion or irreligion that they please. I do not see what the jurisdiction of bishops over their subordinates is to be, or whether they are to have any jurisdiction at all."

(p.163)

So, French Bishops were to be elected by men of any, or of no religion, and what of Burke's Established Church, did not parliament have considerable influence in the choice of its bishops? And were all men in parliament members of the Church of England? But there is more:

"I hope their partisans in England . . . will succeed neither in the pillaging of the ecclesiastics, nor in the introduction of a principle of popular election to our bishoprics and parochial cures. This, in the present condition of the world, would be the last corruption of the Church; the utter ruin of the clerical character; the most dangerous shock that the state ever received through a misunderstood arrangement of religion. I know well enough that the bishoprics and cures under kingly and seigniorial patronage, as now they are in England, and as they have been lately in France, are sometimes acquired by unworthy methods; but the other mode of ecclesiastical canvass subjects them infinitely more surely and more generally to all the evil arts of low ambition which, operating on and through greater numbers, will produce mischief in proportion."

(p.164)

And so, Mr Burke has the answer; an established church may have the appointment of its bishops controlled by religious or irreligious men, as the case may be, as long as they belong to the secular establishment, but not if they are drawn from the populace at large.

"You may suppose that we do not approve your confiscation of the revenues of bishops, and deans and chapters, and parochial clergy possessing independent estates arising from land, because we have the same sort of establishment in England. . . . I see the confiscators begin with bishops and chapters and monasteries, but I do not see them end there."

(p.167)

"With regard to the estates possessed by bishops, and canons, and commendatory abbots, I cannot find out for what reason some landed estates may not be held otherwise than by inheritance. Can any philosophic spoiler undertake to demonstrate the positive or the comparative evil of having a certain, and that too a large proportion of landed property, passing in succession to persons whose title to it is, always in theory, and often in fact, an eminent degree of piety, morals, and learning; and property which by its destination, in their turn, and on the score of merit, gives to the noblest families renovation and support, to the lowest the means of dignity and elevation; a property, the tenure of which is the performance of some duty . . . and the character of whose proprietors demands, at least an exterior decorum, and gravity of manners; who are to exercise a generous but temperate hospitality, part of whose income they are to consider as a trust for charity; and who, even when they fail in their trust, when they slide from their character, and degenerate into a more common secular noble or gentleman, are in no respect worse that those who may succeed them in their forfeited possessions? Is it better that estates should be held by those who have no duty than by those who have one? -by those whose character and destination point to virtues than by those who have no rule and direction in the expenditure of their estates, but their own will and appetite? Nor are these estates held together in the character or with the evils supposed inherent in mortmain. They pass from hand to hand with a more rapid circulation than any other. No excess is good; and therefore too great a proportion of landed property may be held officially for life; but it does not seem to me of material injury to any commonwealth, that there should exist some estates that

have a chance of being acquired by other means than the previous acquisition of money."

(pp.180–1)

This is one of Burke's convoluted and seemingly important paragraphs, which
show him in the guise of advocate, and certainly not philosopher; an advocate
with a brief in which he is not totally confident and which therefore causes
him to exaggerate his arguments. Why can he not simply say that the church
needs to hold some properties, and that it is the institution, rather than the
individual temporary holder of an office, which is the proprietor? If it comes
to that, we are all temporary holders of any property that may come our way,
and institutions are the bodies which most nearly defy mortality. This piece
is not particularly flattering to bishops and other clerical functionaries, it is
even less so to Burke's beloved aristocracy. In his later 'Letter to a Member
of the National Assembly' he compliments King William's choice of bishops
which he contrasts unfavourably with what the French are doing:

> "Burnet tells us, that nothing tended to reconcile the English nation to
> the government of King William so much as the care he took to fill the
> vacant bishoprics with men who had attracted the public esteem by
> learning, eloquence, and piety, and, above all, by their known moderation
> in the state. With you, in your purifying revolution, whom have you
> chosen to regulate the church? Mr Mirabeau is a fine speaker – and a fine
> writer – and a very fine man; but really nothing gave more surprise to
> everybody here, than to find him the supreme head of your ecclesiastical
> affairs. . . . Your assembly addressed a manifesto to France, in which they
> tell the people, with an insulting irony that they have brought the church
> to its primitive condition. In one respect their declaration is undoubtedly
> true; for they have brought it to a state of poverty and persecution. . . .
> Have not men, under this new hope and head of the church, been made
> bishops for no other merit than having acted as instruments of atheists.
> . . . Have not such men been made bishops to administer in temples in
> which the church wardens ought to take security for the alter plate, and
> not so much as to trust the chalice in their sacrilegious hands. . . ."

(Letter to a Member, p.288)

Mr Mirabeau is a "very fine man", but should not be "supreme head of
ecclesiastical affairs" in Catholic France, but Burke does not balk at the Presbyterian William of Orange or the Lutheran George I being head of the Church
of England. **Priestley** is concerned about the direct relationship between the
crown and the church which it pledges itself to guard; he does not believe that
either really benefits; here he is responding to Burke:

> "The *clergy* to be as independent as the *crown* or the *nobility*, should have
> a negative in all proceedings in parliament. But the clergy are, in fact,
> dependent upon the crown and must necessarily be so, while the crown
> has the disposal of all bishoprics, and other great preferments; and the
> effect of this is seen by their voting with the crown. It is also no

compliment to the general disposition of the clergy, that you should tremble for the effects of their *factions*, if they were to depend upon any other than the crown. I should think, however, that, if they be so dangerous a body of men, you might make yourself rather easier if they were to depend on the *whole legislature*, and not upon the crown only, to which they now give a dangerous accession of power."

(Letters to EB, p.121)

"Though the power of the Church was derived from the feudal system, this most absurd of all its parts still remains, when many other parts of it, far more exceptionable and inconvenient, have been abolished. But as the church cannot now subsist of itself, as it did formerly, when it overawed the whole of the state, it gives a vast additional power to the crown, on which it is now wholly dependent; our princes having assumed that *supremacy over the church*, which had been usurped by the popes."

(p.139)

Priestley calls for support for his views from an unexpected quarter, a distinguished and well known catholic priest, but one regarded as something of a stormy petrel in his own church:

"To shew that I am not singular in my opinion of the impropriety of religion, I would more particularly recommend to your notice, and that of my readers, an excellent tract of Mr Berington's titled, *The Rights of Dissenters*; nor is he the only Catholic who sees this business of the *alliance of the church and the state* in the same light that I do. Different as are our systems of religion, in a variety of important respects, we are equally willing that they should stand or fall by their proper evidence, and we ask no aid of the civil power to support them."

(p.141)

The full title of this tract by Rev. Joseph Berington is: *The Rights of Dissenters from the Established Church in relation principally to English Catholics.* (1789) It is quite a lengthy composition of 66 pages (plus xii). He is highly critical of James II:

"When the measure's of James's administration most directly tended to the introduction of the religion of catholics, I condemn them. *It is by no means of human policy that I wish to see my religion established,* (my italics, P O'B) because all such means I consider to be deordinate, and most clearly contrary to the essential spirit of Christianity, exemplified in its first establishment."

(Berington p.10)

"The Catholics were the other body of men, to whom the blessings of the Revolution (of 1688) were not permitted to extend. Were they deserving of the exclusion? – I think they were. They remained attached to another form of government, that is, they were *Jacobites* . . . . But, in the eye of impartial justice, the *Catholics* now stood on the same ground as other *Jacobites*, in nothing differing from them; because, evidently, it was no peculiar tenet of their religion, which prompted them to embrace a political sentiment, in which they had so many associates of the Protestant persuasion. . . . But, it so happened, that, the statutes enacted against the latter, (RCs) even after the Revolution, did not describe them as Jacobites, in which capacity only they were deserving of coercion, but as *Papists*, that is as men punishable for *peculiar religious tenets."*

(pp.16–17)

Berington goes on to argue that "English Catholics are not Papists, nor ever were"; *(p.19)* a proposition which many will regard as somewhat semantic. He then acknowledges that Rome had abused its power in the past, but that "the influence of Rome in this country was not permanently great". It could be opposed when the interests of the state seemed paramount. "Its legates, on these occasions, were treated with marked indifference; nor, at any time, could they enter the kingdom without the consent of the monarch." *(p.27)* Later he asserts that the Protestant religion may be severed from the state as the Catholic was, but that the civil constitution will remain whole, uninjured and unimpaired, it would be equally safe in the hands of Protestant Dissenters, or of Catholics. Penal laws do not belong to the essence of the constitution; Tests and Oaths of Allegiance are unnecessary; and so he approves of what is happening in France. (Again note that the date is 1789.) It is not surprising that Priestley calls on the testimony of this witness. Burke would, of course, be fearful of inviting himself to be branded by any appeal to such a source, and so he ignores the tract, but there is much in it which he would almost certainly have approved, and with which he was probably acquainted.

Priestley has a further comment to make on the influence exerted by church-men upon the secular state:

"Infinite have been the mischiefs in which all nations have been involved on account of *religion*, with which, as it concerns only God and men's own consciences, civil government, as such, has nothing to do. Statesmen misled by ignorant or interested priests, have taken upon them to prescribe what men should believe and practice, in order to get to heaven, when they themselves have often neither believed, nor practised, anything under that description."

(Letters to EB, p.145)

There are echoes here which remind us that in our own time there are priests who profess belief at one level, and yet are quite open in their doubts as to a personal God; so, what do our writers have to say about God and about his relations to us humans. Berington, whom Priestley has introduced to us, had this to say:

"It is not more evident that the founder of the Christian system despised worldly honour, and wealth, and pleasure to teach us that virtue only merited esteem, than that he rejected all means of human power, whereby the truths he came to deliver, might have been propagated or maintained. It was on the persuasive operation of a disinterested and benevolent life, that he relied for success, and on the display of miracles which were then necessary. Had other means, in the order of unerring wisdom, been more expedient, can we think they would have been neglected? But he, who in his private life, and as a member of society, practised the virtues, which alone can give worth to both; so also, in his public capacity, as the great minister of religion, did he pursue the means best adapted to the end. Will this be disputed? I quote not particular texts or passages of those writings, which are believed to contain the certain proofs of his divine mission, and the most beautiful maxims of truth, because they, as usual, might be controverted. The character of the whole cannot, and is irresistible. – In directing his followers how they should act, after he had left them, he prescribes no other rule. He tells them not when kings and potentates, and states shall be converted, to avail themselves of the circumstance, and thereby to shield their faith. Never does he point to human means; because, though all power in heaven and on earth had been given to him, his kingdom was not of this world."

(Berington pp.34–35)

Priestley himself writes in a very similar manner *(pp.67–8)* as we have seen above. Burke has several short passages on the topic:

"We fear God; we look up with awe to kings; with affection to parliament; with duty to magistrates; with reverence to priests; and with respect to nobility. Why? Because, when such ideas are brought before our minds, it is *natural* to be so affected; because all other feelings are false and spurious, and tend to corrupt our minds, to vitiate our primary morals, to render us unfit for rational liberty; and by teaching us a servile, licentious, and abandoned insolence, to be our low sport for a few holidays, to make us perfectly fit for, and justly deserving of, slavery, through the whole course of our lives."

(Reflections, pp.94–5)

"These . . . are . . . the sentiments of not the least learned and reflecting part of this kingdom they think themselves bound, not only as individuals in the sanctuary of the heart . . . to renew the memory of their high origin and cast; but also in their corporate character to perform their national homage to the institutor, and author and protector of civil society; without which civil society man could not by any possibility arrive at the perfection of which his nature is capable, nor even make a remote and faint approach to it. They conceive that He who gave our nature to be perfected by our virtue, willed also the necessary means of its perfection. – He willed therefore the state. – He willed its connexion with the source and original archetype of all perfection."

(p.107)

But Priestley and Berington have reminded us that "His kingdom was not of this world" and that He gave no sign that he wished the church which he was establishing to be hogtied to any secular state.

"Superstition is the religion of feeble minds; and they must be tolerated in an intermixture of it, in some trifling or some enthusiastic shape or other, else you will deprive weak minds of a resource found necessary to the strongest. The body of all true religion consists, . . . in obedience to the will of the sovereign of the world; in a confidence in his declaration; and in imitation of his perfection."

(p.176)

Tom Paine quoting the first of these passages from Burke comments:

"The duty of man is not a wilderness of turnpike gates, through which he is to pass by tickets from one to the other. It is plain and simple, and consists of but two points. His duty to God, which every man must feel; and with respect to his neighbour; to do as he would be done by."

(Rights, p.89)

But Paine's best comment comes when he is making some observations on *The Declaration of the Rights of Man and of Citizens,* adopted by the French National Assembly. Article X states:

"No man ought to be molested, on account of his opinions, provided his avowal of them does not disturb the public order established by the law." He questions: "whether (this) article sufficiently guarantees the right it is intended to accord with; besides which it takes off from the divine dignity of religion, and weakens its operative force upon the mind, to make it a subject of human laws. It then presents itself to Man, like light intercepted by a cloudy medium, in which the source of it is obscured from his sight, and he sees nothing to reverence in the dusky ray."

(p.135)

He expands upon this in a fairly lengthy foot note, where once again we must remind ourselves that this is from Part I of his *Rights of Man,* written and published early in 1791, before agnosticism had overtaken him. This note states:

"There is a single idea, which, if it strikes rightly upon the mind either in a legal or a religious sense, will prevent any man or any body of men, or any government, from going wrong on the subject of Religion; which is, that before any human institution of government was known in the world, there existed, if I may so express it; a compact between God and Man, from the beginning of time; and that as the relation and condition which man in his *individual person* stands in towards his Maker cannot be changed, or anyways altered by any human laws or human authority, that religious devotion, which is a part of this compact, cannot so much as be made a subject of human laws; and that all laws must conform themselves to this prior existing compact, and not assume to make the compact conform to the laws, which besides being human, are subsequent thereto. The first act of man, when he looked around and saw himself a creature which he did not make, and a world furnished for his reception, must have been devotion, and devotion must ever continue sacred to every individual man, *as it appears right to him;* and governments do mischief by interfering."

(p.135)

This is a profound statement, indeed, and Paine does not give any source for it, other than his own musing, although it would be surprising if it was not reflecting ideas which he had discovered from reading, or which he had been taught in earlier years. The notion which he is propounding is that which is known to Christian thinkers as *Natural Law,* and one which is not exclusive to Christianity, since it is quite basic; it is the notion that every creature is created to a design and for a purpose, or purposes, known to the creator. As Paine is stating, governments must be aware, at some level of consciousness, that such a relationship exists between creator and created, and should be wary of any interference with the implied compact. Our other writers would have been aware also of these basic concepts, but it is remarkable that Paine should have been the one to express them so clearly. They do not sit comfortably with some of the thinking in his later *Age of Reason,* nor with that of Robespierre and other advanced Deist 'philosophers' of the French Revolution, who seem to assume that governments have every right to interfere in ways which this statement of Paine precludes. Many a regime, before, at that time, and since, has acted in the same manner, to the detriment of all citizens.

Against Change

Burke is at great pains to maintain that the status quo ante should be maintained at all costs, even it seems at the cost of abandoning what most would consider to be reason itself; he tells us that we should be proud of our prejudices. *(See Reflections p.95 – above)*

Priestley pounces on this paradoxical outburst to ridicule its author, and to explain just where his argument is taking him. *(See Letters pp.113–4 – above.)*

It should be remarked that this Priestley is the same who had defended the first Catholic Relief Act (1778) against Lord George Gordon's riotous mob, and who also had declared that if any religion deserved to be established in Ireland it should be Roman Catholicism and not Anglicanism; and this in spite of the fact that he did not favour an established religion in any state, also that he regarded Catholicism as heretical. He was a man of strong principle who could set aside his own personal prejudices to allow for justice and human rights; he has no illusions about cherishing them because of a certain degree of antiquity.

Tithes, Church Property and its Disposal

From reading the works of some modern writers of repute,
you would fancy a parson's life was passed in gorging himself
with plum-pudding and port wine; and that his Reverence's
fat chaps were always greasy with the crackling of tithe pigs
. . . . Whereas if you take the real man, the poor fellow's
flesh pots are very scantily furnished with meat . . . many
tithes are levied upon his pocket. . . . He has to dine with
the Squire; and his wife must dress neatly; and he must look
like a gentleman, as they call it, and bring up his six great
hungry sons as such.

Thackeray's Book of Snobs.

A tithe is defined as: a tenth of annual produce of agriculture etc., conceived as due to God and hence payable for the support of priesthood, religious establishments, etc. A money payment was substituted for a tithe of produce in 1836, and this was collected after 1936 by the state on behalf of clergy. This has been a levy exacted for support of the established church and as such caused great resentment among all dissenters. Not surprisingly Priestley is the main critic:

"There are also many other things relating to your church establishment, that ought to be attended to, such as giving some of your clergy seats in the House of Lords, by which you debase their proper character, and divert them from their proper pursuits; the enormous disproportion in the provision you make for the clergy, and that most inexpedient method of doing it by tythes . . ."

"The obligation imposed upon the Dissenters to contribute to the maintenance of the public establishment, which you think to be so essential to its support, I think to be equally tyrannical, unnecessary, and disgraceful to it. If it be such as really to recommend itself to a great majority of the people, surely that great majority will be able to support it, without the help of those who have a religion of their own to provide for. This circumstance is one, among many others, which manifestly shows a distrust of its proper basis, on *reason and truth*. Whether you will call it a proper *establishment* or not, it is certainly the most equitable thing in any country, and the best method of getting a true and useful religion, to leave every person at liberty to think and chuse for himself, and to support that which he prefers. There being then no undue bias on the mind, that form of religion will at length establish itself, and becoming universal, which shall be found by experience to be the most deserving of it; and the state will be thereby relieved from a great part of its present care and incumbrance. This has always been the case in a great part of North America, and the history of it will not give you any alarming apprehensions of adopting the same in this country."

(Letter to Pitt, 1787, pp.34–36)

It comes as a surprise that Priestley should have an expectation that one form of religion should eventually become universal, unless of course he has in mind his own supra-rational brand! There has always been an element of diversity in Christianity from the earliest times; and to a degree this is healthy. In a religion, one of the major tenets of which is 'love your neighbour' we should be striving for unity among the followers of Christ, but this is not the same as complete uniformity, which we can never reasonably expect in a free society.

But Priestley has a particular example of abuse in his mind, which should have endeared him to Burke, but even here there was no response forthcoming.

"If we now look to Ireland, you will see, Sir, the most manifest of all abuses, I will venture to say, that ever accompanied any establishment whatever; a thing unknown in England, or any other country in the world. In all other places it is the religion of the *majority*, and that of a very great majority of the inhabitants, that is supported by the state, to which the majority are compelled to contribute; and one argument universally alleged for them, and to which you had recourse, is, that it is the religion of the majority. But in Ireland the religion established by law is that of a small minority, that, I believe, of not more than *one person in ten* of the inhabitants of the country; so that to support the religion of this *tenth man*, the nine are compelled to pay their full tythes. I have been informed that there are even whole parishes, in which the established clergy do no duty at all. It has, moreover, been said, tho' I hope without truth, that in parishes in which there have been but few Protestant families, the clergy have contrived to remove them, that they might enjoy their revenues, without being obliged to any clerical duty."

"It may be said that when this system was adopted there was some hope of bringing over the inhabitants to the religion that was thus imposed upon them; but this pretence must have ceased long ago. With every means in their power, some just, and others shockingly unjust (at which the feelings of human nature must revolt, as much as at any circumstance attending a popish inquisition) the clergy of the established church in Ireland have never been able to convert any considerable number of Catholics in the south, or of Presbyterians in the northern parts of the island. If, sir, you have any regard to common justice, and the most obvious maxims of it, exert yourself to remedy this crying abuse; and be assured that you will not be able to find out any other remedy, that shall be effectual to quell the present disturbances in that country."

"If this conduct was proper with respect to Ireland, why was not the same thing attempted in Scotland; and why is it not carried into execution in Canada, Nova Scotia, or wherever you have *power* to enforce it? As to *justice*, or *mercy*, it is evident that they were not considered in the case."

(pp.36–8)

This was written in 1787, when parliament had rejected a Bill for repeal of the Test Act; a cause dear to the heart of Priestley and his friends, supported on this occasion by Edmund Burke, who would have enjoyed the arguments rejecting the claims of the established church in Ireland. William Pitt, however was of another mind and voted against the bill. Priestley develops his case further in 1791, when writing to Burke and here also, he has further comments on the situation developing in Ireland, as we shall see:

". . . Let it not be said that the Church of England would have the impudence, if it had the power, to collect its tithes from every country in Christendom, though every parish should be a *sinecure,* and all the bishops be denominated *in partibus.* Let there be an appearance at least, which now there is not, of some regard to *religion* in the case, and not to mere *revenue.* Often as I have urged this subject, and many as have been those who have animadverted upon my writings, hardly any have touched upon *this.* They feel it to be tender ground. They can, however, keep an obstinate silence, they can shut their ears, and turn their eyes to other objects, when it is not to their purpose to attend to this."

(Letters to EB, p.59)

". . . There was nothing like a *tax,* levied for the support of religion for many ages, nor is there any such thing at this day in a very great part of the christian world. Tithes are comparatively but a modern invention, the payment of them being first voluntary, and afterwards obligatory; and the compulsory payment of tithes did not take place in the whole of the country till the time of King John, *of glorious and immortal memory,* on that account. There are now no tithes payable in the ecclesiastical states of Italy, or in Sicily; . . ."

(p.81)

Commenting on Burke's statement that: "christian statesmen would first provide for the multitude the first object in the ecclesiastical institution, . . ." and that "the Gospel being preached to the poor was one of the great tests of its true mission", *(Reflections, p.111)* Priestley retorts:

"Here, Sir, your argument, as far as there is anything of argument in it, is, that since the poor cannot afford to pay for religious instruction, the state should provide it for them. . . . but at whose expense is this provision made? If it were at the expense of the rich only, there would be something of charity in it; but is not all property, that of the poor as well as the rich, taxed alike for this purpose? Do not the clergy exact the payment of *small tithes,* and often with the utmost rigour, from their poorest parishioners? Do we not sometimes hear of their being actually turned out of their little tenements, by a distress levied by their spiritual instructors; and are not the poor Irish some of the most destitute and miserable of mankind, driven into almost annual rebellions, by oppression from the exaction of tithes?"

"This, I am told, is the true cause of the rise of those who are called *White Boys*, among the poor catholics of Ireland; and nothing but the terror of military execution can compel them to pay for that instruction which you would give us to understand is so charitably afforded them. Thus, to be compelled to pay for the instruction which they detest, and receive no advantage from, and to be, at the same time, under another kind of necessity of paying for the instruction which they really value, is, indeed a hard case. But this, according to you is *preaching the gospel to the poor."*

(pp.87–8)

This must have been gall indeed for Burke, to be accused of favouring such treatment for poor Irish catholics, whom it was always his interest to defend. We can only wonder if Priestley was aware of this enigma for Burke, the parliamentarian, and whether he was, impishly, rubbing salt into the wounds? He continues:

"The gospel was, in its proper sense, preached to the poor by our Saviour, the apostles, and other primitive christians, who were themselves poor. In those times all the contributions for the maintenance of public worship were made by the rich, and they were as ample as they were voluntary. Those who were less opulent gave as they thought proper, and could afford, and the poor gave nothing; for small tithes were then unknown. The same is the case with us Dissenters. All our places of public worship are open to the poor, accommodated *gratis,* but their wants are attended to as far as the funds of the congregation (and in all of them there is one for this purpose) can go towards their relief."

(pp.88–89)

"A great proportion of the tithes in this country, and, as l am informed, the whole of them in Scotland, is now in the hands of lay proprietors, who, in your opinion, must all be guilty of *sacrilege.* though their conduct be sanctioned by the law of the land."

"If the right of the church to its revenues is not to be affected by any act of a civil legislature, and if it be not derived from any *ordinance of man,* it must come to them from the *ordinance of God.* But where, Sir, do you find any record of this? There is no mention of tithes, or of any permanent church property, in the New Testament; and if it has been by the ordinance of God in any period subsequent to the writing of those books, it is incumbent upon you, Sir, and other advocates for the unalienable property of the church, to shew when the grant was made, and by what miracle (for nothing else can answer the purpose) it was confirmed. But everything relevant to the revenues of the church, is easily traced in history. We very well know *when,* and *whence,* every branch of it arose. It was altogether the ordinance of men, and generally of weak, superstitious and priest-ridden men. And surely the mischiefs which have been found to arise from the folly of one age, ought to be removed by the wisdom of a subsequent one. In one passage, indeed, you allow all that I contend for, when you say, (*p.114*) 'When once the commonwealth has established the estates of the church as property'; for this implies that the estates of the church are the gift of the commonwealth, or state; and what the state has *given*, it may surely *take away*. This is one among the many inconsistencies in your work."

(pp.117–8)

"You have made the provision for the *poor* as sacred as that for the *church*. But certainly this was the institution of *man*, or rather of *woman*, for it took its rise in the time of Queen Elizabeth in this country, and is not known in any other. To many persons, as well as to myself, our method of providing for the poor, is no proof of the wisdom of our ancestors. It takes from man the necessity of *foresight*, and instead of being the most provident, makes him the most improvident of all creatures. So far are our poor laws from encouraging industry, that they encourage idleness, and of course profligacy. Such is the state of this country, burthened with taxes to support the church, and the poor, and to pay the interest (the principal is out of the question) of debts contracted by the folly of our ancestors, that its ability to support itself under them is very problematical."

(pp.119–20)

It may seem strange, at first sight, that Dr. Priestley should be one to decry the poor laws, a provision in which, as he himself indicates, England led the way, but he was a man who always had more than enough to occupy him, and although his income as a minister would be scant, because of his outstanding activities as a scientist and a literary man, from a very early stage, there were always generous patrons willing to fund him. The truth would seem to be that, in his adult life, he had little conception of what real poverty could mean; and that even the most willing individual, when out of work, could not always find alternative employment in the short term, if at all. In fact his attitude is reminiscent of certain politicians and wealthy people in modern times who assume that if people are poor, the problem must, to a large extent, lie with themselves.

Tom Paine, on the other hand, was advocating social provision which was away ahead of his time, but, before considering that, let us hear him on the question of tithes:

"The French constitution has abolished tithes, that source of perpetual discontent between the tithe-holder and the parishioner. When land is held on tithe, it is in the condition of an estate held between two parties; the one receiving one-tenth and the other nine-tenths of the produce: and consequently, on principles of equity, if the state can be improved, and made to produce by that improvement double or treble what it did before, or in any other ratio, the expense of such improvement ought to be borne in like proportion between the parties who are to share the produce. But this is not the case in tithes; the farmer bears the whole expense, and the tithe holders takes a tenth of the improvement, in addition to the original tenth, and by this means gets the value of two-tenths instead of one. This is another case that calls for a constitution."

(Rights, p.107)

This is a nice point, irrespective of the somewhat doubtful arithmetic at the end, (two-tenths should mean one-fifth, but these are tenths of two different sums and so it is still one-tenth of the new combined sum.) It is significant that Paine hammers home his plea for a written constitution on any anvil that presents itself. Priestley has some final points to make on the estates of the church:

"Had our present minister actually entered into the war that some suppose he did not do wisely to provoke,* and the consequence had been as it probably would, the addition of another hundred million to our debt, though *you* might not tremble for what you consider as the *ark of God* in this country, other persons, whose faith was not so strong certainly would."

"You, Sir, appear not to be insensible on the new and critical situation into which immense public debts have brought most European nations, our own not excepted. The apparent stability of these governments has encouraged them to venture upon a system, which, by calling forth the powers of future generations in aid of the present, has enabled them to make extraordinary exertions on particular occasions. Had there been wisdom in these exertions, posterity, being benefited by them, would have had reason to thank their ancestors. But exertions of this kind exceeding the natural powers of the state, have resembled those convulsive motions of the muscles which exhaust their force, and debilitate them with respect to future exertions. And if this system be pursued, as in all probability it will, the time must come when even these extraordinary resources will fail, and we shall then find ourselves in the very same difficulties in which the French are involved at present."

"In this case do you imagine, Sir, that we shall be able to preserve our present government in all its forms, civil and ecclesiastical, any more than the French have been able to preserve theirs? Whatever shall then be thought to be *unsound* in the constitution, and to have contributed, directly or indirectly, to bring us into our difficulties will be marked for excision; . . ."

(Letters to EB, pp.125–6)

"In this necessary reformation of the *civil* government, will it be possible, think you, to prevent all enquiry into *ecclesiastical* matters, which are now

---

* *Minister is what we now call Prime Minister; the war which he had provoked he did enter into, shortly after this.*

so closely connected with things of a civil nature? In this case, is it a certainty that *any* church establishment will be continued; or if there be, will it be precisely that which now subsists? Will the bishops retain their seats in Parliament? Will the spiritual courts be continued? Will the clergy be maintained by tithes? Will the doctrines of the church undergo no change? Will the subscription to all the thirty nine articles be still enforced? Will the universities remain shut to Dissenters, who cannot subscribe to them? Will the test laws remain in force to exclude us from all civil offices, etc. etc.? If this be your opinions, *great*, indeed, Sir, is *your faith*, greater, I imagine, than that of many an archbishop. Though, however, it should be equal to the *removing* of all these *mountains*, you will, I doubt not, imagine this favourite church of yours to be rather safer in times of peace, and without any farther encrease of our national debt, than with a *war* that might double it."

(p.127)

This last paragraph presages most of the changes which have come about gradually and slowly; much more slowly than Priestley and his associates might have expected. It has been a process of gradual erosion, and one which is still operating as the 20th century draws to its close.

CHAPTER XI

Decadence and Failings
in the Established Church

. . . if I had by me the names of those seven or eight Irish
Bishops, the probates of whose wills were mentioned in last
year's journals, and who died leaving behind them some
£200,000 a-piece – I would like to put them up as patrons
of my clerical snobs.

Thackeray's Book of Snobs

PRIESTLEY HITS OUT STRONGLY AGAINST THE TENDENCY TO DECADENCE IN CLERGY of any church which is established under the patronage of the state. Having condemned monasticism as one of the corruptions of Christianity (how he might be surprised at its revival in the 20th century) he goes on to say that they (the monks):

". . . did not sink into contempt till they had acquired what you call the *natural human means of estimation.* The same has been the case with the secular clergy in all countries. They were infinitely more respected, even by the rich and the great, while they were poor, than they have ever been since they have got their present splendid establishments; nor is it difficult to see the cause of this, and how it operates. Ease, affluence, and power, attract persons who have no sense or knowledge of religion; and when mere *men of the world* get ecclesiastical preferment, they will of course disgrace their profession by their vices. It was the unbounded luxury, profligacy, and arrogance, of the court of Rome, possessed as you think of every natural human means of estimation that was one of the principal causes of the reformation."

(Letters to EB, pp.69–70)

There is a beautiful poem, full of irony and humour, written by a young friend and admirer of Dr. Priestley; a close friend of his wife, twenty or more years earlier, and entitled, *The Groans of the Tankard* which expresses these thoughts of Priestley in poetic terms, but with biting wit. Anna Laetitia Aikin, (better known in later years as Mrs Barbauld), a young lady in her twenties, was the daughter of Dr. John Aikin, senior tutor at Warrington Academy, himself a Presbyterian; he possessed an ancient tankard from which he drank water with his meals. His daughter, assuming that this vessel has known better and jollier days, lets her imagination run freely on its past, letting it speak for itself, and her poem has the following lines:

> Unblest the day, and luckless was the hour
> Which doomed me to a Presbyterian's power;
> Fated to serve the Puritanic race,
> Whose slender meal is shorter than their grace;
> Whose moping sons no jovial orgies keep;
> Where evening brings no summons – but to sleep;
> No carnival is even Christmas here;
> And one long Lent involves the meagre year.
> Bear me ye pow'rs! to some more genial scene,
> Where on soft cushion lolls the gouty Dean,
> Or rosy Prebend, with cherubic face,
> With double chin, and paunch of portly grace,
> Who lull'd in downy slumbers shall agree
> To own no inspiration but from me.

(Poems of ALB, 1994 edition, p.61)

Rev. Berington has similar views:

"In the establishment itself, I can discover no plan for the extension of virtue; much for the growth of selfish and worldly passions. Secure in the possession of wealth and preferment, or looking eagerly towards both, the ministers of religion will relax in soft indulgence, or they will be filled with cares, which are not those of a man abstracted from the world, and devoted to his neighbour's service. Ambition, vanity, profusion, will find their way to the soft couch of preferment, while the more indigent and patronless will pine in the humble walk, at the sight of ease and honours, to which they may not reach."

(pp.41–2)

Priestley, Aikin, and Anna Lactitia's husband were ordained Presbyterian ministers, who became Unitarian; the young lady, in later years, tells how Rousseau's *Heloise* had gripped the students, then at the Academy, with romantic fever, which led to her own and other marriages. How this assembly of tutors and students would have relished being around to enjoy Trollope's *Barchester Chronicles!* Concerning his own Unitarianism Priestley has some comments on the orthodoxy or otherwise of many Anglican clergy; these come both in his *Letters to Burke* and his earlier *Letter to William Pitt:*

". . . You ought to make such alterations, as not to exclude from the benefits of it (establishment) any serious professors of Christianity. This, you said, would introduce universal confusion, every parish being divided within itself, in consequence of some persons believing one thing, and others another. But is not this the case at present? Do all the ministers of the Church of England, notwithstanding their subscription to the same thirty-nine articles, purposely framed in order to prevent diversity of opinion, think alike? Nay, is it not notorious that they even preach, and publish as different opinions as the Dissenters themselves?"

"I would also ask, where is the great inconvenience attending this circumstance? Whatever it be, it must grow less and less continually, and would sooner vanish, if that liberty was given to all by law, which some of the clergy will venture to take by connivance. The consequence of free discussion would in time produce a rational and permanent uniformity. For truth, we need not doubt, will finally prevail in every contest, and no person ought to be under any bias in favour of any particular opinion, in consequence of its being favoured by the state; which if it be an error, must greatly protract the prevalence of it. And certainly, Sir, no persons should be under any temptation to wound their consciences, by attempts to reconcile their belief of one doctrine with their subscription to another. This is an evil now existing, of great and growing magnitude, unspeakably greater than anything that can be imagined to result from the abolition of such subscriptions. This makes men of integrity in some things, notoriously insincere in others, and the preachers of truth and virtue to the nation not seldom enter upon their profession with the solemn avowal of a falsehood; *offences will come, but woe to those by whom they come.*"

"If, Sir, you suppose that all the clergy of the church of England really believe what they have subscribed, or ever did believe it, as that there are three persons in one Godhead, that Jesus Christ is a proper object of prayer, and that he is to be adjured by his bloody sweat and passion, and by his *holy nativity and circumcision*; if you suppose they believe that all mankind sinned in Adam, and are punished for his sin; and that all being, on this account, destined to everlasting destruction, God made choice of some of them to be saved, while he left others under an irreversible sentence of damnation, with many other doctrines equally abhorrent to reason, and contradicted by the whole tenor of scripture, you are greatly mistaken. You, Sir, having been educated in one of our universities, have, no doubt, subscribed these doctrines yourself, but perhaps without ever knowing that you did so, certainly before you had considered them. Why then should the obligation to this subscription be continued?"

(Letter to Pitt, pp.25–7)

"Assure yourself, Sir, that the Unitarian doctrine has already taken deep root in the church itself, and it is a plant of strong constitution, and makes vigorous shoots. The present controversy greatly quickens its growth, and in spight (sic) of all the efforts of churchmen, and of all that, as a statesman, you can do to assist them, the doctrines which constitute the peculiar faith of the church of England must fall before it."

(p.30)

A few years later, the French Revolution supervening, he wrote in a somewhat similar strain to Edmund Burke:

"Your clergy themselves force this upon us. (Conformity) For they cannot rail at us as Dissenters, but they must needs glance at our *opinions*, and especially such as they imagine will render us most obnoxious, never forgetting the *unitarianism* of many of us. Consequently, when we defend ourselves (not being apt to entertain doubts of the goodness of our cause) we pursue our antagonists through the whole field of their arguments. We boldly assert the *unity of God*, and the purity and simplicity of his worship. We exclaim against all usurpation of the rights of our only lawgiver Jesus Christ, by priests or kings, by councils or parliaments. On these topics we are always ready *to cry aloud and not spare*. In this manner, Sir, you raise a storm the force of which you and your church will not be able to stand."

(Letters to EB, p.134)

Priestley goes on to discuss the way in which Burke has dealt with the case put up by Dr. Price, and the fact that his main weapon has been ridicule.

"*But ridicule is not the test of truth*, and if reason and common sense is to be heard, it must surely appear even to yourself . . . that upon any other principle than that of Dr. Price, no reformation can be justified. Because, on the very same principle, whatever it be, that any person is authorised to dissent from a mode of worship, set up by *the state*, he is authorised to dissent from any that may be set up by *private persons;* and if he think the public profession of religion, in the form of *public worship*, to be a duty, he is obliged in conscience to set up one of his own, whether more or fewer persons, or any besides his own family will join him in it."

(p.135)

Here, Priestley has placed his finger very firmly on the major difference between himself and Edmund Burke; the latter inclines to pontificate and, if he is not getting the better of an argument, does not hesitate to resort to ridicule, mockery, irony, dismissal, or, the simple ignoring of his adversary, to win his point. Priestley is always willing to debate and discuss points of difference, knowing that there are many around who will disagree with him, and some of them violently so, having many times experienced this. He is sure in his own mind, as we have just seen, that his rejection of the Holy Trinity and the divinity of Christ Jesus must, sooner than later, triumph, because to him it is self evident truth. He had already written and published many works to support such views, but they are little known today, except by a faithful and dwindling band of followers, much as the sect itself has faded almost to oblivion in the present century; full blooded agnosticism and humanism are much more the vogue. Most of the works we are considering here have been deliberately excluded from national consciousness for political motives, whereas his religious writings are ignored because they have largely ceased to interest believers.

There is a strange reflection on this topic of Unitarianism by Rev. Herbert McLachlan in his history of Warrington Academy (1943), where Priestley had taught. It had been around in the guise of Socinianism for many years but came to maturity in the Warrington period. He tells us:

"For an excellent practical reason, then, Warrington was altogether free from religious tests for teachers and pupils alike, the first institution making so wide an appeal to boast such freedom, *after heresy had raised its head in nonconfonnity*, (my italics) until the rise of the modern university colleges."

(McL, WA, p.18)

So, even his own followers and chroniclers did not hesitate to describe Priestley's great movement as 'a heresy', but this adds to his credibility, rather than discrediting him. He had a marked antipathy towards the church of Rome, but this did not prevent him from publishing a forthright pamphlet immediately after the Gordon riots, defending British Catholics and their rights as citizens to public worship and free speech, even though he made it clear he expected they would be laughed out of court as soon as a sensible British public became aware of their ludicrous antics; this would be at the same time that his own ultra-rational followers were taking over the nation, as to a significant extent they did its leadership during the 19th century. But history since that time tells a different story. He would be surprised at how matters have developed, but unlikely to be downcast. He was a great scientist, but clung to some strange outmoded notions (notably the concept of phlogiston) long after others had moved on. None of us is infallible, and a great man, who has contributed so much to mankind, should not be slighted for his failings. He would have been happy to leave his reputation on such grounds.

Returning to the topic of Anglican clergy, apart from their faith, orthodox or tainted, Priestley has other criticisms of their role in society and, in particular, of how they relate to the secular establishment:

"Religion I consider as a thing that requires no civil establishment whatever, and that its beneficial operation is injured by such establishments, and the more in proportion to its riches. I am satisfied that such an establishment, instead of being any advantage, is a great encumbrance to a state, and in general highly unfavourable to its liberties. Civil establishments of Christianity were altogether unknown in the early ages, and gained ground by very slow degrees, as other corruptions and abuses in the system did."

(Letters to EB, p.53)

"On the effect of splendid establishments on the minds of men I have enlarged before, and shall now only observe that, through gross inattention to the principles of human nature, you have neither considered the effect of the clergy of this country on their own minds, or on those of the rich and the great, to whom their ministry is to be adapted. Is it not a fact, that, so far from the former being independent of the latter, that in consequence of having great emolument in continual prospect (which is the case of all the clergy, the bishops themselves not excepted) they must continually look up to them, and court them, in order to advance themselves? Have you never heard of their conniving at, rather than reproving them for, their vices and extravagances, while they have the care of their education at home, and abroad. Is not almost every clergyman, whose talents or connexions encourage him to aspire to a bishopric, or any other great preferment, ready to adopt the maxims, and court the favour, of the great, in whose power alone it is to aid their views? Is it not notorious that the bishops in general fall in with the measures of the court, whatever they are, evidently because they cannot rise higher, or provide for their dependants, by any other means? For whenever the maxims and measures of the court change, the conduct of the bishops almost universally, and even instantly, changes with them."

(pp.91–2)

In a footnote, on the same page, Priestley adds an anecdote to illustrate this tendency, with further comment; the year is 1773:

"When we were introduced to Lord ——, and represented our case to him, he replied in these words, 'Gentlemen, I enter not into the motives and reasons of this application. Are the bishops for you? If they are you may be sure of me. If they are against you, I shall be so too. *They serve us, and we must help them.*' Here we see the real nature of the *alliance between the church and the state*. It is nothing else than a league between two parties in the state against the common liberties of the country."

(p.92)

Priestley quotes Burke at some length, going on to comment on the evils of civil preferment. Addressing him as a *lay divine* who teaches that civil establishments of religion are peculiarly useful in free governments; he gives the floor to Burke *(p.93)*:

"The consecration of the state, by a state religious establishment, is necessary also to operate with a wholesome awe upon free citizens; because, in order to secure their freedom, they must enjoy some determinate portion of power. To them, therefore, a religion connected with the state, and with their duty towards it, becomes even more necessary than in such societies, where the people by the terms of their subjection, are confined to private sentiments, and the management of their own family concerns. All persons possessing any portion of power, ought to be strongly and awfully impressed with an idea that they act in trust to the one great Master, Author and Founder of society."

"This principle ought to be more strongly impressed upon the minds of those who compose the collective sovereignty, than upon those of single princes. Without instruments, these princes can do nothing. Whoever uses instruments, in finding helps, finds also impediments. Their power is, therefore, by no means complete, nor are they safe in extreme abuse. . . . But where popular authority is absolute and unrestrained, the people have an infinitely greater, because a far better founded confidence in their own power. . . . It is therefore of infinite importance that they should not be suffered to imagine that their will, any more than that of kings, is the standard of right and wrong."

(Reflections, pp.101–3)

Priestley then takes up the challenge:

"In all of this, Sir, you as usual, confounded *religion* with the *civil establishment* of it, and hence the manifest inconclusiveness of your whole argument. Religion, no doubt, is useful to all men, of all ranks, in power, or subject to it, as it furnishes an additional motive to good behaviour in every situation. But what has this to do with any civil establishment of it, with its being maintained by the state, the officers of which state will, of course, have the sole power of ecclesiastical as well as civil preferment? How will the members of a popular assembly be overawed by the admonition of men whose salaries are settled, and whose places are disposed of, by themselves, any more than a single arbitrary sovereign? Will not the clergy always look up to that power, which has preferment at its disposal, in whatever hands it be lodged? Are not the established ministers in Holland advocates for their republican government, as much as the English bishops of this day for the limited monarchy of England, and as much as the bishops of Charles I and II were for absolute monarchy, passive obedience, and non-resistance?"

"The clergy, or any other set of men, in the pay of a state, soon perceive what are the maxims of the governing powers in the state, and readily adopt them. Are not the aspiring clergy of the present reign, advocates for higher maxims of government in church and state, than those of the two preceding reigns? The fact is evident, and the difference is to be looked for in the different dispositions of the courts. The former were liberal, and favourable to dissenters, whereas the present is less so. This alone accounts for the whole. If the governors of any country in which religion is established, have no motives to stand in awe of the ministers of religion, which they evidently have not (as they always see the ministers of religion standing in awe of *them*, and courting them) it is of no use to them that it is established at all. If it be of any use, it is simply as *religion*, as a principle acting upon conscience, and influencing individuals, independently of any civil establishment of it."

(Letters to E.B. pp.95–6)

Priestley advises Burke on the dangers threatening his 'dear church'. for which he is 'tremblingly alive all over', first those from without and then those within; we shall concentrate on the latter:

"Danger from *without* is uncertain, and may be warded off; but not so that from *within.* I mean the growing light of the age, in consequence of which we are more and more sensible of the absurdity of the doctrines, the insufficiency of the discipline, and the oppression of the revenues of your church. The people of this country will at length discover that what they have paid so dearly for, as a *benefit*, is really a *nuisance*, that it is hostile to the clearest truth, and subversive of rational liberty for which you, Sir, profess to be a warm advocate."

(p.128)

Priestley comments on secular statesmen meddling in ecclesiastical affairs:

"Statesmen, misled by ignorant or interested priests, have taken upon them to prescribe what men should believe and practice, in order to get to heaven, when they themselves have often neither believed, nor practised, anything under that description. They have set up idols, to which all men, under the severest penalties have been compelled to bow; and the wealth and power of populous nations, which might have been employed in great and useful undertakings, have been diverted from their proper channels, to enforce their unrighteous decrees. By this means have mankind been kept for ages in a state of bondage worse than Egyptian, the bondage of the mind."

(p.145)

On the remuneration of clergy Priestley has also challenged Burke:

"Is it not true that, in all cases of a *civil* nature, every person who receives a salary for any duty whatever, will be more attentive to that duty, when the person who pays the salary, and who is interested in the proper discharge of the duty, has the power of appointing and dismissing him? The reason is obvious. It then becomes the interest of the person who performs the duty, as well as of the person who is benefited by it, that it be *well done*. And can it make any difference, whether the duty be of an ecclesiastical, or of a civil nature, when both are discharged by *men*, beings of the same passions, and subject to the same influences? Every man will do his duty best when he has the eye of a master immediately upon him. Please, Sir, to make the trial. Let your domestic servants, or your domestic chaplain, be appointed, not by yourself, but some other man, or body of men, and let it be as difficult and as slow a process, to obtain a change of them, as it is now for a parish to get rid of a minister whose conduct disgraces them, which is but too often the case. I do not believe that, upon this plan, you would have much expectation of being well served."

(pp.99–100)

Tom Paine also challenges Burke on the discrepancy between the higher clergy and curates in the matter of remuneration. He picks him up on the notion that: The people of England can see some bishops on £10,000 a year, and a curate on £30 or £40 a year, or less, without concern, going on to say:

"No, Sir, they certainly do not see those things without great pain or grudging. It is a case that applies to every man's sense of justice, and is one among many that calls aloud for a constitution."

(Rights, p.106)

Priestley's Birmingham Home Wrecked – 14th July 1791 – by Church & King Mob

Later in Part II of his magnum opus he develops the point further:

"With respect to another class of men, the inferior clergy, I forbear to enlarge upon their condition; but all partialities and prejudices for, or against, different forms and modes of religion aside, common justice will determine, whether there ought to be an income of twenty or thirty pounds a year to one man, and of ten thousand to another. I speak on this subject with more freedom, because I am known not to be a Presbyterian; and therefore the cant cry of court sycophants, about church and meeting, kept up to amuse and bewilder the nation cannot be raised against me."

"Ye simple men, on both sides of the question, do ye not see through this courtly craft? If ye can be kept disputing and wrangling about church and meeting, ye just answer the purpose of every courtier, who lives the while on the spoil of the taxes, and laughs at your credulity. Every religion is good that teaches man to be good; and I know of none that instructs him to be bad."

(p.282)

Reference has already been made to the Gordon Riots of 1780, as arising from religious prejudice and in which Burke himself was one of the prime targets, although he escaped unscathed; Paine takes him up on this matter:

"There is in all European countries a large class of people of that description which in England is called the 'mob'. Of this class were those who committed the burnings and devastation in London in 1780, and of this class were those who carried heads on spikes in Paris. . . . Why then does Mr Burke charge outrages of this kind on a whole people? As well may he charge the riots and outrages of 1780 on all the people of London, or those in Ireland on all his own countrymen."

(p.80)

". . . Governments, so far from being always the cause or means of order, are often the destruction of it. The riots of 1780 had no other source than the remains of those prejudices which the government itself had encouraged. But with respect to England there are also other causes."

(p.188)

This last sentence is somewhat enigmatic and certainly not self-explanatory, however, Paine does go on to mention factors such as inequitable taxation and other injustices which inflame the underprivileged. But in considering this passage, once again dates are crucial; this second passage is from Part II of the *Rights of Man* which was not published until 1792, between this and Part I, in the early months of '91, came the Birmingham riots of July, when Priestley and a number of his friends in and around that town suffered considerable loss of property and were fortunate that some of them did not lose their lives as well. The rioters on that occasion were freely acknowledged as the 'Church and King Mob'. It is not suggested that government had any direct connection with the actions that took place, but there is ample evidence to show that people in high place, right to the throne itself had little sympathy with the victims. Recent research and publications from Birmingham itself bring evidence that certain local magistrates and civic leaders played a very doubtful role in this whole affair. Paine would almost certainly have been aware, at least of suspicions, when he wrote the passage just quoted.[*]

Is Disestablishment Desirable?

Priestley seems to have been the one who argued most vehemently for disestablishment of the church of England; he was certainly highly critical of its position within the state, as we have seen already. He summarises his arguments in Letter VIII which has the title: 'Of a civil Establishment being essential to Christianity', in which he has the following:

"The whole system of the civil establishment of religion had its origin at a time when neither *religion* nor *civil government* was much understood. It was the consequence of the feudal states of Europe becoming Christian in an age where we find little of Christianity, besides the name; its genuine *doctrines* and its *spirit* having equally disappeared."

"Every article therefore within the compass of the civil establishment of Christianity, is evidently an innovation; and as systems are reformed by reverting to their first principles, Christianity can never be restored to its pristine state, and recover its real dignity and efficiency, till it be disengaged from all connexion with civil power. . . . This establishment therefore may be compared to a *fungus,* or a *parasitical plant,* which is so far from being coeval with the tree on which it has fastened itself, that it seized upon it in its weak and languid state, and if it be not cut off in time, will exhaust all its juices and destroy it."

"Writing to an orator, I naturally think of metaphors and comparison, and therefore I will give you two of three more. So far is a civil establishment from being friendly to Christianity that it may be compared to an animal called the *sloth,* which, when it gets upon any tree, will not leave it till it has devoured even the leaves and the bark, so that it presently perishes. Rather it is the animal called a *Glutton* which falling from a tree (in which it generally conceals itself) upon some noble animal, immediately begins to tear it and suck its blood; and if it be not soon shaken off . . . it infallibly kills its prey."

"Now when I see this *fungus* of an *establishment* upon the noble plant of *Christianity,* draining its best juices; when I see this sloth upon its stately branches, gnawing it, and stripping it bare; or to change my comparison, when I see the Glutton upon the shoulders of this noble animal, the blood flowing down, and its vitals in danger; if I wish to preserve the tree or the animal, must I not, without delay, extirpate the

---

[*] See V. Bird and Alderman Martineau.

fungus, destroy the sloth and kill the Glutton. Indeed, Sir, say, or write, what you please, such vermin deserve no mercy. You may stand by, and weep for the state of your favourite fungus, your sloth, or your Glutton, but I shall not spare them."

"In your idea, a civil establishment, is the very *basis, or foundation* of religion. But when any structure is to be raised, the foundation is the first thing that is laid; whereas this was evidently the very last. Instead therefore, of its being *the foundation,* or even the *buttress,* it may rather be said to resemble the heavy *stone roof* pressing with enormous weight upon the walls, which on that account require many buttresses to support it, and after all proves to be so heavy, and is now become so ruinous, that it will be found absolutely necessary to take it all down, if the building is to be preserved. Nay, as in the late taking down of the cathedral, I think, of Hereford, if the greatest care be not taken, the attempt to meddle with this cumbrous roof will be hazardous, both to those who remove it, and those who stand near it."

(Letters to EB, pp.83–5)

In this essay Priestley is heavy-handedly imitating the style of Burke, but whereas Burke was able to get away with such a venture and even to excite admiration; it is his metier and his audience expect it of him, Priestley merely managed to inflame his enemies and his critics even further. He frankly acknowledges that in addressing himself to an orator, he has been tempted to use metaphors and comparisons, but oratory is not his art; he is a philosopher and is much more effective when he maintains that persona. However, amidst all the verbiage, his case against a civil establishment of religion stands, but it has been better expressed in some of the other letters.

The Church in Danger

> *The Christian ideal has not been tried and found wanting;*
> *it has been found difficult and left untried.*
> G K Chesterton – *The Unfinished Temple*

'The Church in Danger' was an urgent cry around that period, especially with the perceived threat, posed by the revolution in France. Like much else at the time this threat was grossly exaggerated, especially since the situation in the two countries was so different. England had a nationalised church, closely tied into the state establishment; a church not quite sure whether it was truly protestant, or a nationalised branch of the old pre-reformation universal church. In France the national church was Catholic; it was not established, but its links with the secular state were close, reflecting a long tradition. In both, the clerical hierarchy was, to a large extent, part of the aristocracy. Each had its dissenters; in England these were the truly protestant sects, together with the Catholics; in France the Huguenots predominated, probably closer to the Presbyterians of Scotland than to other sects, reflecting something of the 'auld alliance'.

The danger for Catholicism in France came primarily from within, being due to its own decadence, apathy and abuses, especially at the higher levels of organisation; the level to which the nation should have been looking for leadership. In England there was decadence also, especially when compared with the nonconformist sects. But parliament, at that time, was strongly favouring the established church, so that any threat which existed was not from within, but from a fear that the social disorder in France might spread. This excited some of the more voluble clergy, and enthusiastic laymen, such as Edmund Burke. Priestley heaped great scorn on this climate of fear and hysteria, which, it must be acknowledged, his own writings and sermons were doing their share to foment:

> "The cry of the *church being in danger,* is almost as old as the church itself, has been kept up by its friends, and physicians, whenever it has suited their purpose . . . . This has served as an excuse for every outrage upon others; as if nothing was ever meant by them, but to secure itself. And thus the most bloody and *offensive* wars are often made under the cover of being merely *defensive* ones which are always held to be lawful. The *church of Christ* is built upon a rock, and we are assured that *the gates of hell shall not prevail against it.* Now, had this church of yours, whose fears and cries have always been the signal of alarm to all its neighbours, been made of proper materials, and constructed in a proper manner, had it been built upon this rock of *truth,* it would never have had anything to fear. Its own evidence and excellence would have supported it. Should the state itself be overturned, the people would, of themselves, and from predilection, reinstate their favourite church in all its former rights and privileges. But you are sensible it has not this hold on the minds of the people, and you justly suspect that, if any misfortune should happen to it, they would never rebuild it, but, if left to their own free choice, would adopt some other plan more useful and commodious."

> "Time was when your church pretended to fear where no fear was, and being then vigorous her cries were heard as the roaring of a lion. Of late she has been so feeble, that we only amuse ourselves with them; and now the danger is really transferred from us to herself."
>
> *(Letters to EB, pp.123–4)*

"You, Sir, who with many others have lately joined in the cry of the church being in danger, have thought to guard it by laws and tests, excluding Dissenters from all places of trust and profit. Paying our full share of the public taxes, and having always distinguished ourselves by our industry, in manufactures and commerce (all our trading towns abounding with Dissenters), we thought it not unreasonable to request a right of admission, at the will of the crown, or the election of our fellow subjects, to such advantages as arise from that flourishing state of the country to which, it is not denied that we have eminently contributed. Thrice, we have made the application, and twice you, Sir, made no opposition to us. We therefore flattered ourselves that, having been in other respects a friend to *equal liberty,* especially in America and Ireland, where, as well as in Scotland, no such tests are known, you would have been a friend to us. But it seems that after deeply ruminating on the subject, and having, no doubt, prayed for, and, as you though, obtained, more light than you had before, you most unexpectedly, and with peculiar warmth and fierceness, opposed us."

(p.131)

Once again Priestley is rubbing salt into Burke's wounds by drawing attention to his sentiments regarding Ireland, as well as his activities on the American front, which contrast with the stance he has now adopted on France, and his spiteful, new found opposition to repeal of the Test and Corporation Acts. Regarding his change of heart Priestley quotes this paragraph from *Reflections* back at him:

"You do not imagine, that I wish to confine power, authority, and distinction to blood, and names, and titles. No, Sir. There is no qualification for government but virtue and wisdom, actual or presumptive. Wherever they are actually found, they have in whatever state, condition, profession or trade, the passport of heaven to human place and honour. Woe to the country which would madly and impiously reject the service of the talents and virtues, civil, military, or religious, that are given to grace and to serve it; and would condemn to obscurity everything formed to diffuse lustre and glory around a state."

(Reflections, p.54)

So according to Burke and his associates, Dissenters were to remain excluded 'from all places of trust and profit' throughout the kingdom; whereas, shortly afterwards Burke is saying to his correspondent in France that there should be 'no qualification for government but virtue and wisdom'. In spite of such contradictions, Burke still has his constituency, even to this day, that hotly rejects any charge of inconsistency at that time.

Another contemporary who is strongly critical of the Established Church is William Cobbett, but with this significant difference, that he is himself a member of that same church. However, it is the political establishment rather than the confessional church with which he is quarrelling. In his conclusion he states:

"Born and bred a Protestant of the Church of England, having a wife and numerous family professing the same faith, having the remains of most dearly beloved parents lying in a Protestant church-yard, and trusting to conjugal or filial piety to place mine by their side, I have in this undertaking had no motive . . . but a sincere and disinterested love of truth and justice. It is not for the rich and powerful of my countrymen that I have spoken; but for the poor, the persecuted, the proscribed."

(History of Reformation, para.478)

Priestley was deceased more than 20 years and Paine somewhat less when these words were penned by Cobbett and, though each had a somewhat different stance, there is much in this book that the other two would have approved. Not only the contents, but even more so the style, would have incensed the sophisticated and politically correct Burke.

CHAPTER XII

Aspects of Dissent

What, gentlemen, can't we, even in the Church, acknowledge a republic? There, at least, the Heralds College itself might allow that we, all of us, have the same pedigree, and are direct descendants of Eve and Adam, whose inheritance is divided amongst us.

Thackeray's Book of Snobs

Priestley is on firm and very familiar ground when dealing with nonconformity and dissent; here he speaks with authority. In parliament Burke had supported moves to have the iniquitous Test and Corporation Acts repealed, and this was in line with his efforts to get relief for Catholics from the even more severe Penal Laws, that effort which culminated in the Catholic Relief Act of 1778, and which, as previously noted, had provoked the Gordon Riots of 1780. In the eyes of the law, Catholics were dissenters just as much, if not even more so, than any other nonconformists. It was therefore no surprise that the Catholics having gained a modicum of relief, those other dissenters should soon mount a campaign to have their own disabilities removed. The first bill was rejected by a substantial margin – 176 to 98, in March 1787, at which time Priestley wrote his *Letter to William Pitt;* a second attempt two years later almost succeeded, the margin being reduced to 122 against 102; this was in May 1789, as revolution in France was beginning to get into its stride, and just two months before the Bastille fell.

The hopes of dissenters were raised, and another attempt was made to have a bill passed in March 1790, but reaction had set in strongly, and this time defeat was by 294 to 105. It is noteworthy that almost double the number of members voted on this occasion, compared with the previous year, but what is even more remarkable, in the present context, is that Edmund Burke, who had previously voted in favour of repeal, now voted against. It has to be remembered that the *Dissertation* by Richard Price, which provoked Burke's *Reflections on the Revolution in France,* had intervened and started his reaction against old friends, who now became his *unspeakable* opponents. The movement for repeal was now dead and did not arise again until 1828, when it was carried in the year before Catholic Emancipation. Priestley's views are firm and tinged with bitterness:

"Infidelity has made considerable progress in this country, and especially in the upper classes of life, persons to whom you imagine the wealth of the clergy would naturally recommend their religion. But these men do not frequent your churches, and they regard your establishment no farther than they can avail themselves of its emoluments, as it is a means of providing for their younger sons and brothers. If the Houses of Lords and Commons were fairly polled, after voting according to their *real opinion*, whether, think you, would the majority be in favour of Christianity, or against it? Many, and those not inattentive observers, think the latter."

"If riches and power have the charms which you ascribe to them in the business of religion, how came the *Reformation* to take place? The power and spleandour of the church of Rome was at its height in the time of Luther and his followers, yet, without any aid of this kind to oppose it, in Germany, in this country, or in Scotland, it gave way to the efforts of men who had no advantage but what they derived from reason and piety. Surely, Sir, the bulk of mankind do not see with your eyes. If they did, how can you account for the great number of Dissenters in this country from the time of Queen Elizabeth (who had the same ideas that you have on these subjects) down to the present time; and what can be the cause of the amazing increase of methodism? Neither their ministers nor ours are rich. We have not the style of *my lord*, nor have we seats in parliament. But, destitute as we are of all these advantages, I will venture to say, that our ministers, as a body, are much more respected by their congregations than yours, possessed, in your idea, of all the *natural human means of estimation*. Judging of us by yourselves, you naturally suppose, that it is only through envy and malignity, that we declaim against the wealth and power of the clergy."

(Letters to EB, pp.73–5)

Here he quotes from Burke's *Reflections* a passage which has already been included, and which concludes:

"We shall believe these reformers then to be honest enthusiasts, not, as we now think them, cheats and deceivers, when we see them throwing their own goods into common, and submitting their own persons to the austere discipline of the early church."

(Reflections, p.114)

Priestley continues:

"This, Sir, is a paragraph of which it is to be hoped you will some time hence be ashamed. You do not give us the alternative of being either knaves or fools. You will not allow us any place in this more respectable, or rather less contemptible, class of men. None of us who disapprove of establishments, Dr. Price, or myself, can have the honour of being ranked with *honest enthusiasts*. We are all absolutely, and without a single exception, *cheats* and *deceivers*, that is, persons who are saying one thing, and at the same time meaning another. But we are happy in an appeal from your judgement, as you are from ours; though, judging from myself, we are by no means disposed to censure you with so much severity as you do us. I do not say that we are so mortified to the world, as that the good things with which you tempt us, have no charms for us. We are *men*, and have the feelings of men, as well as yourselves. But if they struck our imagination as forcibly as they do yours, and if we were the *knaves* and *hypocrites* that you suppose us to be, why do we not make greater efforts to obtain them? The market is open, but we do not chuse to give the price. If these things be accessible to *some*, they are no doubt to *others*, in proportion to their ability or interest, or whatever it be that assists their preferment."

"As to subscription to your articles, etc., if I be such a person as you have described, why might I not declare my unfeigned assent and consent to them, as well as others? Besides, if the advantages of an establishment were the things that we are aiming at, why are we labouring at the subversion of all establishments, exposing their inutility, and even their mischievous nature and tendency? If the tree be cut down, how are we to live upon the fruit of it? And, there are now, I believe, very few Dissenters, who, if the present establishment was overturned, would wish to substitute any other in its place.

(Letters to EB, pp.76–8)

Comparing conditions in the first millennium, with more recent conditions in certain forms of Christianity, Priestley confronts his accuser again:

"You dread a scene of *faction* and low *intrigue* among the clergy who should be candidates for places in the church. But what was the fact for more than a thousand years in the christian church in general, when all the bishops and clergy were elective, when *men* were the same that they are now, and, when whatever you imagine of peculiar zeal, and disinterestedness in the primitive times of the church, was certainly abated? Or what is now the case with Dissenters in this country, and through all the states of North America, where the officiating clergy of all denominations are now, and ever have been elective? . . . There are more than a thousand dissenting ministers in this kingdom, and they are all elected by their respective congregations; but any great inconvenience attending an election of this kind very seldom occurs. It is probable that you, though living in the country, and acquainted with Dissenters, never heard of any such thing, any more than in America, or in Ireland."

"So far is there from being any cabal or intrigue, to obtain places with us, that the person chosen seldom hears of it, till his invitation is sent to him; and anything like canvassing would be an effective bar to his election. Indeed, it very seldom happens that there is more than one candidate named at one time, and the members of any congregation are considered as very imprudent if they admit of two. Besides, if any improper proceedings should occur, it will be easy to provide remedies."

"You say, that no person liberally educated, or any other than those in the lowest classes in life, will be candidates for church preferment. This, Sir, goes upon the idea that no person will officiate in a christian church but for the sake of the temporal emolument which he receives from it, which is a most unjust and ill-founded reflection on christianity, and the ministers of it. It may, indeed, be the case with a church, the articles of which men of sense cannot subscribe, and the stated duty of which is against their consciences. For such services as *these* men must be *paid,* and well paid too; and in general it will be done for nothing but the pay. But this is not the case with *us,* nor was it *so* in the early ages of the church. Though few of our salaries will more than half maintain us, there are never wanting persons of independent fortune, and the most liberal educations, who voluntarily devote themselves to the work of our ministry. From unbiased choice they give their time, and their fortunes to an employment which they deem to be most honourable and important, in whatever light it may appear to *you;* and our situation is such, that few besides persons of some ability and piety will think of the profession."

"So respected is the character of a minister with us, though the case may be different with you, that whatever was his original rank in life, it places him on a level with the most opulent of his congregation; and it rarely happens but that in all our congregations, there are some persons of as good fortunes, and as polished manners as any others in the town or neighbourhood. On this account, as well as from a principle of genuine piety and benevolence, the situation of a dissenting minister has many attractions, especially to a person of a serious and studious turn of mind. We think it greatly preferable to that of the generality of the established clergy, with all their prospects of preferment, which often produce a cringing and servile disposition. And I will venture to say, that, independent of the private fortunes which many of our ministers have, their character and conduct render them as truly respectable, and independent in mind, as any set of clergy in the world; far more so, I am confident than yours, with all the advantages you boast."

(pp.100-3)

Priestley is reluctant to credit Anglican clergy with any virtue, either collectively or individually, but it is worth considering the passages quoted from Thackeray's *Book of Snobs.* He can be critical of his church, but he is also conscious of a great deal of unsung virtue among its parish clergy. Considering the academic quality and achievements of established clergy and of nonconformist ministers, Priestley makes an unflattering comparison:

". . . The dignified clergy, whom the court makes independent of the people, are not those who, in any country, produce learned theological works, but generally men in the lower orders, and who have no motive to chuse their profession besides an attachment to the duties and studies peculiar to it, and who wish to distinguish themselves in it. Very few bishops in your church have been writers, at least after they were made bishops. The greatest works your church has to boast of were the productions of obscure clergymen; and despicable as our situation may appear to you, who certainly know very little about us, an application to the studies suited to our profession, appears, by the number of our writings, to be much greater than among the clergy of the established church. The relation we stand in to our congregations insures a respectable private character, and in a manner obliges us to devote the leisure we have, to literature, to science, and to professional studies. How strangely, Sir, must you be, blinded by your high church prejudices, not to perceive that this both *is*, and necessarily *must* be the difference between the clergy of the established church, and ministers with us; a difference greatly to our advantage; and it arises wholly from our people having the choice of their ministers, and of course a power of dismissing them when, on any account, they do not approve of them."

" . . . Though you clearly see that a splendid church establishment, with bishops appointed by the court, actually makes many of the clergy mere *men of the world,* so that they have nothing of the *christian minister,* besides the name, and the consequence of this has been disbelief and utter contempt of christianity in men of rank and fortune, you would pretend that the abolishing of christianity would be the consequence of their dissolution. Indeed, Sir, both the nature of the case, and facts, which are obvious to the most careless eye, show that christianity cannot be preserved along with them. They are a disease that must be extirpated, or the subject will be destroyed."

(pp.103–5)

In a later section, Priestley expresses his disquiet at the way in which the established clergy are remunerated, and the way in which this disturbs their ministry:

" . . . Only take away the emoluments of the clergy, and leave them to subsist, as we dissenting ministers do, and as the apostles and bishops in primitive times did, on the voluntary contributions of those who are benefited by their ministry, and you will effectively remove all cause of trembling on their account. Let them be naturally as quarrelsome as dogs, they will be as quiet as lambs, if no bone of contention be thrown among them. What danger arises from our divisions, or those of the many discordant sects which have ever existed in North America? Be they ever so great we never trouble the state with them, and we are unanimous and hearty in every common cause, respecting either christianity or public liberty."

(pp.121–2)

The growth of dissent, both the older forms, and the newly emerging Methodism, is another problem for the established church which Priestley raises:

"The increase of dissenters is a fact that you and your clergy are either wholly ignorant of, or are strangely inattentive to. I shall mention only one instance. I have resided in Birmingham only ten years, and there are now building the eighth, the ninth, and the tenth, new places of dissenting or methodist worship, in this town, all within this short period, nine of them for new congregations, and the others for increased ones. Another is talked of, and many have been built in the neighbourhood; and in this time there has not been one additional church, or chapel, for the members of the church of England. The increase of the dissenters and methodists, in Sheffield, in Leeds, and I have no doubt, in other manufacturing towns, has been nearly in the same proportion."

"Every controversy in which churchmen have meddled, has been to their disadvantage. The heads of the church therefore now wisely avoid all controversy. But even this policy will not avail them long. Every clergyman is not wise, and *fools*, as they say, *will be meddling*, and every meddling is to their hurt, and that of their cause."

(p.129)

Priestley is not convinced that an increase in sects is to be deplored, on the contrary he sees some advantage therein:

"You, Sir, seem to dread a *number of sects* among christians. But what serious inconvenience would arise from their being increased even tenfold? It would be much better for the state, than if there were only two. Religious bigotry would also be diminished by this means, and the members of these sects would sooner learn to exercise charity for each other, distinguishing the great things in which all christians agree, from the comparatively smaller things in which any of them differ. In this way, also, they would soon arrive at a *rational uniformity;* the points of difference being freely canvassed, and truth prevailing, and establishing itself, as no doubt it will in the end."

(p.136)

There is little doubt that two centuries on Priestley would be gratified to find that a growing number of Christians of many denominations are seeing the differences which still divide us, in much the way that he has set out; there are the basic tenets (not all of which he himself held), and many other features which are peculiar to one denomination but not to another. **Methodism** was a new feature in the 18th century, and therefore is commented upon for its own merits; Priestley, in particular, is complimentary. We have already noted the question he poses *(p.74):* "What can be the cause of the amazing increase in Methodism?" Later he goes on to comment:

"The instruction of the poor is more attended to by the Methodists than by any other class of christians in this country. They not only make them welcome, but they seek out, they invite and press them to receive instruction; and if those of them who are comparatively poor, tax themselves for the maintenance of their preachers, and the building of their places of worship, it is in such a manner as promotes industry, and checks profligacy and extravagance. By this means, becoming more sober and more frugal, they become comparatively rich and are better able to contribute, their penny, their two-pence, or six-pence a week, to supply the wants of others. I honour their wisdom and oeconomy, and think most highly of those persons whose education and habits dispose and enable them to adapt themselves to the instruction of the lowest and poorest of the vulgar. They are civilising and christianising that part of the community, which is below the notice of your dignified clergy, but whose souls, as the common phrase is, are as *precious in the sight of God,* as those who are called *their betters.* Such men will have their reward in heaven. I only wish they had more knowledge, and more charity along with their zeal; and *these* also, will come in due time."

(pp.89–90)

"Dissenters of one denomination or another, are very much increased of late years, and many of them are avowedly hostile to every establishment. The Methodists are by no means attached to it. Few of them ever trouble your churches, and frequently in great bodies become dissenters."

(p.128)

In these passages Priestley highlights the outstanding social achievement of the Wesley brothers and their associates in the Methodist movement; they catered for the poor, producing a devout and articulate class of artisan, 'sober and frugal', who, in time, developed a thirst for reform, but whose solution was not a rush to take the Tower of London, erecting guillotines in the forecourt of St. Paul's and of Westminster Abbey, then spreading to other cities and towns throughout the kingdom. No, but they rushed to learn from Tom Paine's *Rights of Man,* a more peaceful activity, which they would never have achieved in the conditions prevalent at the beginning of that century. The closest Britain got to bloody revolution was in the year in which Edmund Burke died – 1797, when the naval mutinies at Spithead and the Nore almost brought the government down. *(Roger Wells, 1986, ch.V)* These naval ratings were the most oppressed and abused group in the whole of British society, pushed beyond endurance, who achieved a blockade of the port of London, almost strangling the nation, but this is another feature of our history which is swept under the carpet, lest it should disturb and enlighten the populace at large; much safer to concentrate upon such things as the splendid, but improbable victory of Henry V's army at Agincourt, or the defeat of the Spanish Armada by the elements of the heavens, which console the collective psyche.

What a pity that Edmund Burke and other members of the establishment, both secular and clerical, could not appreciate these benign forces which were operating in their midst; the government would not then have panicked; great social abuses might have been tackled; the British would have given a much more positive lead in Europe, instead of resorting to war, and a half hearted Reform Act would not have been delayed until 1832.

It is interesting to consider, in this connection, Winston Churchill's assessment of the contribution from Methodism, and of Dissent in general; he is much closer to Priestley than to Burke:

"The religious revival of John Wesley had broken the stony surface of the Age of Reason. The enthusiasm generated by the Methodist movement and its missions to the poor and humble accelerated the general dissolution of the 18th century world. The Dissenters, who had long supported the Whig party, increased in wealth and importance and renewed their attack on the religious monopoly of the Established Church. Barred from parliament and from the franchise, fertile in mind, they formed an intelligent, thrustful, and unsatisfied body of men."

(WSC, Age of Revolution, p.199)

It is interesting to reflect on Tom Paine's evolution in the religious sphere; his parents had a mixed marriage. His mother being of the established church, he was baptised and confirmed as an Anglican, but his father was a Quaker and young Tom frequently attended meetings with him. Before leaving home it appears that he heard John Wesley preach, being impressed by him and his movement which had such a powerful influence with the *common people*. In his early twenties, first in Kent then in London, he operated for a time as a Methodist preacher and teacher, learning there from much of his skill as a communicator across a wide spectrum of humanity. Methodists and Quakers would lament his later lapse into agnosticism. *(Keane, pp.16–25, 46–49, 60–62)*

Concluding his Rights of Man, Paine addresses himself to the part which religion should play in society, a topic which he has eschewed up to that point, saying:

"Throughout this work, various and numerous as the subjects are, which I have taken up and investigated, there is only a single paragraph upon religion, viz. *'that every religion is good that teaches man to be good'*.

"I have carefully avoided to enlarge upon the subject, because I am inclined to believe, that what is called the present ministry wish to see contentions about religion kept up, to prevent the nation turning its attention to subjects of government. It is as if they were to say, *'Look that way or any way, but this'*.

"But as religion is very improperly made a political machine, and the reality of it is thereby destroyed, I will conclude this work with stating in what light religion appears to me."

"If we suppose a large family of children, who, on any particular day or particular circumstance, made it a custom to present to their parent some token of their affection and gratitude, each of them would make a different offering, and most probably in a different manner. Some would pay their congratulations in themes of verse or prose, by some little devices, as their genius dictated, or according to what they thought would please; and perhaps, the least of all, not able to do any of those things, would ramble into the garden, or the field, and gather what it thought the prettiest flower it could find, though, perhaps, it might be but a simple weed. The parent would be more gratified by such variety, than if the whole of them had acted upon a concerted plan, and each had made exactly the same offering. This would have the cold appearance of contrivance, or the harsh one of control. But of all unwelcome things, nothing could more afflict the parent than to know, that the whole of them had afterwards gotten together by the ears, boys and girls, fighting, scratching, reviling and abusing each other about which was the best or the worst present."

"Why may we not suppose, that the great Father of all is pleased with variety of devotion; and that the greatest offence we can act is that by which we seek to torment and render each other miserable. For my own part, I am fully satisfied that what I am now doing, with an endeavour to conciliate mankind, to render their condition happy, to unite nations that have hitherto been enemies, and to extirpate the horrid practice of war, and break the chains of slavery and oppression, is acceptable in his sight, and being the best service I can perform, I act it cheerfully."

"I do not believe that any two men, on what are called doctrinal points, think alike, who think at all. It is only those who have not thought who appear to agree. It is in this case as with what is called the British Constitution. It has been taken for granted to be good, and encomiums have take the place of proof. But when the nation comes to examine into its principles, and the abuses which it admits, it will be found to have more defects than I have pointed out in this work and the former."

"As to what are called national religions, we may with as much propriety, talk on national Gods. It is either political craft, or the remains of the pagan system, when every nation had its separate and particular deity."

(Rights, pp.292–4)

There are many differences between Priestley and Paine in this sphere, but in the sentiments expressed here there is much of harmony. As a footnote, it is interesting to note the analysis of G K Chesterton in respect of Puritanism, as it developed in Scotland, in contrast with England:

"In Scotland Puritanism was the main thing, and was mixed with Parliamentary and other oligarchies. In England Parliamentary oligarchy was the main thing, and was mixed with Puritanism. When the storm began to rise against Charles I, after the more or less transitional time of his father, the Scotch successor of Elizabeth, the instances commonly cited mark all the differences between democratic religion and aristocratic politics. The Scotch legend is that of Jenny Geddes, the poor woman who threw a stool at the priest. The English legend is that of John Hampden, the great squire who raised a county against the King. The Parliamentary movement in England was, indeed, almost wholly a thing of squires, with their new allies the merchants. They were squires who may well have regarded themselves as the real and natural leaders of the English; but they were leaders who allowed no mutiny among their followers. There was certainly no village Hampden in Hampden village."

(Short History, p.170)

CHAPTER XIII

Education and the Churches

If you consider, . . . what profound snobbishness the University system produced, you will allow that it is time to attack some of those feudal middle-age superstitions. . . . Because a lad is a lord, the University gives him a degree at the end of two years which another is seven years in acquiring. Because he is a lord, he has no call to go through an examination.

Thackeray's Book of Snobs

T HE EDUCATIONAL DISABILITY OF DISSENTERS, and progress they had made, is another topic further to be explored. Let us first hear Burke on the virtues and advantages of British education at that time, and then hear Priestley on its disadvantages for all of those outside the charmed circle of the establishment. Burke is, in the main, addressing himself to France:

"Nothing is more certain than that our manners, our civilisation, and all the good things which are connected with manners, and with civilisation, have, in this European world of ours, depended for ages upon two principles; and were indeed the result of both combined; I mean the spirit of a gentleman, and the spirit of religion. The nobility and the clergy, the one by profession, the other by patronage, kept learning in existence, even in the midst of arms and confusions, and whilst governments were rather in their causes, than formed. Learning paid back what it received to nobility and priesthood; and it paid with usury, by enlarging their ideas, and by furnishing their minds. Happy if they had all continued to know their indissoluble union and their proper place! Happy if learning, not debauched by ambition, had been satisfied to continue the instructor, and not aspired to be the master! Along with its natural protectors and guardians, learning will be cast into the mire, and trodden down under the hoofs of a swinish multitude."

"If, as I suspect, modern letters owe more than they are always willing to own to ancient manners, so do other interests which we value full as much as they are worth. Even commerce, and trade, and manufacture, to the gods of our economical politicians, are themselves, perhaps, but creatures; are themselves but effects, which, as first causes, we choose to worship. They certainly grew under the same shade in which learning flourished. They too may decay with their natural protecting principles. With you, for the present at least, they all threaten to disappear together.

Where trade and manufactures are wanting to a people, and the spirit of nobility and religion remains, sentiment supplies, and not always ill supplies, their place; but if commerce and the arts should be lost in an experiment to try how well a state may stand without these old fundamental principles, what sort of a thing must be a nation of gross, stupid, ferocious, and, at the same time, poor and sordid barbarians, destitute of religion, honour, or manly pride, possessing nothing at present, and hoping for nothing hereafter."

(Reflections, pp.86–7)

"Our education is in a manner wholly in the hands of ecclesiastics, and in all stages from infancy to manhood. Even when our youth, leaving schools and universities, enter that most important period of life which begins to link experience and study together, and when with that view they visit other countries, instead of old domestics whom we have seen as governors to principal men from other parts, three fourths of those who go abroad with our young nobility and gentlemen are ecclesiastics; not as austere masters, nor as mere followers; but as friends and companions of a graver character, and not seldom persons as well born as themselves. With them, as relations, they most commonly keep up a close connexion through life. By this connexion we conceive we attach our gentlemen to the church; and we liberalise the church by an intercourse with the leading characters of the country."

(p.109)

"To destroy any power, growing wild from the rank productive force of the human mind, is almost tantamount, in the moral world, to the destruction of the apparently active bodies in the material. It would be like the attempt to destroy the expansive force of fixed air in nitre, or the power of steam, or of electricity, or of magnetism. These energies always existed in nature, and they were always discernible. They seemed, some of them unservicable, some noxious, some no better than a sport to children; until contemplative ability, combining with practical skill, tamed their wild nature, subdued them to use, and rendered them at once the most powerful and the most tractable agents, in subservience to the great views and designs of men."

(p.175)

It would be good to think that Burke had in mind his erstwhile friend, Joseph Priestley, when he was writing on the world of physics, electricity, chemistry, etc., or when he is suggesting a necessary connection between the world of manufacturing, trade and commerce with education. Priestley had many connections, across the board, in all these fields; his *Essay on a course of Liberal Education for Civil and Active Life,* published in 1765, when he was a tutor at Warrington Academy, was a classic; one of the first attempts to explore the style of education required for men engaging in industry, commerce, and manufacture, as distinct from the more academic subjects. He wrote on the

Theory of Language and Universal Grammar; on *Oratory and Criticism;* on *History and General Policy;* on *The Constitution and Laws of England;* on religion, and on many other topics, but no, Burke was not about to cast any bouquets in that direction.

Burke's thoughts on English education are positively Utopian, but unrealistic; it is difficult to reconcile his remarks with the comments of various contemporaries who reveal the English universities in a state of advanced decadence; for instance Edward Gibbon, who as a Gentleman Commoner, was admitted to the Fellows' table at Magdalen College, Oxford, in 1752, says of the students there: "From the toil of reading, or thinking or writing they had absolved their conscience. Their conversation stagnated in a round of College business, Tory politics, personal stories and private scandal; their dull and deep potations excused the brisk intemperance of youth". *(Trevelyan, Illustrated English Social History, vol 3, p.71)* (Burke's own university career was more distinguished. As the Irish historian Lecky says, "He appears to have found (in Trinity) an amount of intellectual activity considerably greater than that which Gibbon . . . found at Oxford." *The Great Melody* (p.31)) At Cambridge, no lecture was delivered by any Regius Professor of Modern History between 1725 and 1773; somewhere around the latter date, when Priestley's lectures on History were published, John Symonds, the then Professor, commended this work to his students.[*] So what does Priestley himself have to say on Education? Like so many of the other topics he might have been living in a different world from Burke; his comments, however, are not made to Burke, the subject already having been addressed, when writing to William Pitt in 1787, where he said:

"Another circumstance relating to the establishment of this country calls loudly for redress. It is utterly incapable of defence, and yet will probably be retained as long as possible, in consequence of its being necessary to *keep things as they are.* I mean the subscription to the thirty-nine articles of the church of England, at the time of matriculation in our universities. This is an absurdity peculiar to this country. In all others the universities are open to all the world, while yours are shut to all except yourselves. As if it were from a dread of free enquiry, you take care to fetter the mind at the very time when you ought most of all to favour its expansion, and to remove every obstruction to the attainment of truth."

"By thus shutting the door of the universities against all sectaries, and keeping the means of learning to yourselves, you may think to keep us in ignorance, and therefore less able to give you disturbance. But though ignominiously and unjustly excluded from the seats of learning, which, as maintained by the public funds ought to be open to all the community, and driven to the expedient of providing, at great expense, for scientific education among ourselves, we have had this advantage, that our institutions, being formed in a more enlightened age, are more liberal, and

---

[*]   *O'Brien, Warrington Academy, 1989, for these references*

therefore better calculated to answer the purpose of a truly liberal education. Thus while your universities resemble pools *of stagnant water* secured by dams and mounds and offensive to the neighbourhood, ours are like *rivers*, which, taking their natural course, fertilise a whole country. Our plans of education embrace a much greater variety of objects; and the minds of our youth, being unfettered by subscription, are certainly more open to the impression of truth."

"If you, Sir, have the discernment and courage becoming a great statesman in this country, do you yourself, as a representative of one of the universities, propose the removal of this great evil, abolish subscription at the time of matriculation, lay open the advantages of Oxford and Cambridge to us Dissenters, equally with the other members of the same community, and if you still think it necessary that your own clergy should believe such doctrines as those above mentioned, let the subscription be confined to *them,* and let it be made at the time of their leaving the university, or entering upon any church preferment. They will then subscribe with their eyes open, a greater proportion of the clergy will most probably really believe the system they teach, and then, although ignorant and mistaken, yet, being *honest,* they will, with more advantage, recommend honesty and integrity to others."

(Letter to Pitt, pp.31–3)

There is a considerable and growing literature on the merits of dissenter education and its significant contribution to the advent and spread of new red brick universities through the 19th and 20th centuries. This operated from the Restoration right through to the 18th century. Anyone wishing to understand Priestley's outstanding position at the climax of this achievement needs to consult these works. (See Bibliography.)

Burke would probably be outraged at the thought that principles of law should be taught anywhere other than the universities and the Inns of Court, but Priestley had, as far back as the early 1760s, been lecturing on these topics in the Dissenter Academy at Warrington in Lancashire. It is worth considering his introduction to *A Syllabus of Lectures on the Constitution and Laws of England* (the third part of his *Essay on a Course of Liberal Education for a Civil and Active Life)* and then to look at his agenda for a couple of lectures from the *History of England* section:

"**The General Division of the Subject:**
To exhibit as distinct a view as possible on the whole state of the country, I shall first consider its CIVIL and then its ECCLESIASTICAL constitution and laws. In laying down what relates to the civil state of the kingdom, I shall be guided by a view to the great objects of all civil policy; relating in the first place, those institutions which tend to make us HAPPY, and consequently POPULOUS at home; then those which tend to make us FORMIDABLE abroad, and lastly show the manner in which the EXPENSES OF OUR GOVERNMENT are defrayed. In explaining the provision there is made, in our constitution and laws, for securing the internal peace and

happiness of the state, I shall consider, I. The LEGISLATIVE power of the state. II. The EXECUTIVE power. III. The LAWS of the state. IV. The METHOD OF PROCEEDING IN THE COURTS, in order to obtain the benefit of the laws. When I consider the laws of the state, I shall, in the first place, explain those regulations which are of a PUBLIC or more general nature; and then the mutual obligations of INDIVIDUALS to one another. Under the former of these heads, I shall place those laws which have for their immediate object the preservation of the government itself, for those which relate to trade and commerce, and to public conveniences of various kinds. Under the latter head I shall shew the provision which our laws have made to guide our lives, limbs, liberty, reputation, and property, real and personal; also those which relate to the commerce of the sexes, and the domestic relations. After exhibiting the state of the laws respecting natives, I shall consider how they regard ALIENS; and when everything relating to law has been discussed, the business of EQUITY will be explained."

(Essay on Liberal Education, pp.99–101)

Almost any example of an agenda for a lecture from Priestley's syllabus will suffice for illustration. Lectures 51 and 53 have been chosen:

Lecture 51
"Use of colonies to a commercial state. Difference between ancient and modern colonies. Importance of our American colonies. The entire subservience of a colony to the mother country. The situation in Ireland. Unreasonable Jealousy of it. The Isle of Man. Uniformity of weights and measures. Maxims with respect to money. Of the nature of Exchange. In what cases a great quantity of money is useful or hurtful to a state, and how the increase of it operates to produce an improved state of society."

(p.60)

Lecture 53
"The consequences of a flourishing state of society deduced. What kinds of luxury are hurtful. How far the country in which luxury prevails is hereby rendered incapable of self defence or the contrary. The temper of mind in luxurious and barbarous ages compared. The mischiefs of idleness. The state of virtue in the earlier and later periods of most histories. Effects of large capital cities. The dreadful consequences of a total depravity of manners. Gaming. Education."

(p.61)

It should be obvious from these examples how profound and far reaching was the education provided by Priestley to his students, and being still quite a young man at that time, how detailed had been his own education and reading. He has told us himself that, when he associated with Burke, they discussed little other than politics, and that he believed Burke would have been unlikely to be familiar with his writings. If that be so, what a pity it was; these two, if they had entered into a broad and continuing dialogue, could have been a

Priestley's statue. Scientist, philosopher, Priestley College, Warrington (Original at Birstall, W.Yorks)

tremendous positive force, at such a crucial time as in the days of the French Revolution.

When Professor Bronowski produced his *Ascent of Man* in 1973 (the book following the BBC TV series) he was obliged to select a tiny handful of outstanding individuals who had contributed significantly to human progress from earliest recorded time. Among these he included Priestley, singling out his discovery of oxygen, and the difference between animal and plant respiration. (He is quite wide of the mark in assessing his character.) ... (pp.144–8) He mentions the Lunar Society but not Priestley's membership. He mentions Paine as author of *Rights of Man* but primarily as having produced the first model of an iron bridge. (pp.272–3)

Both Priestley and Burke are convinced that a broad education, whether at University or Academy, should be firmly based in Divinity, a view that persisted well on into the 19th century, until so called 'higher education' became narrower and more specialised, since when those with a more practical bent have tended to neglect not only Divinity but also the humanities as a whole to the detriment of a broader understanding.

A good example of one who combined the best of these 18th century thinkers regarding education, is John Henry Newman (1801–90) born when Priestley and Paine were still living, and active till almost the end of the century. Like them, and Burke as well, he had rather a mixed background, his mother being of Huguenot stock, and his father of Dutch. He had no firm denominational roots in early life and tells among other things that he enjoyed reading Paine's *Age of Reason*, and "found pleasure in thinking of the objections which were contained in them". In later years he set forth views in his *'Idea of a University'* which linked those of the dissenter Priestley with Burke's Anglicanism:

"If the various branches of knowledge, which are the matter of teaching in a university, so hang together that none can be neglected without prejudice to the perfection of the rest, and if Theology be a branch of knowledge . . . to withdraw (it) from the public schools is to impair the completeness and invalidate the trustworthiness of all that is actually taught in them."

But he did not neglect the secular element and this would be much in harmony with the ideals of Priestley, without upsetting Burke:

"If then a University is a direct preparation for this world, let it be what it professes. It is not a convent, it is not a seminary; it is a place to fit men of the world for the world. We cannot possibly prevent them plunging into the world, with all its ways and principles and maxims when their time comes; but we can prepare them for what is inevitable; and it is not the way to learn to swim in troubled waters, never to have gone into them. . . . Cut out from your class books all broad manifestations of the natural man; and those manifestations are waiting for your pupil's benefit at the very doors of your lecture room in living and breathing substance. They will meet him there in all the charms of novelty, and all the fascination of genius or of amiableness. . . . You have refused him the masters of human thought, who would in some sense have educated him, because of their incidental corruption; Homer, Ariosto, Cervantes, Shakespeare, because the old Adam smelt rank in them; and for what have you reserved him? You have given him 'a liberty unto' the multitudinous blasphemy of his day; you have made him free of its newspapers, its reviews, its magazines, its novels, its controversial pamphlets. . . . You have succeeded but in this, – in making the world his University."

Just ahead of Priestley, Philip Doddridge at his Northampton Academy was putting forward similar views, warning his students against the risk of isolating themselves from the world at large. He told them to:

"Cultivate an extensive and candid acquaintance with the world. Take heed of immuring yourselves too much in your studies. Think not the time lost which is spent out of them. Despise not common christians – free converse with them may be attended with many good consequences. Acquaintance with the world of men will be better learnt by converse, as anatomy is better learnt by dissection than by books alone."

On reflection it is obvious that although Priestley and Burke diverged in many ways, and had quite different intellectual formation, in a basic common sense approach to education they would have had much in common. But the broad approach has dwindled greatly in British education in this present century, specialisation being the order of the day in most third level courses, being pushed downwards into the high schools as well. The scientist and the economist cannot spare time for the arts, and would not even think of divinity as part of a rounded education, although ministers of religion by and large would now consider themselves ill prepared without a basic knowledge of science and other practical subjects.

We need a new Priestley to write a new syllabus of education for civil and active life, just as the nation could benefit from a new spiritual leader with the energy, integrity and drive of a John Wesley.

Chapter XIV

Religion in America and France before and after Revolution

All religions united with government are more or less in-
imical to liberty. All separated from government are compatible with liberty.
Henry Clay, to the House of Representatives, United States (1818)

FINALLY, we come to a consideration of the position of religion in the revolutionary states of America and France. At once there is a contrast between America, where no establishment ties had ever occurred, from the start of immigration by Europeans onwards, and France where the secular state and the Catholic church had enjoyed close and cordial relations for many centuries, but the church was not formally established as in Britain. This distinction is perhaps more philosophical than practical.

Churches in America

"Happy is such a country as America, where no such *alliance* as that of *church and state* was ever formed, where no such unnatural mixture of ecclesiastical and civil policy was ever made. They see our errors and wisely avoid them. We also may see them, but when it will be too late".
(Letters to EB, pp.130–1)

At the close of his penultimate letter, Priestley quotes from Dr. Ramsay's *History of the American Revolution*, his comments on this issue, as it applied to new forms of government in the newly formed United States:

"It was one of the peculiarities of these forms of government, that all religious establishments were abolished. Some retained a constitutional distinction between Christians and others, with respect to eligibility to office; but the idea of supporting one denomination at the expense of others, or of raising any one sect of Protestants to a legal pre-eminence, was universally reprobated. The alliance between church and state was completely broken, and each was left to support itself independent of the other."
(Ramsay, vol.I p.355)

The constitutional distinction between Christians and others, which seemed appropriate at that time, could not expect to survive in a newly emerging nation whose immigrants were coming from an ever wider ethnic spectrum; there would be Jews, Muslims, Humanists and many other varieties. This provision could have been invoked against Tom Paine when he returned to America, after publication of his *Age of Reason*, if he had sought public office, on the grounds that he was no longer a true Christian believer. His erstwhile Quaker brethren obviously believed this to be the case when they refused him burial, but if church and state were truly separated, would this have been just, to bar him from office; a man who had contributed so much to founding the nation, in the quite recent past? The question is hypothetical, as Paine did not seek involvement, and was in fact almost totally ignored by his new fellow countrymen!

There was little consciousness of, or attention to, the plight of the indigenous native American population, caricatured as savage, uncivilised Red Indians. But these people had a highly developed culture of their own, which the more sophisticated Europeans found it difficult to understand. Paine became involved when, early in 1777, he was engaged as secretary to a commission representing Pennsylvania's Council of Safety, which was set up to negotiate with a group from the Iroquois tribes as to their status under the new republican government. The meeting lasted four days, but its apparent success was short lived. Paine was favourably impressed. "He seemed magnetised by what he saw as the natural beauty, prudence and intelligence of the Native Americans. . . . He praised their love of natural liberty . . . and their stubborn refusal . . . to give up their autonomy to any earthly power." (*Keane, pp.147–50*) Their egalitarianism impressed him, and their Deist philosophy also had a natural appeal in the light of his own spiritual evolution.

Priestley has a further quotation from Ramsay on religious trends in America:

"The world will soon see the result of an experiment in politics, and be able to determine whether the happiness of society is increased by religious establishments, or diminished by the want of them."
(vol.II, p.317)

Ramsay is here adopting a rather detached view; prepared to await the outcome, and Priestley reflects this; probably the only reasonable attitude in these circumstances:

"It is an experiment . . . on a sufficiently large scale, and in a very reasonable time, we may expect to see the result of the process."
(Letters to EB, p.142)

In his final letter Priestley returns to this theme with some rather interesting observations:

"After the noble example of America, we may expect, in due time, to see the governing powers of all nations confining their attention to the *civil* concerns of them, and consulting their welfare in the present state only; in consequence of which they may all be flourishing and happy. *Truth* of all kinds, and especially *religious truth,* meeting with no obstruction, and standing in no need to heterogeneous supports, will then establish itself by its own evidence; and whatever is *false* and delusive, all the forms of superstition, every corruption of true religion, and all usurpation over the rights of conscience, which have been supported by power or prejudice, will be universally exploded as they ought to be."

(p.146)

This final letter is Priestley's Utopian climax and, as with some of his other predictions, nobody would be more surprised than he at strange developments in American religion, as we approach the millennium; developments which belie much of the above paragraph. Many cynical citizens of that 'brave new world' would challenge him and ask with Pilate: 'What is truth'?

The Church in France

The more priests there are, the more they sin against me
their dignity I shall turn into dishonour.
They feed on the sin of my people and batten on their iniquity.
But people and priests will fare alike.
I shall punish them for their conduct and repay them for their deeds.

Hosea 4:7–9

In the matter of religion, revolutionary France was not starting with a clean slate like America, nor did it have a church 'by law established' as in England. It was, however, much closer to the English model except that the close bonds between church and state were assumed rather then formal, deriving mainly from custom and tradition, the pattern prevalent in most of Western Europe, including England, before the Reformation. Various comments have already been quoted, but since the works in consideration here are centred on the French Revolution, and as the decaying relationship became crucial, there is naturally far more comment than in the case of America, and much still to be considered. The words of Hosea are only too apt: a multiplicity of high ranking clergy with assumed dignity which was, in the main, social rather than spiritual, feeding on the sins of the people, especially aristocratic people, and battening on their iniquity. Burke is not impressed, however, with the quality of the lower clergy taking places in the new National Assembly:

"Having considered the composition of the third estate as it stood in its original frame, I took a view of the representatives of the clergy. There too it appeared that full as little regard was had to the general security of property, or to the aptitude of deputies for their public purposes, in the principles of their election. That election was so contrived as to send a very large proportion of mere country curates to the great and arduous work of new-modelling a state; men who had never seen the state so much as in a picture; men who knew nothing of the world beyond the bounds of an obscure village; who immersed in hopeless poverty, could regard all property, whether secular or ecclesiastical, with no other eye than that of envy; among whom must be many, who for the smallest hope of the meanest dividend in plunder, would readily join in any attempts upon a body of wealth, in which they could hardly look to have any share, except in a general scramble. Instead of balancing the power of the active chicaners in the other assembly, these curates must necessarily become the active coadjutors, or at best the passive instruments, of those by whom they had been habitually guided in their petty village concerns. They too could hardly be the most conscientious of their kind who, presuming upon their incompetent understanding, could intrigue for a trust, which led them from their natural relation to their flocks, and their natural spheres of action, to undertake the regeneration of kingdoms. This preponderating weight, being added to the force of the body of chicane in the *Tiers Etat*, completed that momentum of ignorance, rashness, presumption, and lust of plunder, which nothing has been able to resist."

(Reflections, pp.49–50)

It is obvious that his main problem with these men is that they are of the lower order of clergy, men of no property, who must of necessity be ignorant of affairs of state, because hitherto precluded from any participation, and who are ousting those much better placed, in the hierarchy, soundly based in the landed gentry, irrespective of real faith or commitment. We have already considered the experience and reports of Priestley, Mrs Barbauld, Arthur Young and other British observers, who were far from impressed at the quality of the higher clergy with whom they came in contact. If Burke's curates are of such inferior quality, how much can this be attributed to a lack of sound leadership from their own hierarchy? And should we not consider whether compassion for their flocks, with a modicum of faith, might not be more suitable for the task in hand, than those 'higher qualities' so much prized by Edmund Burke. But he has more to say on the parlous state of religion in France:

"Where trade and manufacturers are wanting to a people, and the spirit of nobility and religion remains, sentiment supplies, and not always ill supplies, their place; but if commerce and the arts should be lost in an experiment to try how well a state may stand without these old fundamental principles, what sort of a thing must be a nation of gross, stupid, ferocious, and at the same time, poor and sordid barbarians, destitute of religion, honour, or manly pride, possessing nothing at present, and hoping for nothing hereafter?"

(p.87)

Now we come to what is undoubtedly one of Burke's most profound and philosophic reflections; it merits careful and quiet contemplation:

"History consists, for the greater part, of the miseries brought upon the world by pride, ambition, avarice, revenge, lust, sedition, hypocrisy, ungoverned zeal and all the train of disorderly appetites which shake the public with the same '. . . troublous storms that toss the private state, and render life unsweet'. These vices are the *causes* of those storms. Religion, morals, laws, prerogatives, privileges, liberties, rights of men, are *the pretexts*. The pretexts are always found in some specious appearance of real good. You would not secure men from tyranny and sedition, by rooting out of the mind the principles to which these fraudulent pretexts apply? If you did you would root out everything that is valuable in the human breast. As these are the pretexts, so the ordinary actors and instruments in great public evils are kings, priests, magistrates, senates, parliaments, national assemblies, judges and captains. You would not cure the evil by resolving that there should be no more monarchs, nor ministers of state, nor of the Gospel; no interpreters of law; no general officers; no public councils. You might change the names. The things in some shape must remain. A certain *quantum* of power must always remain in the community, in some hands, and under some appellation. Wise men will apply their remedies to vices, not to names; to the causes of evil which are permanent, not to the occasional organs by which they act, and the transitory modes in which they appear. Otherwise you will be wise historically, a fool in practice. Seldom have two ages the same fashion in their pretexts, and the same modes of mischief. <u>Wickedness is a little more inventive</u>. Whilst you are discussing fashion, the fashion is gone by. The very same vice assumes a new body. The spirit transmigrates; and far from losing the principle of life by the change of its appearance, it is renovated in its new organs with the fresh vigour of a juvenile activity. It walks abroad, it continues its ravages, whilst you are gibbeting the carcass, or demolishing the tomb. You are terrifying yourselves with ghosts and apparitions, whilst your house is the haunt of robbers. It is thus with all those who, attending only to the shell and husk of history, think they are only waging war with intolerance, pride and cruelty, whilst, under colour of abhorring the ill principles of antiquated parties, they are authorising and feeding the same odious vices in different factions and perhaps in worse."

(pp.155–6)

This lengthy passage is included here, not because it applies specifically to the church in France; it does, however, include religion, morals and priests in its rather comprehensive catalogue, which embraces church and state, whilst commenting on events in France. One might argue with Burke as to the further application of these profound observations, but there is no doubt as to their philosophic soundness. It shows to what heights he could rise when he chose, and what a pity it was that he fell below his own high standards, when blinded by prejudice. This he demonstrates on the very next page when he refers to the "infamous massacre of St. Bartholomew" with its slaughter of the Huguenots, and the Cardinal of Lorraine, in his robes, "ordering general slaughter". This horror had recently been re-enacted, on stage, in Paris and Burke asks:

"Was this spectacle intended to make the Parisians abhor persecution, and loathe the effusions of blood? – No; it was to teach them to persecute their own pastors; it was to excite them, by raising a disgust and horror of their clergy, to an alacrity in hunting down to destruction an order, which if it ought to exist at all, ought to exist not only in safety, but in reverence."

(p.157)

In a later passage he goes on to pose a relevant question:

"Undoubtedly, the natural progress of the passions, from frailty to vice, ought to be prevented. . . . But, is it true that the body of your clergy had passed those limits of a just allowance?"

(p.159)

He then proceeds with a virtual litany of supplementary questions, the answers to which, if they were affirmative, would prove the French to be "a sort of monsters; a horrible composition of superstition, ignorance, sloth, fraud, avarice, and tyranny". But, it seems, these questions are only posed for ridicule, and so that the vices listed may be thrown back "to several of the churchmen of former times, who belonged to the two great parties, which then divided and distracted Europe"

Burke's judgement is right, in that showing that spectacle on stage, of which he complains, at that particular time, was bound to be inflammatory, as the equally horrible excesses of the September massacres in 1792 demonstrate only too well, in which many clergy, among others, were done to death by a 'lynch mob'; in some cases even after the self appointed 'court' had exonerated and freed them. But Burke, having brought forward one of the vilest episodes in French history, cannot seem to see that these dreadful acts, from the past, connived at and worse, by leading French clergymen, are now coming home to roost, with vengeance visited on the children's children, and with as little justice (never mind compassion) as that which had been meted out to the Calvinists in a previous age. Had the clergy in the late 18th century been, on the whole, devout men of integrity, themselves giving a whole-hearted example of compassion and restraint, can we believe that the people as a whole, would have tolerated such loathesome excesses? To weep for them, and especially those who were truly innocent, is one thing, but to pretend that they were entirely innocent and blameless flies in the face of history. However, Burke looks to a more glorious future, with almost the Utopian vision of Priestley or Paine:

"But history, in the 19th century, better understood and better employed, will, I trust, teach a civilised posterity, to abhor the misdeeds of both these barbarous ages. . . . It will teach posterity not to make war upon either religion or philosophy, for the abuse which the hypocrites of both have made of the two most valuable blessings conferred upon us by the bounty of the universal Patron, who in all things eminently protects and favours the race of man."

(p.158)

Would that any of these Utopian visionaries had been proved right, but the history of our own century, soon drawing to its close, makes a mockery of their most hopeful predictions. Burke goes on to relate his own personal experience in France, which although somewhat out-of-date, he uses to justify its churchmen over all.

"When my occasions took me into France, towards the close of the late reign, the clergy, under all their forms, engaged a considerable part of my curiosity. So far from finding, (except from one set of men, not then very numerous, though very active) the complaints and discontents against that body, which some publications had given me reason to expect, I perceived little or no public or private uneasiness on their account. On further examination, I found the clergy, in general, persons of moderate minds and decorous manners. I include the seculars, and the regulars of both sexes. I had not the good fortune to know a great many of the parochial clergy; but in general I received a perfectly good account of their morals and of their attention to their duties. With some of the higher clergy I had a personal acquaintance; and of the rest, in that class, a very good means of information. They were, almost all of them, persons of noble birth. They resembled others of their own rank; and where there was any difference it was in their favour. They were more fully educated that the military noblesse; so as by no means to disgrace their profession by ignorance, or by want of fitness for the exercise of their authority. They seemed to me, beyond the clerical character, liberal and open; with the hearts of gentlemen and men of honour; nor insolent nor servile in their manners and conduct. They seemed to me rather a superior class; . . . I saw among the clergy in Paris . . . men of great learning and candour; and I had reason to believe that this description was not confined to Paris. What I found in other places, I know was accidental, and therefore to be presumed a fair sample. . . . Some of these ecclesiastics of rank, are by their titles, persons deserving of general respect."

(pp.160–1)

Here Burke is writing at considerable length, almost as if he had gone to France as a sort of one man commission to review the state of the church there. We know that he spent about four weeks there in February-March 1773, and that he fulfilled other social engagements apart from the ecclesiastical, at the same time placing his teenage son in a household to acquire the language. It is hard to believe that he acquired such a comprehensive and favourable view, as this passage suggests, without encountering some of the failings, which other visitors from England report in the pre-revolutionary period, and which we have already considered. He seems greatly impressed by the fact that most of the higher clergy he met were persons of noble birth; but why should ecclesiastics of rank be deserving of respect, mainly because of their families? Such a view might have gone unchallenged in his day, but few in the western world today would openly admit to such a prejudice; it is almost as if this qualification quite over-rules any other, or that its absence would need to be considered. It is not surprising, however, when we take into consideration Burke's almost hypnotic obsession with a 'natural aristocracy' and the advantages of 'noble birth'; he does however have some qualifying remarks to smooth over difficulties, before proceeding to more recent degeneration:

"You had before your Revolution about a hundred and twenty bishops. A few of them were men of eminent sanctity and charity without limit. When we talk of the heroic, of course we talk of rare virtue. I believe the instances of eminent depravity may be as rare amongst them as those of transcendent goodness. Examples of avarice and of licentiousness may be picked out, I do not question it, by those who delight in the investigation which leads to such discoveries. A man as old as I am will not be astonished that several, in every description, do not lead that perfect life of self denial, with regard to wealth or to pleasure, which is wished for by all, by some expected, but by none exacted with more rigour, than by those who are attentive to their own interests, or the most indulgent to their own passions. When I was in France, I am certain that the number of vicious prelates was not great. Certain individuals among them, not distinguishable for the regularity of their lives, made some amends for their want of the severe virtues, in their possession of the liberal; and were endowed with qualities which made them useful in the church and state. I am told that, with few exceptions, Louis XVI had been more attentive to character, in his promotions to that rank, than his immediate predecessor and I believe (as some spirit of reform had prevailed through the whole reign) that it may be true."

(p.162)

This reads as something of an overall whitewash; a want of spirituality, devotion, or even of faith itself may be excused and overlooked providing the individual clergyman has liberal virtues, whatever that may mean, or that he serves church and state faithfully. Burke certainly does not tell us what he means by liberal virtues. He is impressed by Louis XVI's attention to character in making promotions within the hierarchy of the church, and, in so far as this is an improvement on what had gone before, this is good; also remarkable is Burke's throw away line admitting that a spirit of reform has prevailed throughout this king's reign. But Priestley has other thoughts on royal involvement in ecclesiastical preferment, and on the changes taking place in France:

"Another important article in *our* ecclesiastical establishment, is the right of our kings to the nomination of bishops. But it is well known that the right of chusing the bishops was originally, and for many centuries, in their respective churches, the metropolitans of a province shewing their approbation by joining in the ordination, and that even the emperors themselves, after they became Christians, never assumed any such authority.It was first usurped by the popes, in the plenitude of their power, and by the feudal princes of Europe, in consequence of their investing bishops with their *temporalities,* and making them *lords of territory.* The National

Assembly of France have, to their immortal honour, restored to all the Christian churches in that country, their original right of appointing their own pastors, both the ordinary clergy and the bishops."

"As to the claim of our princes to be *heads of the church* (which is an usurpation from an usurper, the pope) and that of our parliament, to enact what shall be deemed *articles of faith*, and to give a form and constitution to the whole church, it is a thing not so much as pretended to by any other temporal power in the world, and a greater absurdity and abuse than anything subsisting in the system of popery, where at least the judges in ecclesiastical affairs, are ecclesiastical persons."

(Letters to EB, pp.81–3)

Ecclesiastical Changes in Revolutionary France

Burke is very disturbed at what is happening to the church in France, as we have previously noted; he comments:

". . . The present ruling power has shown a disposition only to plunder the church. It has punished *all* prelates; which is to favour the vicious, at least in point of reputation. It has made a degrading pensionary establishment, to which no man of liberal ideas or liberal condition will destine his children. It must settle into the lowest classes of the people. As with you the inferior clergy are not numerous enough for their duties; as these duties are, beyond measure, minute and toilsome, as you have left no middle classes of clergy at their ease, in future nothing of science or erudition can exist in the Gallican church. To complete the project, without the least attention to the rights of patrons, the assembly has provided in future an elective clergy; an arrangement which will drive out of the clerical profession all men of sobriety; all who can pretend to independence in their function or their conduct; and which will throw the whole direction of the public mind into the hands of a set of licentious, bold, crafty, factious, flattering wretches of such condition and such habits of life as will make their contemptible pensions (in comparison of which the stipend of an exciseman is lucrative and honourable) an object of low and illiberal intrigue. Those officers, whom they still call bishops are to be elected to a provision comparatively mean, through the same arts, (that is, electioneering arts,) by men of all religious tenets that are known or can be invented. The new law givers have not ascertained anything whatsoever concerning their qualifications, relative either to doctrine or to morals; no more than they have done with regard to the subordinate clergy; nor does it appear but that both the higher and the lower may, at their discretion practise or preach any mode of religion or irreligion they please. I do not see what the jurisdiction of bishops over their subordinates is to be, or whether they are to have any jurisdiction at all."

(Reflections, pp.162–3)

Burke's concern is a very legitimate one, but leaving aside his beliefs about the new constitution and the new regime in France, is he really equipped to judge whether the changes in church government are *so much* for the worse? They are certainly not ideal, and the concern of legislators is not primarily with faith and morals, but were their predecessors so much better? And if so why was the church so weak in itself, not even attempting to fight back until it was far too late and the changes were already firmly established? Priestley has some questions to pose:

"Has the splendour of the ecclesiastical establishment in France, which is much superior to anything of the kind in this country, prevented the spread of the Reformation on the one hand, or of infidelity on the other? By your own account, France is almost a nation of infidels, at least their National Assembly, in your idea, consists chiefly of them. Have the remains of this splendour, respectable still in your eyes, prevented the rejection of Christianity altogether *here?* If you know the world and even what passes at home, you must know the contrary."

(Letters to EB, p.73)

". . . You condemn the French National Assembly, for innovating in *their* religion, which is Catholic, as much as you could blame the English Parliament, for innovating in *ours*, which is Protestant. You condemn them for lowering the state of Archbishops, bishops, and abbots, though they have improved that of the lower orders of the clergy."

(p.60)

Burke continues to express his concern for the future:

" . . . It seems to me, that this new ecclesiastical establishment is intended only to be temporary, and preparatory to the utter abolition, under any of its forms, of the Christian religion, whenever the minds of men are prepared for this last stroke against it, by the accomplishment of the plan for bringing its ministers into universal contempt. They who will not believe that the philosophical fanatics, who guide in these matters, have long entertained such a design, are utterly ignorant of their character and proceedings. These enthusiasts do not scruple to avow their opinion, that a state can subsist without any religion better than with one; and that they are able to supply the place of any good which may be in it, by a project of their own – namely, a sort of education they have imagined founded in a knowledge of the physical wants of men; progressively carried to an enlightened self interest . . . a *Civic Education.*"

(Reflections, pp.163–4)

Is he not falling into the philosophical trap which imagines that civic and scientific education must always be at odds with Christian faith and doctrine, and that tension will persist until one or the other is overthrown; the rationalists believing that it is faith which will fade away. In their day, Priestley was a leading rationalist and scientific discoverer, but he held his faith in balance with his other and very wide knowledge. Burke would object that his faith was flawed, and so would the majority of Christians today, but we know from

his autobiography that he upheld his Christianity fearlessly in face of the
scepticism and astonishment he encountered from high ecclesiastics on his
travels in France before the revolution. These tensions, which Burke rightly
identifies, were to grow during the 19th century, but there were leading
educationalists coming up, such as John Henry Newman, with his "Idea of a
University" who made a strong case for a balanced course which would
accommodate both traditions; Burke would probably have been reassured, but,
in the final analysis, man is a creature with freewill and each individual will
follow his own bent.

   In considering the faith of larger communities, which Burke sees as being
so much at risk in France, it is surprising that he does not find greater
consolation in the record of his own beloved motherland. Priestley, in a passage
already quoted, could appreciate that the oppressed people in Ireland, who
were mainly Catholic, had managed to uphold their faith, in opposition to a
powerful establishment determined to 'convert' them. The truth, in regard to
France, was that the church was weak and infidelity rife. There is much to
learn from the Old Testament, from the Books of Kings and the Chronicles,
which portray the chosen people swinging backwards and forwards between
firm monotheism and the worship of Pagan Deities, often attempting to com-
bine both in a sort of ecclesiastical bigamy; the verses from Hosea, quoted
above, provide a neat summary. Priestley adds:

> "You insinuate that the scheme to render the clergy of France elective, is
> preparatory to an intended abolition of Christianity, as if Christianity did
> not exist, and exist in infinitely greater purity, before any of the clergy
> were otherwise than elective. On the contrary, it is the system of church
> establishments that always has produced, and that ever must produce,
> unbelievers. You make it a mere engine of state, a source of *wealth* to
> some of the clergy, and of *power* to those who have the nomination of
> them; and in both cases the proper interests of *religion* are never thought
> of. In consequence of this, it is notorious that the superior clergy in France
> and Italy have long been generally considered as unbelievers, as well as
> those who procure them their preferment."
>
> *(Letters to EB, pp.104–5)*

Paine also has some notable strictures on the church in France:

> "In France, the cry of the Church! The Church! was repeated as often as
> in Mr Burke's book, and as loudly as when the dissenters' bill was before
> the English parliament; but the generality of the French clergy were not
> to be deceived by this cry any longer. They knew that whatever the
> pretence might be, it was themselves who were one of the principle objects
> of it. It was the cry of the high beneficed clergy, to prevent any regulation
> of income taking place between those of ten thousand pounds a year and
> the parish priest. They, therefore, joined their case to those of every other
> oppressed class of men, and by this union obtained redress. . . . The

French constitution has abolished tithes, that source of perpetual discontent between the tithe holder and the parishioner."

(Rights, pp.106–7)

He has an interesting comment on one leading churchman who played a prominent part at an early stage in the revolution:

"The Archbishop of Toulouse was appointed to the administration of the finances, soon after the dismission of Calonne. He was also made Prime Minister, an office that did not always exist in France. . . . The Archbishop arrived to more state authority than any minister since the Duke de Choiseal, and the nation was strongly disposed in his favour; but by a line of conduct scarcely to be accounted for, he perverted every opportunity, turned out a despot, sunk into disgrace, and a Cardinal."

(p.121)

As Lord Acton was to say a century or so later: "All power corrupts, and absolute power corrupts absolutely", but it is sad to see in this instance the universal church appearing to award, or was it to console, the villain. And now Burke again in defence of traditional forms:

"I know well enough that the bishoprics and cures, under kingly and seigniorial patronage, as now they are in England, and as they have been lately in France, are sometimes acquired by unworthy methods; but the other mode of ecclesiastical canvass subjects them infinitely more surely and more generally to all the evil arts of low ambition which, operating on and through greater numbers, will produce mischief in proportion."

(Reflections, p.164)

So he is not so blinkered as some of his previous comments might suggest, nor entirely oblivious to ecclesiastical abuses, as this next piece confirms to a surprising degree when reflecting upon degeneracy in the French church.

"Burnet says, that when he was in France, in 1683, 'The method which carried over the men of the finest parts to popery was this: they brought themselves to doubt of the whole Christian religion. When that was done, it seemed a more indifferent thing of what side or form they continued outwardly'. If this was then the ecclesiastical policy of France, it is what they have since but too much reason to repent of. They preferred atheism to a form of religion not agreeable to their ideas. They succeeded in destroying that form, and atheism has succeeded in destroying them. I can readily give credit to Burnet's story; because I have observed too much of a similar spirit (for a little of it is 'much too much') amongst ourselves."

(p.165)

Next, he commends toleration to his correspondent in Paris:

"Impious men do not commend themselves to their community by iniquity and cruelty towards any description of their fellow creatures. We hear these new teachers continually boasting of their spirit of toleration. That those persons should tolerate all opinions, who think none to be of estimation, is a matter of small merit. Equal neglect is not impartial kindness. The species of benevolence which arises from contempt, is not true charity. There are in England abundance of men who tolerate in the true spirit of toleration. They think the dogmas of religion, though in different degrees, are all of moment; and that amongst them there is, as amongst all things of value, a just ground of preference. They favour therefore, and they tolerate. They tolerate not because they despise opinions, but because they respect justice. They would reverently and affectionately protect all religions, because they love and venerate the great principle upon which they all agree, and the great object to which they are all directed. They begin more and more plainly to discern that we have all a common cause, as against a common enemy. They will not be so misled by the spirit of faction, as not to distinguish what is done in favour of their subdivision, from those acts of hostility which, through some particular description, are aimed at the whole corps, in which they themselves, under another denomination are included."

(p.166)

Noble sentiments, and beautifully expressed, and who should know better than Burke; after all it was only a decade since London was held to ransom, in the vicious outbreak known as the Gordon Riots. He himself would have had short shrift from the mob, as a parliamentarian who was a behind-the-scenes promoter of the Catholic Relief Act (1778) which stoked their anger. Priestley too, as author of an anonymous pamphlet defending the act, calling for fairness and toleration (as above) was vulnerable, but the outbreak had been crushed before he was unmasked.

   Sadly, however, this is another instance in which Burke's actions, or rather inaction, failed to measure up to his own declared sentiments, at this crucial juncture; it was little more than half a year, from the publication of his *Reflections*, when the 'Church and King Mob' ran riot in Birmingham, and Priestley was, this time, an undoubted victim. Burke was silent; all the justice, charity, toleration, etc., was forgotten; not only did he fail to respond to the *Letters*, but he could not even find a word of sympathy for his erstwhile friend; in fact it is said that privately he expressed satisfaction, like his new found friend, the king. Friends and enemies have been switched in a short time, but we are told that in no way was Burke inconsistent; he is only fearful of the great threat posed by the wild elements in France and their friends in Britain:

"We cannot be ignorant of the spirit of atheistical fanaticism that is inspired by a multitude of writings, dispersed with incredible assiduity and expense, and by sermons delivered in all the streets and places of public resort in Paris. . . . The spirit of proselytism attends this spirit of fanaticism. They have societies to cabal and correspond at home and abroad for the propagation of their tenets. . . . England is not left out of the comprehensive scheme of their malignant charity: and in England we find those who stretch out their arms to them, who recommend their example from more than one pulpit, and who choose, in more than one periodical meeting, publicly to correspond with them, to applaud them, and to hold them up as objects for imitation; who receive from them tokens of confraternity, . . ·. who suggest to them leagues of perpetual amity, at the very time when the power to which our constitution has exclusively delegated the federative capacity of this kingdom, <u>may find it expedient to make war upon them.</u>"

(pp.169–70)

It is intolerable to Burke that pulpits on both sides of the channel should be used to explore and to propagate the doctrine of human rights, but it is also a shocking revelation that, *as early as 1790, he is already warmongering.* However, having declared war, on his own account, he quickly changes the subject, in the next paragraph, and makes no attempt to justify or to explain this awesome pronouncement. So, let us move on with him to relations between royalty and episcopacy, and on to more recent constitutional developments.

"Kings, even such as are truly kings, may and ought to bear the freedom of subjects that are obnoxious to them. They may too, without derogating from themselves, bear even the authority of such persons, if it promotes their service. Louis XIII mortally hated the Cardinal de Richelieu; but his support of that minister against his rivals was the source of all the glory of his reign and the solid foundation of his throne itself. Louis XIV, when he came to the throne, did not love the Cardinal Mazarin; but for his interests he preserved him in power. When old, he detested Louvois; but for years, whilst he faithfully served his greatness, he endured his person. When George II took Mr Pitt, who certainly was not agreeable to him, into his councils, he did nothing which could humble a wise sovereign. But these ministers, who were chosen by affairs, not by affection, acted in the name of, and in trust for, kings; and not as their avowed, constitutional, and ostensible masters. I think it impossible that any king, when he has recovered his first terrors, can cordially infuse vivacity and vigour into measures which he knows to be dictated by those, who, he must be persuaded, are in the highest degree ill affected to his person. Will any ministers who serve such a king with but a decent appearance of respect cordially obey the orders of those whom, but the other day, in his name, they had committed to the Bastille?"

(pp.222–3)

This is a fascinating passage, moving from the 'glory days' of the 'sun king' and his predecessor, with all the inherent tensions, then on to Hanoverian England. Burke, as a long standing and sophisticated parliamentarian, well knew that whoever was in command, whether monarch or prime minister, often had to endure supporters who were opposed in various ways, and uncongenial as well. He himself, though never a minister, had wielded great power, and been a thorn in the flesh of George III, especially during the

American crisis, but now he was the king's good friend. Why then was he so blind to the potential for peaceful and orderly transition to a constitutional monarchy in France, similar to the English model; the French king was agreeable and adaptable, and was far better placed for that role than George I had been. The objective of the National Assembly in 1790, was little different to that of the English parliament in 1714; it was to gain firm control of the monarch who should thenceforth become an obedient figurehead. Incidentally, who were these fearful potential officers of state, recently released from the Bastille, who would intimidate ministers; Burke must have known, together with most other reasonably informed citizens, that the few poor wretches set free had no such figure among them. Was he truly ill informed, or, once again, was he merely shroud waving?

Church property and its disposal was a thorny problem and one addressed by Burke in considerable detail; a few highlights from his *Reflections* should suffice:

"What had the clergy to do with these (financial) transactions? What had they to do with any public engagement further than the extent of their own debt? To that, to be sure, their estates were bound to the last acre. Nothing can lead more to the true spirit of the assembly, which fits for public confiscation, with its new equity, and its new morality, than an attention to their proceeding with regard to this debt of the clergy. The body of confiscators, true to that monied interest for which they were false to every other, have found the clergy competent to incur a legal debt. Of course they declared them legally entitled to the property which their power of incurring the debt and mortgaging the estate implied; recognising the rights of those persecuted citizens, in the very act in which they were thus grossly violated."

(p.124)

"When they (the members of the Assembly) had finally determined on a state resource from church booty, they came on the 14th of April, 1790, to a solemn resolution on the subject; and pledged themselves to their country, 'that in the statement of the public charges for each year, there should be brought to account a sum sufficient for defraying the expenses of the R.C.A. religion, the support of the ministers at the altars, the relief of the poor, the pensions of the ecclesiastics, secular as well as regular, of the one and of the other sex, *in order that the estates and the goods which are at the disposal of the nation may be disengaged of all charges, and employed by the representatives, or the legislative body, to the great and most pressing exigencies of the state.*"

(p.262)

"At length they have spoken out, and they have made a full discovery of their abominable fraud, in holding out the church lands as a security for any debts, or any service whatsoever. They rob only to enable them to cheat; but in a very short time they defeat both the ends of the robbery, and the fraud, by making out accounts for other purposes, which blow

up their whole apparatus of force and deception. . . . These are the calculating powers of imposture! This is the finance of philosophy!"

(p.263)

"In order to persuade the world of the bottomless resource of ecclesiastical
confiscation, the assembly have proceeded to other confiscations of estates
in offices, which could not be done with any common colour without being
compensated out of this grand confiscation of landed property. . . . Have
they ever given themselves the trouble to state fairly the expense of the
management of the church lands in the hands of the municipalities to whose
care, skill, and diligence, and that of their legion of unknown underagents,
they have chosen to commit the charge of the forfeited estates, and the
consequence of which had been pointed out by the Bishop of Nancy?"

(pp.264–5)

"In all this procedure I can discern neither the solid sense of plain dealing,
nor the subtle dexterity of ingenious fraud. The objections within the
assembly to pulling up the floodgates for this inundation of fraud are
unanswered; but they are thoroughly refuted by a hundred thousand
financiers in the street. These are the numbers by which metaphysic
arithmeticians compute. They are the grand calculations on which a philosophical public credit is founded in France. They cannot raise supplies;
but they can raise mobs."

(pp.265–6)

A fine irony here, when we consider the 'Church and King Mobs' about to
be raised in England within the year. There is little doubt that the church in
France had been truly bamboozled, but it had been profligate in its management
and did not look to secure its own interest in good time. What Burke does
not acknowledge was the hopeless state of the nation's finances before the
revolution; in fact, this was a major cause of the whole upheaval. The new
people taking over were naturally lacking in experience of an operation at this
level; the 'experts' who had preceded them were not notable for their success
either; hostility from surrounding nations compounded the problem and as we
have seen Burke was urging Britain to go to war. This was a strange recipe for
achieving solutions in any of the countries concerned, and inevitably brought
much devastation, as well as piling up debts all round. In his *Letter to a Member
of the National Assembly* the following year, Burke makes a strange and
unexpected offer; he says:

"A certain intemperance of intellect is the disease of the time, and the
source of all its other diseases. I will keep myself as untainted by it as I
can. Your architects build without a foundation. I would readily lend a
helping hand to any superstructure, when once this is effectively secured."

(Letter to a Member, p.317)

A handsome offer; we can only wonder why it was never taken up! But what
sort of superstructure was he envisaging for a building with no foundation.

This letter was dated January 1791, in the following December Burke published his *Thoughts on French Affairs*, in which he gives further consideration to the financial scene:

". . . They have shot out three branches of revenue to supply all those which they have destroyed, that is, the *Universal Register of all Transactions*, the heavy and universal *Stamp Duty*, and the new *Territorial Impost*, levied chiefly on the reduced estates of the gentlemen. These branches of the revenue, especially as they take assignats in payment, answer their purpose in a considerable degree, and keep up the credit of their paper; for as they receive it in their treasury, it is in reality funded upon all their taxes and future resources of all kinds, as well as upon the church estates. As this paper is become, in a manner, the only visible maintenance of the whole people, the dread of bankruptcy is more apparently connected with the delay of a counter-revolution, than with the duration of this republic; because the interest of the new republic manifestly leans upon it; and, in my opinion, the counter-revolution cannot exist along with it. The above three projects ruined some ministers under the old government merely for having conceived them. They are the salvation of the present rulers."

"As the assembly has laid a most unsparing and cruel hand on all men who have lived by the bounty, the justice or the abuses of the old government, they have lessened many expenses. The royal establishment, though excessively and ridiculously great for *their* scheme of things, is reduced at least one half. . . . As to the ecclesiastical charge, whether as a compensation for losses, or a provision for religion, of which at first they made a great parade, and entered into a solemn engagement in favour of it, it was estimated at a much larger sum than they could expect from the church property, movable or immovable; they are completely bankrupt as to that article. It is just what they wish; and is not productive of any serious inconvenience. The non-payment produces discontent and occasional sedition; but it is only by fits and spasms, and amongst the country people who are of no consequence. These seditions furnish new pretexts for non-payment to the church establishment, and help the assembly wholly to get rid of the clergy, and indeed of any form of religion which, is not only their real but avowed object."

". . . The great confiscation of the church and of the crown lands, and of the appendages of the princes, for the purchase of all of which their paper is always received at par, gives means of continually destroying and continually creating, and this perpetual destruction and renovation feeds the speculative market, and prevents and will prevent, till that fund of confiscation begins to fail, a *total* depreciation. . . . The world of contingency and political combination is much larger than we are apt to imagine. We can never say what may or may not happen, without a view to all the actual circumstances."

(Thoughts on French Affairs, pp.350–2)

The world of high finance, national and international, is a great mystery to the majority of citizens, and probably even to many who are more immediately involved, but what seems to emerge from this complex passage is that a new regime is struggling, as best it can, to get the finances back on an even keel. One complaint, overall, would appear to be summed up in the phrase that the administration is attempting to solve its problem by 'selling off the family silver'. If this is anything like a true assessment, then others since that time have been good scholars, and we can only wonder what Mr Burke might have had to say about modern Britain, together with many other states around the world. One further general comment on the character of the revolution comes in the same essay:

"The present revolution in France seems to me to be of quite another character and description; and to bear little resemblance or analogy to any of those which have been brought about in Europe, upon principles merely political. It is *a revolution of doctrine and theoretic dogma.* It has a much greater resemblance to those changes which have been made upon religious grounds, in which a spirit of proselytism makes an essential part."

"The last revolution of doctrine and theory which has happened in Europe is the Reformation. . . . the effect was *to introduce other interests into all countries than those which arose from their locality and natural circumstances.* The principle of the Reformation was such as, by its essence, could not be local or confined to the country in which it had its origin . . . . Questions of theoretic truth and falsehood (are not) governed by circumstances any more than by places. . . . These divisions, however, in appearance merely dogmatic, soon became mixed with the political; and their effects were rendered much more intense from its combination. Europe was for a long time divided into two great factions. . . . These factions, wherever they prevailed, if they did not absolutely destroy, at least weakened and distracted the locality of patriotism. The public affections came to have other motives and other ties."

(pp.328–9)

It is a nice distinction that Burke draws between doctrine, theoretic dogma, and mere politics, but surely politics is that which stems from policy. Admittedly most politicians seem to be more at ease when dealing with the practical and the pragmatic, that is until they wish to engage the minds and the support of their constituencies and then we are showered with *policy documents.* Burke himself had played this dual game throughout his career and nobody understood it better. What he is really concerned about, and he has expressed this earlier in his *Reflections,* is that the virus of theoretic dogma and doctrine is crossing the channel and infecting large numbers of Britons, just as the protestant virus did in the past. But he himself is not entirely divorced from such activity; notably in his involvement with American affairs he had raised hares which came to run in France alongside those of the dreaded philosophers, who were such a source of unease to him and to his allies. This brings us neatly to one final topic:

The Role of the Press in French Affairs

> Four hostile newspapers are more to be feared than a thousand bayonets.
>
> *Napoleon I – Maxims*

Now Burke again:

"Along with the monied interest, a new description of men had grown up, with whom that interest formed a close and marked union; I mean the political men of letters. Men of letters, fond of distinguishing themselves, are rarely averse to innovation. . . . What they lost in old court protection, they endeavoured to make up by joining in a sort of incorporation of their own; to which the two academies of France, and afterwards the vast undertaking of the Encyclopaedia, carried on by a society of these gentlemen, did not a little contribute.

"The literary cabal had some years ago formed something like a regular plan for the destruction of the Christian religion. This object they pursued with a degree of zeal which hitherto had been discovered only in the propagators of some system of piety. They were possessed with a spirit of proselytism in the most fanatical degree; and from thence, by an easy progress, with the spirit of persecution according to their means. What was not to be done towards their great end, by any direct or immediate act, might be wrought by a longer process through the medium of opinion. To command that opinion, the first step is to establish a dominion over those who direct it. They contrived to possess themselves, with great method and perseverance, of all the avenues to literary fame. Many of them indeed stood high in the ranks of literature and science . . . (their) narrow, exclusive spirit has not been less prejudicial to literature and to taste, then to morals and true philosophy. Those atheistical fathers have a bigotry of their own; and they have learned to talk against monks with the spirit of a monk. But in some things they are men of the world. The resources of intrigue are called in to supply the defects of argument and wit. . . . To those who have observed the spirit of their conduct, it has long been clear that nothing was wanted but the power of carrying the intolerance of the tongue and of the pen into a persecution which would strike at property, liberty and life."

". . . what with opposition and what with success, a violent and malignant zeal, . . . had taken an entire possession of their minds, and rendered their whole conversation perfectly disgusting . . . as controversial zeal soon turns its thoughts on force, they began to insinuate themselves into a correspondence with foreign princes; in hopes through their authority, which at first they flattered, they might bring about the changes they had in view. To them it was indifferent whether these changes were to be accomplished by the thunderbolt of despotism, or by the earthquake of popular commotion . . . they cultivated, . . . the monied interest of France; and partly through the means furnished by those whose peculiar offices gave them the most extensive and certain means of communication, they carefully occupied all the avenues of opinion."

"Writers, especially when they act in a body, and with one direction, have great influence on the public mind; the alliance, therefore, of these writers with the monied interest had no small effect in removing the popular odium and envy which attended that particular species of wealth. These writers, like the propagators of all novelties, pretended to a great zeal for the poor, and the lower orders, whilst in their satires they rendered hateful, by every exaggeration, the faults of courts, of nobility, and of priesthood. They became a sort of demagogue. They served as a link to unite, in favour of one object, obnoxious wealth to restless and desperate poverty."

"As these two kinds of men appear principal leaders in all the late transactions, their junction and politics will serve to account not upon any principles of law or of policy, but as a *cause*, for the general fury with which all the landed property of ecclesiastical corporations has been attacked; and the great care which, contrary to their pretended principles, has been taken, of a monied interest originating from the authority of the crown. All the envy against wealth and power was artificially directed against other descriptions of riches."

(Reflections, pp.121–3)

And then about twelve months later Burke is concentrating his fire upon the press:

"The seeds are sown, almost everywhere, chiefly by newspaper circulations, infinitely more efficacious and extensive than ever they were. And they are a more important instrument than generally is imagined. They are a part of the reading of all, they are the whole of the reading of the far greater number. There are thirty of them in Paris alone. The language diffuses them more widely than the English, though the English too are much read. The writers of these papers, indeed, for the greater part, are either unknown, or in contempt, but they are like a battery in which the stroke of any one ball produces no great effect, but the amount of continual repetition is decisive. *Let us only suffer any person to tell us his story, morning and evening, but for one twelve month, and he will become our master.*"

(Thoughts, p.335)

These are fascinating reflections, and to a large extent topical today. We can but wonder what Burke would have to say about the multiplicity of media, with which we are now inundated and the insidious influence which they have upon our lives, our aspirations, our attitude to others, to government, to authority, to the supernatural, etc. etc. The last sentence, above, is particularly significant for us now, in these days of large multinational corporations, which in many instances are more powerful and more influential than national governments, or the large international unions. Some of these multinationals gaining control of a range of media all at once, are threatening to have an effective stranglehold on society even greater than what Burke was seeing in the France of his time.

At that time the problems were not so widespread, but the power and influence, which he describes, was greatly concentrated. The papers circulating, particularly in Paris, had a tremendous inflammatory effect, especially on less discriminating minds, which drew such people into mobs, whose actions were often unpredictable and vicious, once they were formed. Burke was well aware of this danger from his experience during the Gordon Riots, and later during the Birmingham Riots of 1791, shortly before the last paragraph, above, was written. He also had experience of the power and influence of a periodical, much nearer to home, with Wilkes and his famous *North Briton* which had thrown the monarchy, the administration, and parliament into great turmoil; a matter in which he himself was, to some considerable extent, involved.

In Paris, *L'ami du Peuple*, edited by Jean Paul Marat,* was the most obnoxious and notorious, of all the periodicals of which, Burke tells us, there were about 30 at that time. In the end this scurrilous writer provoked his own assassination; he had owed some of his experience to a prolonged residence in England, around the time of the Wilkes' controversy, and no doubt learned some lessons therefrom.

One final reflection on the evolution of media since then and their influence. The trouble now is not just that Big Brother is watching us, but that we are forever watching Big Brother, and being mesmerised; or as Wendell Phillips told it in 1852: "We live under a government of men and morning newspapers".

---

* Among other activities whilst in England, Marat had taught French at Warrington Academy for a year in the early '70s, shortly after Priestley had left; elsewhere in Britain he engaged in medicine, human and veterinary, as well as some dubious criminal activities, including a theft from the Ashmolean Museum at Oxford. *(Gottschalk)*

CHAPTER XV

Utopia – 1791

Ah love could thou and I with fate conspire
To grasp this sorry Scheme of Things entire,
Would not we shatter it to bits – and then
Remould it nearer to the Heart's Desire.

Rubaiyat of Omar Khaam

E DMUND BURKE WAS AN EXPERIENCED AND PRACTICAL POLITICIAN, of an independent mind and something of an idealist, as witnessed in the great causes to which he had given generously of his time and effort: India and the affair of Warren Hastings; the revolt of the American colonies; Ireland and the Catholic interest. But the land called Utopia was to him Terra Incognita; not so however with his adversaries in 1791.

Paine had some very practical ideas for the future, albeit that well over a century elapsed before they even began to be realised. The last of Priestley's letters to Burke is so Utopian as sometimes to enter the realms of fantasy.

Paine's Social Agenda

"Revolutions, then, have for their object, a change in the moral condition of governments, and with this change the burden of public taxes will lessen, and civilisation will be left to the enjoyment of that abundance, of which it is now deprived."

"In contemplating the whole of this subject, I extend my views into the department of commerce. In all my publications, where the matter would admit, I have been an advocate for commerce, because I am a friend to its effects. It is a pacific system, operating to cordialise mankind, by rendering nations, as well as individuals, useful to each other. As to mere theoretical reformation, I have never preached it up. The most effectual process is that of improving the condition of man by means of his interest; and it is on this ground that I take my stand."

(Rights of Man, p.234)

It is interesting that Paine eschews theoretical reformation; his personal history bears this out; he is ever a practical man rather that a starry-eyed idealist. His basic view on commerce would be true in an ideal world; however it was scarcely true, in practice, in his own time, which, to its shame, was engaged in a very thriving slave trade. In other respects it is even less true since, and right down to our own day.

"If commerce were permitted to act to the universal extent it is capable, it would extirpate the system of war, and produce a revolution in the uncivilised state of governments. The invention of commerce has arisen since those governments began, and is the greatest approach toward universal civilisation, that has yet been made by any means not immediately flowing from moral principles."

(pp.234–5)

Two centuries on, Paine would be horrified to find that, rather than commerce extirpating war, the most thriving and lucrative trade today is in engines of war, closely followed by the evil trade in noxious drugs which insidiously attack the moral fibre of nations, as well as of individuals.

In his critique of poor-rates, at that time, he tells us that these amount to a direct tax, levied mainly on poor labourers and disguised in articles bought; in other words they were similar to what we now know as Value Added Tax. He advocates a more even equitable distribution of wealth. He is aware of terrible poverty and deprivation in large towns and cities; conditions portrayed in works such as Daniel Defoe's *Moll Flanders* and others of that era.

"Many a youth comes up to London full of expectations and with little or no money, and unless he gets immediate employment he is already half undone; . . . A world of little cases are continually arising, which busy or affluent life knows not of. . . . Hunger is not among the postponable wants. . . ."

(p.268)

He would find some changes were he now to return, but the problems he outlined are by no means fully extirpated. Much of the improvement which has come about is owed to proposals which Paine put forward, at that time, when they were obviously considered wildly impractical and utopian; but, in fact, it was well over a century before even the mildest and least contentious began to be implemented. These included: children's allowance; basic education for all; old age pensions; maternity benefit; a marriage grant; a funeral grant for workers dying away from home; provision of 'employment, at all times, for the casual poor in the cities of London and Westminster'.

"By the operation of this plan, the poor laws, those instruments of civil torture, will be superseded, and the wasteful expense of litigation prevented. The hearts of the humane will not be shocked by ragged and hungry children, and persons of seventy and eighty years of age begging for bread. The dying poor will not be dragged from place to place to breathe their last, as a reprisal of parish upon parish. Widows will have a maintenance for their children, and not be carted away, on the death of their husbands, like culprits and criminals; and children will no longer be considered as increasing the distresses of their parents. The haunts of the wretched will be known, because it will be to their advantage; and the number of petty crimes, the offspring of distress and poverty, will be lessened. The poor, as well as the rich, will then be interested in the support of government, and the cause and apprehension of riots and tumults will cease. – Ye, who sit in ease, and solace yourselves in plenty, and such there are in Turkey and Russia, as well as in England, and who say to yourselves, 'Are we not well off', have ye thought of these things? When ye do, ye will cease to speak and feel for yourselves alone."

(p.270)

A bright and rosy prospect and not unattainable; we have moved considerably in that direction, but would that it were so in its entirety by now, especially in the matter of law and order, where much remains to be achieved. Little enough progress has been made since that other 18th century idealist, John Howard, achieved his great advance in prison reform around that time. The practical reforms listed above are readily understood, and would no longer be considered utopian, but Paine goes beyond these in his closing pages, regarding the French Revolution, at 1791, as *fait accompli*, and making further predictions in that light:

"The fraud, hypocrisy, and imposition of governments, are now beginning to be too well understood to promise them any long career. The farce of monarchy and aristocracy, in all countries, is following that of chivalry, and Mr Burke is dressing for the funeral. Let it then pass quietly to the tomb of all other follies, and the mourners be comforted."

"When it shall be said in any country in the world, my poor are happy; neither ignorance nor distress is to be found among them; my jails are empty of prisoners, my streets of beggars; the aged are not in want, the taxes are not oppressive; the rational world is my friend, because I am the friend of its happiness: when these things can be said, then may that country boast its constitution and its government."

"Within the space of a few years we have seen two Revolutions, those of America and France. In the former, the contest was long, and the conflict severe; in the latter the nation acted with such a consolidated impulse, that having no foreign enemy to contend with, the revolution was complete in power the moment it appeared. From both those instances it is evident, that the greatest forces that can be brought into the field of revolutions, are reason and common interest. Where these can have the opportunity of acting, opposition dies with fear, or crumbles away by conviction. It is a great standing which they have now universally obtained; and we may hereafter hope to see revolutions, or changes in governments, produced with the same quiet operation by which any measure, determinable by reason and discussion, is accomplished."

"When a nation changes its opinion and habits of thinking, it is no longer to be governed as before; but it would not only be wrong, but bad policy, to attempt by force what ought to be accomplished by reason. Rebellion consists in forcibly opposing the general will of a nation, whether by a party or by a government. There ought, therefore, to be in every nation a method of occasionally ascertaining the state of public opinion with respect to government. On this point the old government of France was superior to the present government of England, because, on extraordinary occasions, recourse could be had to what was then called the States General. But in England there are no such occasional bodies; and as to those who are now called Representatives, a great part of them are mere machines of the court, placemen and dependants."

(pp.286–7)

There is a nice distinction posed here between revolution and rebellion, and philosophically the distinction holds, but in practical terms how much does it really mean, and would Paine have made this point a few years later. His great error at that moment was to believe that the French *'revolution was complete in power the moment it appeared';* he still had many years to live; the Reign of Terror was just ahead, in which he reaped his reward for his services to that revolution by being imprisoned, and almost losing his life. He lived to see Napoleon become Emperor, but had passed on before Waterloo. However, still in 1791, he has some further reflections on amity and alliances:

"The objects that now press on the public attention are, the French Revolution, and the prospect of a general revolution in governments. Of all nations in Europe, there is none so much interested in the French Revolution as England. Enemies for ages, and that at a vast expense, and without any national object, the opportunity now presents itself of amicably closing the scene, and joining their efforts to reform the rest of Europe. . . ."

"In the preceding part of this work, I have spoken of an alliance between England, France, and America, for purposes that were to be afterwards mentioned. Though I have no direct authority on the part of America, I have good reason to conclude, that she is disposed to enter into a consideration of such a measure, provided, that the governments with which she might ally, acted as national governments, and not as courts enveloped in intrigue and mystery. That France as a nation, and a national government, would prefer an alliance with England, is a matter of certainty."

(p.288)

Paine's dream of an alliance between England, France and America did not materialise at that time, but he would obviously have appreciated the present North Atlantic Treaty Organisation.

"With how much glory, and advantage to itself, does a nation act, when it exerts its powers to rescue the world from bondage, and to create itself friends, than when it employs those powers to increase ruin, desolation and misery. The horrid scene that is now acting by the English government in the East Indies, is fit only to be told of Goths and Vandals, who destitute of principles, robbed and tortured the world they were incapable of enjoying."

(p.289)

Here Paine puts his finger on a common cause which he shares with Burke; while he had been struggling for Human Rights, first in America, then in France, Burke had been engaged in a similar struggle on behalf of the Indian subcontinent and its peoples. Would that Burke could have seen the merit in Paine's analysis of French aspirations for a harmonious relationship with Britain, and had the good sense to advise Pitt and his cabinet accordingly. Some, at least, of Paine's utopia might have arrived much sooner, and thus he continues:

"Never did so great an opportunity offer itself to England, and to all Europe, as is produced by the two revolutions of America and France. By the former, freedom has a natural champion in the western world; and by the latter, in Europe. When another nation shall join France, despotism and bad government will scarcely dare to appear. . . . The insulted German and the enslaved Spaniard, the Russ, and the Pole, are beginning to think. The present age will hereafter merit to be called the Age of Reason, and the present generation will appear to the future as the Adam of a new world."

(p.290)

Here, perhaps, we have the chink in Paine's Utopian armour: the faith which he had cherished as an Anglican with Quaker connections, and which manifests itself in earlier writings, such as his *Common Sense,* had become eroded, and his Deist evolution, which he would outline in his *Age of Reason,* was gradually ousting that earlier faith. In former times he would have remembered Chapter 11 of Genesis with its story of the Tower of Babel, and God's vengeance upon man's arrogance, who, having survived The Flood, believed he could now insure his future without further reference to his maker.

In his preface to Part II of the *Age of Reason,* Paine gives us his reaction to the sad turn about in French affairs during the *Reign of Terror,* and his analysis of its causes. Referring to circumstances existing in France in 1793 he states:

"The just and humane principles of the revolution, which philosophy had first diffused, had been departed from. . . . The intolerant spirit of church persecutions had transferred itself into politics; the tribunal, styled revolutionary, supplied the place of an inquisition; and the guillotine and stake outdid the fire and faggot of the church. I saw many of my most intimate friends destroyed; others daily carried to prison; and I had reason to believe, and had also intimations given me, that the same danger was approaching myself."

A sad disillusionment! Much has been revealed, in the writings here reviewed, of the decadence in mainline Christianity throughout Europe. In this climate men were again assuming that because they found so many failings in organised religion they could the better achieve success, relying solely upon themselves and their well informed, better organised *Reason.* In two centuries since then, with a tremendous leap forward in human knowledge, we have much evidence of our own fallibility when arrogance tempts us to go it alone!

Priestley's Utopia

Priestley's background and evolution were rather different from those of Paine, and his Arianism never swept him onwards into Deism, like some of his followers in the 19th century, so his Utopia has a somewhat different hue. We have observed how he witnessed to his Christianity, flawed though it was in the eyes of the orthodox, when he was in France before the revolution. We have seen him demolish many of Burke's *Reflections* in his *Letters* and now in the last one we get his own daydreams; contemplating the changes that have taken place in France, up to then, he tells Burke:

> "These great events, in many respects unparalleled in all history, make a totally new, a most wonderful, and important, area in the history of mankind. It is, to adopt your own rhetorical style, a change from darkness to light, from superstition to sound knowledge, and from the most debasing servitude to a state of most exalted freedom. It is a liberating of all the powers of man from that variety of fetters, by which they have hitherto been held. So that, in comparison with what has been, now only can we expect to see what men really are, and what they can do."
>
> "The generality of governments have hitherto been little else than a combination of *the few,* against *the many;* and to the mean passions and low cunning of these few have the great interest of mankind been too long sacrificed."
>
> *(Letters to EB, pp.143–4)*

> "How glorious is the prospect, the reverse of all the past, which is now opening upon us, and upon the world. Government, we may now expect to see, not only in theory, and in books, but in actual practice, calculated for the general good, and taking no more upon it than the general good requires; leaving all men the enjoyment of as many of their *natural rights* as possible, and no more interfering with matters of religion, with men's notions concerning God, and a future state, than with philosophy or medicine."
>
> *(p.145)*

> "Together with the general prevalence of the true principles of civil government, we may expect to see the extinction of all *national prejudice* and enmity, and the establishment of *universal peace* and goodwill among all nations. When the affairs of the various societies of mankind shall be conducted by those who shall truly represent them, who shall feel as they feel, and think as they think, who shall really understand, and consult their interests, they will no more engage in those mutually offensive *wars,* which the experience of many centuries has shown to be constantly expensive and ruinous. They will no longer covet what belongs to others,

and which they have found to be of no real service to them, but will content themselves with making the most of their own."

(p.146)

This last paragraph is close indeed to Tom Paine, and like him Dr. Priestley certainly has a very starry eyed view of the perfectability of human nature; we know that the potential is there, but we also know, from hard experience, that even with the best will, perfection is hard to maintain. The history of the past two centuries makes nonsense of his beautiful dream. But now, he moves on to consider imperial lust:

"The very idea of *distant possessions* will be even ridiculed. The East and West Indies, and everything *without ourselves* will be disregarded, and wholly excluded from all European systems; and only those divisions of men and of territory, will take place, which the common convenience requires, and not such as the mad and insatiable ambition of princes demands. No part of America, Africa, or Asia, will be held in subjection to any part of Europe, and all the intercourse that will be kept up among them, will be for their mutual advantage."

"The causes of *civil wars*, the most distressing of all others, will likewise cease, as well as those of foreign ones. They are chiefly contentions for *offices*, on account of the power and emoluments annexed to them."

(p.147)

Little did Priestley realise that Europe was on the verge of the greatest imperial expansion the world has ever known; this has been reversed again in the present century, and in this regard at least his dream has come true. But civil strife, such as that in the Balkans, is a running sore that he would have expected, long since, to have been healed. He next passes on to economics:

"If there be a superfluity of public money, it will not be employed to augment the profusion, and increase the undue influence, of individuals, but in works of great public utility, which are always wanted, and which nothing but the enormous expenses of government, and of wars, chiefly occasioned by the ambition of kings and courts, have prevented from being carried into execution. The expense of the late American war only would have converted all the waste grounds of this country into gardens."

(p.148)

Some of these factors may have changed in the meantime, but the economy of nations is nothing like so idealistic as is here envisaged, and there is more to come on the matter of wars:

"Another cause of civil wars has been the attachment to certain persons and families, as possessed of some *inherent right* to kingly power. Such were the bloody wars between the houses of York and Lancaster, in this country. But when, besides the reduction of the power of crowns within their proper bounds . . . that kind of respect for princes which is founded on mere superstition . . . shall vanish as all superstitions certainly will

before real knowledge, wise nations will not involve themselves in war
for the sake of any particular persons of families, who have never shewn
an equal regard for them."

(pp.148-9)

If royal persons or families are seldom the cause of wars in recent times there
have been other persons and other families who have caused as much trouble
to their communities, as for instance Hitler, Idi Amin, Stalin, Saddam Hussein,
Ferdinand and Imelda Marcos, Papa Doc, and Baby Doc, to mention just a
few. It is the well known phenomenon of power corrupting, especially when
it becomes absolute. People do not choose to confer this species of power upon
rulers, but when it has once been grasped it is very difficult to break that grasp.

"If *time* be allowed for the discussion of differences, so great a majority
will form one opinion, that the minority will see the necessity of giving
way. Thus will *reason* be the umpire in all disputes, and extinguish civil
wars as well as foreign ones. The empire of reason will ever be the reign
of peace."

"This, Sir, will be the happy state of things, distinctly and repeatedly
foretold in many prophecies, delivered more than two thousand years
ago; when the common parent of mankind will *cause wars to cease to the
ends of the earth, when men shall beat their swords into ploughshares,
and their spears into pruning hooks; when nation shall no more rise up
against nation, and when they shall learn war no more. (Isaiah 2:4, Micah
4:3)* This is a state of things which good sense and the prevailing spirit
of commerce, aided by Christianity, and true philosophy cannot fail to
effect in time."

(pp.149-50)

Sadly the *empire of reason*, and the *spirit of commerce*, are only too happy to
operate independently of Christianity, or any spiritual force, and so this bright
future of Dr. Priestley seems little nearer now than it was in his own time.
Human wisdom, as knowledge accumulates, has a tendency to arrogance, which
is destructive of the ends which the good doctor envisages; he goes on:

"I mention this topic in a letter to *you*, on the idea that you are a real
believer in revelation, though your defence of all church establishments,
as such, is no argument in favour of this opinion; the most zealous abettors
of *them*, and the most determined enemies of all reformation, having been
unbelievers in all religion, which they have made use of mainly as an
engine of state."

(p.150)

And so, we see here again some common ground between Priestley and Burke;
the latter was wont to argue that French philosophers, together with their
followers in Britain and elsewhere were a Godless breed; Priestley comes close
to that same position in the passage just quoted. Then on he goes to the abuse
of monarchy:

"In this new condition of the world, there may still be *kings*, but they will be no longer *sovereigns*, or *supreme lords*, no human beings to whom will be ascribed such titles as those of *most sacred, or most excellent majesty*. There will be no more such profanation of epithets, belonging to God only, by the application of them to mortals like ourselves."

(p.151)

These antagonists are very close, and once again it is quite clear that Priestley is not the regicide that Burke and his friends like to portray him. Both are accepting of constitutional monarchy, providing there is tight democratic control; the monarch's powers being strictly limited. This was clearly Burke's position during and even before the American upheaval. Priestley envisages a simpler and a purer type of administration:

"Government being thus simple in its objects, will be unspeakably *less expensive* than it is at present, as well as far more *effectual* in answering its proper purpose. There will then be little to provide for besides the administration of justice, or the preservation of the peace, which it will be the interest of every man to attend to, in aid of government."

"They are chiefly our vices and follies that lay us under contribution, in the form of the *taxes* we now pay; and they will, of course, become superfluous, as the world grows wiser and better."

(p.152)

In this conclusion Priestley seems surprisingly short sighted, looking only to those elements of expenditure which he expects to wither away, but he himself as a leading member of the Lunar Society and thus at the forefront of the Industrial Revolution, was helping to create new services and public utilities which would inevitably be expensive to develop and maintain. Furthermore, he does not even begin to consider the community services which must inevitably flow from Tom Paine's vision. But, now, in conclusion there is a final sarcastic swipe at Burke:

"If you, Sir, together with your old or your new friends, can steer the ship of state through the storm, which we all see to be approaching, you will have more wisdom and steadiness than has yet been found in any that have hitherto been at the head of our affairs. And if in these circumstances, you can save the *church*, as well as the *state*, you will deserve no less than *canonisation*, and ST. EDMUND will be the greatest name in the calendar."

(p.154)

Canonisation and sainthood could have little significance for Priestley except as weapons of scorn to heap upon his adversary and so must be seen as his final expression of contempt for Burke's *Reflections on the Revolution in France*. It would be interesting to have had Burke's reflections on the Utopian vision of both Priestley and Paine, as well as on their detailed criticism of the case he himself had put forward; but this was not to be!

Paine has foreshadowed a North Atlantic Treaty Organisation (NATO), whilst Priestley would eagerly welcome a European Union; on this latter theme, however, Burke would delight our latter day Eurosceptics with his warmongering pamphlet, of November 1792, entitled: *Heads for Consideration on the Present State of Affairs*, where he tells his audience, and in particular Pitt's government:

"There never was, nor is, nor ever will be, nor ever can be, the least rational hope of making an impression on France by any Continental powers, if England is not a part, is not the directing part, is not the soul, of the whole confederacy against it."

"This, so far as it is an anticipation of future, is grounded on the whole tenor of former history."

(Heads . . ., p.397)

"Her chief disputes must ever be with France; and if England shows herself indifferent and unconcerned, when these other European powers are combined against the enterprises of France, she is to look with certainty for the same indifference on the part of these powers when she may be at war with that nation. This will tend totally to disconnect this kingdom from the system of Europe, in which if she ought not rashly to meddle, she ought never wholly to withdraw herself from it."

(p.398)

Albeit that history has moved on apace, have any of our modern Eurosceptics, better encapsulated their doctrine than in this last sentence; if and when they form a breakaway party, they must surely do so under the banner of Priestley's: 'St. Edmund'.

J E Hobsbawm gives it a somewhat different slant where he speaks of:

"Edmund Burke, whose economic ideology was one of pure Adam-Smithianism, retreated in his politics into a frankly irrationalist belief in the virtues of tradition, continuity and slow organic growth, which have ever since provided the theoretical mainstay of conservatism . . .

(The Age of Revolution, pp.291–2)

We have seen Paine's expression of disillusionment with the degeneration which had taken place in the French Revolution; Priestley was no less frank. In his farewell sermon on 28th February 1794, before emigrating to America, he had this to say:

"What could have been more unexpected than the events of any one of the last four years, at the beginning of it? What a total revolution in the ideas and conduct of a whole nation! What a total subversion of principles, what reverses of fortune, and what a waste of life! In how bloody and eventful a war we are now engaged, how inconsiderable in its beginnings, how rapid and wide in its progress, and how dark with respect to its termination! At first it resembled Elijah's cloud, appearing no bigger than a man's hand; but now it covers, and darkens, the whole European hemisphere!"

(p.31)

Burke, on the other hand, had nothing to retract; had he not, after all, been proved entirely right in his gloomy prognostications?

CHAPTER XVI

Debate Aborted

How and Why?

My errors, if any, are my own.
My reputation alone is to answer for them.

Burke's Reflections, p.3

THIS DEBATE ABOUT THE REVOLUTION IN FRANCE may be said to have started with the *Discourse* by Dr. Price in November 1789, which provoked the ire of Edmund Burke, expressed in his *Reflections* the following year. Price, in terminal illness, was no longer fit to respond and so Burke's arguments were taken up by Priestley at the beginning of 1791 and by Paine the following month. It was Burke's turn to reply; he had been strongly challenged and, being a doughty debater, must have been expected to rise to the occasion, but instead he chose scornfully to ignore these 'radical miscreants' and to reserve his fire for the leader and a majority of members of the Whig establishment ranged against him.

In April '91 parliament debated the Quebec Bill and Burke grasped the opportunity it presented to bring on a discussion about developments in France, on the pretext that Quebec being a French- speaking province of Canada, might perhaps pursue a constitution on the new French model. The Whig leader Charles J. Fox tried his best to turn Burke away from this course, but to no avail, and the result was that a wide breech opened up between these two men who had been friends for many years, a breech which was never to be repaired.

In August Burke produced one of the strangest pamphlets he was ever to write, entitled: "*An Appeal from the New to the Old Whigs*, in consequence of some late discussions in parliament – relative to the *Reflections* on the French Revolution". The publication was anonymous, and refers to Burke throughout in the third person, but it was soon known to be from his own pen; nor was this ever denied. The title, alone, is confusing, and requires careful study to unravel its mysteries; it purports to represent the Whig party of his own day, from which he had virtually cut himself off, and appeals to the example of their predecessors, back in the early days of the century, during the reign of Queen Anne.

He cites the impeachment of Rev. Dr. Sacheverel, an otherwise insignificant clergyman of the established church, who had dared to preach a sermon querying the virtues of the 'great and glorious revolution of 1688'. The Whigs, who were in power at this time, adjudged this to be a heinous offence which merited dragging him before the House of Lords, where their prosecution was eventually successful. *(pp.54–84)* It is extraordinary that Burke, who was still engaged in the much more significant impeachment of Warren Hastings, should even have considered this earlier case appropriate to cite. In fact the purpose of these great and glorious 'Old Whigs' was to deny to the wretched Doctor the right of free speech, so it becomes clearer how Burke wished to dispose of those who were becoming thorns in his own flesh.

It is interesting to note that Winston Churchill was scornfully dismissive of this notorious cause when he states:

"The political crisis of Queen Anne's reign moved steadily to its climax. The Church of England was astir, and the Tory clergy preached against the war and its leaders, especially Godolphin. Dr. Sacheverell, a High Church divine, delivered a sermon in London in violent attack upon the Government, the Whigs, and the Lord Treasurer. With great unwisdom the Government ordered a state prosecution in the form of an impeachment. Not only the Tories, but the London mob rallied to Sacheverell, and scenes were witnessed recalling those which had attended the trial of the Seven Bishops, a quarter of a century before. By narrow majorities nominal penalties were inflicted upon Sacheverell. He became the hero of the hour."

(W S C, History of English Speaking Peoples, vol.III, p.70)

Paine asks:

". . . Who are those to whom Burke has made his appeal? A set of childish thinkers and halfway politicians born in the last century; men who went no farther with any principle than it suited their purpose as a party; the nation was always left out of the question; and this has been the character of every party from that day to this. The nation sees nothing in such works, or such politics worthy of its attention. A little matter will move a party, but it must be something great that moves a nation."

(Rights, p.176)

It is strange how this very righteous man set about lauding some of the leading Whigs taking part in such a notorious and ill judged procedure. Robert Walpole was the prime example; Burke relates how: "A careless, coarse, and over-familiar style of discourse, without sufficient regard to persons or occasions, and an almost total want of political decorum, were the errors by which he was most hurt in the public opinion; and those through which his enemies obtained the greatest advantage over him." But, never mind, "Justice must be done," we are told, and "The prudence, steadiness, and vigilance of that man, joined to the greatest possible lenity in his character and his politics, preserved the crown to this royal family . . ." *(p.64)* All this is akin to attitudes in these, our own, days of bread and circuses, when popular sporting idols guilty of serious misdemeanour, or even crimes, must still be adjudged blameless, precisely because those who idolise them would otherwise be upset and might revolt. These are strange attitudes, indeed, in Burke, the prosecutor of Warren Hastings; and it

AN

APPEAL

FROM

THE NEW

TO

THE OLD WHIGS,

IN CONSEQUENCE OF SOME LATE

DISCUSSIONS IN PARLIAMENT,

RELATIVE TO THE

Reflections on the French Revolution.

By [*Edmund Burke*]

THE THIRD EDITION.

LONDON:

PRINTED FOR J. DODSLEY, PALL-MALL.

M.DCC.XCI.

(94)

up the million sterling a year, which the country gives the person it stiles a king. Government with insolence, is despotism; but when contempt is added, it becomes worse; and to pay for contempt, is the excess of slavery. This species of government comes from Germany; and reminds me of what one of the Brunswick soldiers told me, who was taken prisoner by the Americans in the late war: ' Ah!' said he, ' America is a fine free country, it is worth the people's fighting for; I know, the difference by knowing my own; in my country, *if the prince says, Eat straw, we eat straw.*' " God help that country, thought I, be it England or elsewhere, whose liberties are to be protected by German principles *of government, and princes of Brunswick!*"

" It is somewhat curious to observe, that although the people of England have been in the habit of talking about kings, it is always a Foreign House of kings, hating Foreigners, yet governed by them. —It is now the House of Brunswick, one of the petty tribes of Germany."

" If Government be what Mr. Burke describes it, ' a contrivance of human wisdom,' I might ask him, if wisdom was at such a low ebb in England, that it was become necessary to import it from Holland and from Hanover? But I will do the country the justice to say, that was 'not the case; and even if it was, it 'mistook the cargo. The wisdom of every country, when properly exerted, is sufficient for all its purposes; *and there could exist no more real occasion in England to have sent for a Dutch Stadtholder, or a German Elector, than there was in America to have* done a similar thing. If a country does not understand its own affairs, how is a foreigner to understand them, who knows neither its laws, its " manners,

(95)

" manners, nor its language? If there existed a national " so transcendantly wise above all others, that his " wisdom was necessary to instruct a nation, some " reason might be offered for monarchy; but when " we cast our eyes about a country, and observe " how every part understands its own affairs; and " when we look around the world, and see that of all " men in it, the race of kings are the most insigni- " ficant in capacity, our reason cannot fail to ask us " —What are those men kept for?"*

These are the notions which, under the idea of Whig principles, several persons, and among them persons of no mean mark, have associated themselves to propagate. I will not attempt in the smallest degree to refute them. This will probably be done (if such writings shall be thought to deserve any other than the refutation of criminal justice) by others, who may think with Mr. Burke, and with the same zeal. He has performed his part. I shall content myself with shewing, as shortly as the matter will admit, the danger of giving to them, either avowedly or tacitly, the smallest countenance.

There are times and circumstances, in which hot to speak out is at least to connive. Many think it enough for them, that the principles propagated by these clubs and societies enemies to their country and its constitution, are not owned by the *modern Whigs in parliament*, who are so warm in condemnation of Mr. Burke and his book, and of course of all the principles of the ancient constitutional Whigs of this kingdom. Certainly they are not owned. But are they condemned with the same zeal as Mr. Burke and his book are condemned? Are they condemned at all? Are they rejected or discountenanced in any way whatsoever? Is any man who would fairly examine into the de-

* Vindication of the Rights of Man, recommended by the several societies.

G 7   mcanour

"An Appeal from the New to the Old Whigs" (August 1791) With two relevant pages – quotations from *'Rights of Man'* (Tom Paine) confused with Mary Wollstonecraft's *'Vindication of the Rights of Man'*

can come as no surprise that this pamphlet would fail dismally to heal the wide rift opening up in the party of the New Whigs.

But this essay could be ignored, were it not for the far more strange and significant passage which follows. *(pp.84–96)* Here Burke tells us that he is choosing from *certain books,* but he does not identify any particular book, author, or authors; he attributes ideas expressed to the contemporary (Foxite) Whigs, from whom he has seceded, and refers to *'doctrine . . . propagated by these societies',* without naming any in particular, but obviously had in mind societies such as that addressed by Dr. Price in '89, together with the various *constitutional* and *corresponding societies* springing up throughout the land, in sympathy with the French Revolution.

J.E. Hobsbawm in his *Age of Revolution (p.103)* writing of the Corresponding Societies says that they, "can claim to be the first independent political organisations of the labouring class." Such a view would scarcely have endeared them to Burke; more likely it would have increased his antipathy. In the same passage Hobsbawm refers to Paine as "a voice of unique force." All Burke's attributions are wrong and quite misleading.

On close examination, *all the passages* quoted in these pages are taken from Paine's Rights of Man, without any due acknowledgement. Then to confound the reader and compound the insult, the last of these paragraphs bears an asterisk, guiding us to a footnote *(on p.95)* which simply states: "*Vindication of the Rights of Man,* recommended by the several societies."But this is the title of Mary Wollstonecraft's book, (except that it was Men – not Man) written in response to Burke's *Reflections . . .* and published in 1790, even before Priestley or Paine.

The *Appeal . . .* continues: "These are the notions which, under the idea of Whig principles, several persons, among them persons of no mean mark, have associated themselves to propagate. *I will not attempt in the smallest degree to refute them".* *(my italics, P. O'B.) But* neither Paine nor Mary Wollstonecraft was a member of the Whig party, nor did either have any commission from that party to write a tract on its behalf; they were totally independent thinkers and writers. We have already noted that Paine's ideas had originally appeared in a shorter, simpler version entitled *Common Sense* in 1776, at the outset of the American War of Independence, at a time when he was in favour with Burke.

What can have been Burke's object in this *deliberate deception;* all the works of his and those of his three adversaries, the only significant books worth mentioning, had been published within a short span of four or five months, and intelligent, well informed readers would know exactly which was which. They would also know that Burke was not slipshod in such matters, with his training and experience he must have known exactly what he was doing. No, this passage *(pp.84–96)* is complicated and skilfully crafted to create maximum confusion, and that confusion was not Burke's. His pamphlet was almost certainly aimed at a less perceptive, less sophisticated audience; at a class of readers who pay attention only to works emanating from their own camp, not wishing to be contaminated by contrary views, however logical or informative.

Such readers would readily be confused by Burke's tactic, and might easily conclude that the passages quoted were, in the main, from the pen of Mary Wollstonecraft, who could more readily be dismissed, especially as being *a mere woman* and therefore having no real right to *opinions on such profound and manly matters!*

So! Who was this incorrigible young woman, this literary hack, employed by Johnson, the publisher; former governess and schoolmarm, barely into her 30s? How did she dare tackle this eminent and revered parliamentarian, the nation's conscience and prophylactic physician protecting it from the dreaded French disease? She dares to address herself to him as an equal; she is frank and bold, though without abandoning courtesy or dignity, but makes it clear that he is not to expect obsequiousness or crawling deference. She tells him that she believes him to be "a good man, though vain", and she will not be "intimidated by the horse laugh that (he has) raised", nor is she impressed by "the compassionate tears which (he has) elaborately laboured to excite". She tells him: "I war not with an individual when I contend for the **rights of men** and the liberty of reason". (*Vindication p.5*)

Much further on she flatters Burke that he is "an exception" in the Commons, "raised ... by the exertion of abilities", and that he has "ever been an ornament" in the House. Then she taunts him that in the "present crisis" – "since you could not be one of the grand movers, the next **best** thing that dazzled your imagination was to be a conspicuous opposer". (*p.45*)

Her *coup de grace* comes when she accuses him of "contempt for the poor" who "must respect that property of which they **cannot** partake". (*p.58*) How would his poorer relations in Ireland have viewed that verdict? Further, on that topic, she tells him: "Envy built a wall of separation, that made the poor hate, whilst they bent to their superiors; who, on their part, stepped aside to avoid the loathsome sight of human misery". (*p.62*) This was true in Britain, in France, in Ireland, and Burke knew it. (*Cambridge Texts in the History of Political Thought.*)

So, is this lady merely a hack journalist, engaged in a personal vendetta at quite a superficial level, attempting to take on a gentleman whose assured and lofty status was far above her wild imaginings? Indeed, not so, this is a well educated and widely read individual, as we can see from her well ordered presentation and the range of sources from which she quotes. In this short work alone she uses: the Gospels, Shakespeare, Milton, Pope, John Locke, David Hume, Judge Blackstone, Henry Fielding, Rousseau, and Burke's own writings back to 1757 and his essay on the *Sublime* and *Beautiful*. Obviously she could not match Burke himself in respect of knowledge, with his vast experience and being twice her age, but there were many in parliament and among the *upper classes* in general who could not hold a candle to her erudition. She was a friend of Richard Price, from whom she had learned much, and so it is natural that she should have leapt to his defence when he was attacked and belittled by Burke, even before Priestley and Paine took him on.

Mary's biographer, Claire Tomalin, had this to say about the book:

Vindication . . . was a ragbag into which Mary stuffed the ideas she had picked up over the past few years in her reading and conversation, without any attempt to sort them out or reason with Burke at the level he required. The tone was impatient, the arguments sketchy. But it was redeemed by its dominating emotion, a humanitarian sympathy for the poor, and by a passionate contempt for the wilful blindness of the privileged to what kept their system going. If anything held the writing in shape, it was this, from the early pages where she exclaimed 'Security of property! Behold, in a few words, the definition of English liberty,' to the end, where she suggested that waste land should be reclaimed and large estates divided into small farms as a "cure for urban poverty."

"When she came to theorize about the good society, she imagined one in which 'talents and industry' should be encouraged and enabled to win just rewards, in which younger children should not be sacrificed to eldest sons, in which women should aspire to something more than the wish only to be loved, in which press gang and game law and slavery should be abolished, and the poor succoured as of right, not for charity's sake. All this was admirable no doubt, but so rapidly and allusively set down that it cannot have been expected to do more than dazzle readers already in agreement with her point of view. It could not make converts; the impression was of a mind darting to and fro over its own experience, so sure of its conclusions that it dispensed with discussion."

"She leapt over logical hurdles and indulged all her personal obsessions: feckless parents, noble ladies who neglected their children, tutors ignominiously treated by their aristocratic employers. There was even a reference to the consoling power of religion in the lives of those who had lost their youthful friends. It may have been this personal emphasis and wild indulgence in anger and enthusiasm that made Priestley ignore Mary's book rather pointedly, although he expressed a keen interest in seeing all the answers to Burke. Fuseli too was unimpressed, but the general public was easier to please than either of these gentlemen, and much more interested in the tone of the work than the detail of the argument."

"Mary's was the first reply to Burke to be printed, and it was manifestly written out of a good heart and generous indignation."

Tomalin pp.125–6

Tomalin is somewhat severe, and obviously Mary's work did not have the philosophical weight of either Priestley or Paine, but it was by no means lightweight. It had instant success and quite a vogue as an early contribution to the great debate. It wounded Burke's pride and almost certainly hurt his feelings more than any of the others. It is little wonder therefore that he should have resorted to his underhand ruse, appearing to confuse Paine with Wollstonecraft.

If others might be fooled in such a simple fashion, Paine himself was certainly not. In February 1792, almost a year after he published the first part of his

Rights of Man, he produced the second. In his preface to this he expresses his contempt for Burke's shabby dissimulation:

"A great field was opening to the view of mankind by means of the French Revolution. Mr Burke's outrageous opposition thereto brought the controversy into England. He attacked principles which he knew (from information) I would contest with him, because they are principles I believe to be good, and which I have contributed to establish, and conceive myself bound to defend. Had he not urged the controversy, I had most probably been a silent man."

"Another reason for deferring the remainder of the work *(RoM)* was, that Mr Burke promised in his first publication to renew the subject at another opportunity, and to make a comparison of what he called the English and the French constitutions. I therefore held myself in reserve for him. He has published two works since without doing this; which he would certainly not have omitted, had the comparison been in his favour."

"In his last work, his *Appeal from the New to the Old Whigs*, he has quoted about ten pages from the *Rights of Man*, and having given himself the trouble of doing this, says, 'He shall not attempt in the smallest degree to refute them,' meaning the principles contained therein. I am enough acquainted with Mr Burke to know, *that he would if he could (my italics, P O'B)* But instead of contesting them, he immediately after consoles himself with saying that, 'He has done his part'. – He has not done his part! He has not performed his promise of a comparison of constitutions. He started the controversy, he gave the challenge, and has fled from it; and he is now *a case in point* with his own opinion, *the age of chivalry is gone!*"

"The title as well as the substance of his last work, his *Appeal* is his condemnation. Principles must stand on their own merits, and if they are good they certainly will. To put them under the shelter of other men's authority, as Mr Burke has done, serves to bring them into suspicion. Mr Burke is not very fond of dividing his honours, but in this case he is artfully dividing the disgrace."

(Rights, pp.175–6)

The surprising thing about Paine's observation is that although he notes the fact that Burke was using his material without due acknowledgement, he ignores the more significant fact that the views are attributed to certain unnamed societies and a majority in the Whig party opposed to Burke. Even more surprising, however, is the fact that he appears to be missing the point that the title given, in a backhand fashion, for the last paragraph quoted, is that of Miss Wollstonecraft's book. Perhaps it was just a case of 'Homer nods'!

That Burke could be hard and vindictive is again borne out for us, and by another young lady, a more detached individual. Fanny Burney, at the start of the trial of Warren Hasting in 1788, although herself in sympathy with the accused, had great admiration for Burke's performance as chief prosecutor, but concludes with reservations about his personal attitude and motives. This was at a time when his powers had reached their zenith and before he felt rejected and threatened, in 1791. Miss Burney tells us:

"The sentiments he interspersed were as nobly conceived as they were highly coloured; his satire had a poignancy of wit that made it as entertaining as it was penetrating, his allusions and quotations . . . were apt and ingenious; and the wild and sudden flights of his fancy, bursting forth from his creative imagination in language fluent, forcible, and varied, had a charm for my ear and my attention wholly new and perfectly irresistible."

"Were talents such as these exercised in the service of truth, unbiased by party and prejudice, how could we sufficiently applaud their exalted possessor? But though frequently he made me tremble by his strong and horrible representations, his own violence recovered me, by stigmatising his assertions with personal ill-will and designing illiberality."

(Fanny Burney's Diary IV, pp.95–6, 16 Feb.1788)

These are the comments of an intelligent and perceptive observer, from the opposite camp in this instance, who is bowled over by the man's amazing talent, but who can also perceive that there was another, less attractive side to him. She obviously saw that he could manipulate and misrepresent when it suited his purpose; comment which is entirely relevant in this matter of abusing Paine's writing.

If Paine and Wollstonecraft could be dismissed in such a cavalier fashion, it would seem that Priestley did not even deserve to be noticed apart from an outburst in parliament when Burke condemned his Unitarianism. It could be objected that such a reaction was understandable and justified from an orthodox, committed Trinitarian, but Burke had known Priestley for at least 16 years by then, and surely he must have known also the nature of his dissent. But there is another significant anonymous pamphlet, published also in 1791, entitled: *An Answer to Dr. Priestley's Letters to the Rt. Hon. Edmund Burke, by a Layman of the Established Church.* Was this layman some friend of Burke's, taking up the cudgels on his behalf? Or was it, once again, Burke himself writing in the third person, in the fashion of Julius Caesar? After all, he was indeed "a layman of the established church", and had already set a precedent with his anonymous *Appeal . . . to the Old Whigs.* We shall probably never know, and this is not the only mystery arising in connection with attitudes to Priestley at that time, but Burke's authorship is at least a possibility in view of circumstantial evidence.

In a letter to the Morning Chronicle of 7 March 1793, Priestley defends himself against Burke's attack upon him, in the privileged circumstances of parliamentary debate; he states:

"Taking it for granted that your account of Mr Burke's speech . . . may be depended upon, I beg leave . . . to ask him, what authority he had for asserting . . . that I gave my name to the sentiments in the Correspondence of the Revolution Society in England with the Jacobin Society in France, sentiments adverse to our constitution? . . . I am not, nor ever was, a member of any political society whatever, nor did I ever sign any paper originating with any of them. This I do not say because I have any objection to such societies, but my studies and pursuits have been of a different kind."

"I also ask Mr Burke what authority he has for asserting that I was made a citizen of France, because I had declared hostility to the Constitution of England? This assertion, like the preceding is nothing else than a malignant calumny; being an untruth, which, in the present state of things, is calculated to do me the greatest injury. I was made a citizen of France at the same time with Mr Wilberforce, and several others; and I had no more previous knowledge of the measure than he had; and will Mr Burke say that Mr Wilberforce was made a citizen of France, because he had declared hostility to the Constitution of this country?"

"Though few of my publications relate to politics, I have more than once expressed myself in favour of our Constitution, and I call upon Mr Burke to shew that I have ever written anything that can by any fair construction, be said to be *against* it. I conceive myself to be a much better friend to the true principles of it than he now is. When Mr Burke and I were acquainted, and we used to converse on the subject of politics (for we had hardly any other common topic), our sentiments respecting the Constitution, and the principles of liberty in general were, as I then conceived, the same.

"I would observe . . . that I do not see the wisdom of making persons enemies of the Constitution whether they will or not . . ."

"Mr Burke sneering at me for not having been rewarded for my great services in Philosophy, Politics, and Religion, is a mean insult, in one basking in the sunshine of power, on one who is under its frowns. What does Mr Burke know of my services in philosophy or religion; when the probability is, that he is utterly unacquainted with anything that I have written on these subjects? . . ."

(signed) J. Priestley

Edmund Burke was certainly still basking in the sunshine of power at that time, although clouds were gathering in the sky overhead as he severed his ties with old friends, admirers and supporters. Even today however, he still has a solid coterie of admirers who argue his case in spite of all evidence to the contrary, but, in fact, their conviction is achieved by ignoring most of this evidence, just as he convinced himself of righteousness by spurning his opponents in 1791 and onwards, refusing to engage any further in the debate which he himself had initiated.

Priestley, on the other hand, as he states in his letter, was frowned upon by those in power and has largely been written out of the record, in spite of his very significant contributions to that same debate. We can only hope that by bringing his works back into focus again there will be a proper reassessment, according him the credit and appreciation he deserves. Mrs Barbauld, a

Priestley family friend, of long standing, wrote to him in December 1792 on this theme:

> "To thee the slander of a passing age
> Imports not. Scenes like these hold little space
> In his large mind, whose ample stretch of thought
> Grasps future periods. – Well can'st thou afford
> To give large *credit* for that debt of fame
> Thy country owes thee. Calm thou can'st consign it
> To the slow payment of that distant day,
> If distant, when thy name, to freedom's join'd,
> Shall meet the thanks of a regenerate land."
>
> *(Poems of ALB, p.125)*

Or as Chesterton wrote in 1917:

> "There are many silences in our somewhat snobbish history; and when the educated class can easily suppress a revolt, they can still more easily suppress the record of it."
>
> *(Short History, p.216)*

Conclusion

> Whigs and Tories dim their glories,
> *Giving an ear to all his stories –*
> *Lords and Commons are both in the blues!*
> *(Edmund) makes them shake in their shoes!*
>
> *from Iolanthe, with apologies to W S. Gilbert*

BLEST WITH THE WONDROUS GIFT OF HINDSIGHT, how should we judge the participants in this complex debate on the Revolution in France, its background, and its repercussions. Having considered their Utopian vision, we can but sympathise with Priestley and Paine; their analyses, though lacking hard realism at times, were still sound, but their hopes were frustrated, and it must have been a bitter experience for them to observe the sorry deterioration in this movement, which seemed initially to hold out such great hope. Neither lived to see his expectations realised, but both looked to a time when the nations of Europe would co-operate in peace and harmony. They would have been amazed to know that two centuries later; centuries peppered with further revolutions, other upheavals, and great European conflicts, far more horrendous than anything they had known; only now is their dream-child going through a lengthy and often painful parturition, and might still expire in the nursery.

But, it is Burke, mainly, who stands to be judged, as he himself stresses in opening his *Appeal from the New to the Old Whigs*. He scorns to mention such adversaries as Paine, Priestley and Wollstonecraft, but is deeply wounded

by criticism emenating from Charles J. Fox and other former friends in parliament who, he tells us, have concluded: *"That by one book he has disgraced
the whole tenour of his life"*, *(p.1)* whereas he had "proposed to convey to a
foreign people, not his own ideas, but the prevalent opinions and sentiments
of a nation. . . ." *(p.3)* He goes on to declare: "That it is clear he is not disavowed
by the nation whose sentiments he had undertaken to describe. His representation is authenticated by the verdict of his country." *(p.4)*

He is piqued by the almost unanimous opposition to his *Reflections* . . . by
members of his own Whig party, realising that he is being driven into the arms
of the Tories, whose leader, William Pitt, is treating him with scant respect,
but is prepared to harness the power of his considerable talents. This would
be galling for any man jealous of his own reputation and status. He tries to
convince himself, if not others, that he has not changed tack from the period
leading up to and during the American revolt, but neither his parliamentary,
nor his extra-parliamentary, adversaries are prepared to share this conviction.

In those earlier times he was seized with the necessity to curb the growing
tendency of the British monarchy to claw back something of the power and
glory of absolute rule, as it was believed to have existed at least up until the
accession of the Stuarts. The king's illness and his defeat at the hands of the
American colonists had, however, changed all that. So Burke could rejoice in
a new, non-threatening model of constitutional monarchy. He was not alone
in this perception, and the nation as a whole could rejoice; but could he, at
the same time, lay aside memories of the struggle in which he had played such
a leading part, to obtain justice for the colonies, as well as his opposition to
the folly of war in that same cause.

Of course Burke was right in that the American revolt and the French
Revolution were different in many fundamental respects, but in both cases
there was a people struggling against oppression. The Americans, initially, were
not aiming to break with the monarchy, for which they had a sentimental
regard, nor indeed were the French determined to get rid of theirs; but in
Britain an obstinate and oppressive government had been urged on and backed
to the hilt by a reactionary monarch, whereas in France what was initially a
reforming administration had the support and understanding of its king.
Burke's great error was that he failed to appreciate that situation and treated
the reformers in France, as well as their sympathisers in Britain, as if they had
been regicides from the start.

Because he had miscalculated in this manner, he encouraged all the forces
of reaction in both countries, and throughout Europe, thereby bringing to the
surface covert regicides who might otherwise never have come to power. The
emergence of this tendency fostered panic, and even hysteria, in France, which
culminated in the flight to Varennes, of the king and his family, in June of '91,
that year of maximum debate in England. Not surprisingly, those who wished
to see the end of the monarchy were able to present this as a betrayal and a
virtual abdication. Having dragged the king back from the frontier, they then
made him the prisoner which Burke and others had wished to tell the world
he had been before the flight, although not so. The influence he had wielded

up to that moment and the genuine affection heretofore expressed by so many of his people, evaporated overnight and his fate was sealed.

If Burke, at this time, had come again under the spell of monarchy, in spite of previous experience and reservations, he was, and had apparently always been, besotted by aristocracy, a sentiment which is crystallised in that remarkable paragraph on a *Natural Aristocracy* in his *Appeal . . . to the Whigs*. *(pp.107–8)* Heredity, primogeniture, and the landed interest were sacrosanct. In Britain at that time, and for long after, this was an attitude which permeated society at all levels (Thackeray's *Book of Snobs* should be read by anyone who does not fully understand the phenomenon.) In British society equilibrium of a kind was maintained, but Burke was failing to appreciate that profound changes had occurred in France, where arrogance, and almost total lack of compassion on the part of the aristocracy, were way ahead of what was normally experienced on the other side of the channel. Profligacy and greed were making life intolerable for the lower orders in society; a large and growing national debt was bringing famine, or near famine, upon many of these people; resentment and anger were rising; features which are brilliantly captured in Charles Dicken's *A Tale of Two Cities*.

A new tide began to flow, the tide of emigrée nobility, leaving France in fear for their lives, but only guilty conscience could have brought them to abandon their chateaux and vast landed properties. A tide of sympathy welled up in Britain, and also in many other European countries; much of which was selfless and truly compassionate. Many people were swept along on this tide and notably Edmund Burke, but sympathy and emotion blurred his vision. Had he allowed himself to realise that the people of France had every good reason to rise up, he might have appreciated that the revolution was not only a creation of the philosophers, for whom he had such great contempt, and he might then have directed public opinion in England in a way similar to that which he had espoused during the American revolt. Did he ever reflect that the American colonists were far better placed to provide for themselves and protect their own interests than the common people of France? In America, at that time, there was no aristocracy, which had simplified the problem for Burke when it was under consideration, and economic prospects were far better, at all levels of society than they were in France.

What Burke had to say about the Church of England must be judged on its own merits, but had little direct relevance for the situation in France. The Catholic church there was not an established church, even though it had very close personal, family and operational ties with the secular state. When the States General met in '89 the clergy took an independent line, the majority electing to join the Third Estate; by the end of that year church property had been nationalised, and July '90 saw a *Civil Constitution of the Clergy*. Too late the church saw its error, but the fault was its own; it had been in a strong tactical position when it decided to support the Commons, but there was no clear strategy to take advantage of this position and events were moving fast. Ineptitude, apathy and lassitude on the part of the hierarchy had sealed its fate.

In summary, therefore, how is Burke to be judged: in his introduction to *An Appeal . . . he exaggerates grossly* when he claims almost universal support for his views in Britain; views which he has the audacity to declare are "not his own ideas, but the prevalent opinions and sentiments of a nation". Even William Pitt did not see eye to eye with him at that stage, and for a certainty the opposition in parliament, his own party, rejected his views quite vehemently; also what he refers to enigmatically as "these societies". He does not name any society, nor give any idea of their strength or influence. How then can he claim, in all honesty to be expressing "the prevalent opinions and sentiments of a nation"?

When he took his stand on the American revolt he could have supported the British establishment against the colonies, and should have done so, had he, at that point, entertained the opinions and sentiments which he was expressing so forcefully in the 1790s, but he did not do so. Instead he campaigned *for justice* and *against war*.

When it came to the French Revolution, however, he threw all his weight into supporting a far worse establishment than Britain and America had ever known. He ignored the cries for justice from a downtrodden nation, and in the end *promoted war*. Does he tell us that this is consistent with his stance on America? And do we still support his claim?

In spite of Paine's taunt that: "I am enough acquainted with Mr Burke to know that he would if he could" (refute the arguments of his critics) *(Rights, pp.175–6)*, Burke's supporters, then and now, would protest that he was a man of superior intellect, with training and experience quite capable of undertaking the task. This was not Burke's problem, which was in fact emotional, and not intellectual. Any man who could blatantly assert:

> "That in this enlightened age I am bold enough to confess, that we are men of untaught feelings; that instead of casting away all our old prejudices, we cherish them to a very considerable degree, and to take more shame to ourselves, we cherish them because they are prejudices; and the longer they have lasted and the more generally they have prevailed, the more we cherish them."
>
> *(Reflections, p.95)*

This man must have had a large mental block! It is on such considerations that he must be judged.

If this man is confounded, if words fail him, are we to wait because *he does not speak, because he stands there stuck for an answer?*
adapted from the Book of Job, 32:15–16

Bibliography

O F THE WORKS USED IN THIS COMPILATION, quite a number are originals; some are personal copies; others have been consulted in libraries: Warrington Public Library, The British Library, Dr. William's Library, Manchester College, Oxford, Newcastle Literary & Philosophical Society; The Leeds Library; others again are reprints of original texts from the 19th and 20th centuries. Page references given in this present text which are numerous, are from the editions or reprints herein listed. A particular problem has arisen in the case of Priestley's Letters to Edmund Burke in which he quotes extensively from Burke's *Reflections...* using, of course, the original; as the pagination is quite different from the reprint used, the page numbers have been altered accordingly to avoid confusion.

Originals

Price. Richard DD, LL.D, FRS
A Discourse on the Love of our Country to the Soctety for Commemorating the (1688) Revolution in Great Britain. 2nd edition (1789), printed by G Stafford for T Cadell in the Strand

Priestley. Joseph, LL.D, FRS
Lectures on the Theory of Language and Universal Grammar. (1762) Warrington, printed by William Eyres
An Essay on a Course of Liberal Education for Civil and Active Life. With plans of lectures on: I *The Study of History and General Policy;* II *The History of England;* III *The Constitution and Laws of England.* (1765) Printed by William Eyres for Joseph Johnson & Davenport in Paternoster Row, London.
A Course of Lectures on Oratory and Criticism. (1778) London, printed for Joseph Johnson in St. Paul's courtyard.
A Free Address to those who have petitioned for the Repeal of the Late Act in Parliament in favour of Roman Catholics. By a Lover of Peace and Truth (JP) (1780) London, printed for J. Johnson St. Paul's Courtyard.
A Letter to the Rt. Hon. William Pitt on . . . .. Toleration and Church Establishments, occasioned by his speech against the Repeal of the Test and Corporation Acts. (1787) London, printed for J. Johnson in St. Paul's Courtyard, and J Debrett, Piccadilly.
Letters to the Rt. Hon. Edmund Burke, occasioned by his Reflections on the Revolution in France, etc. (1791) 3rd edition corrected. Birmingham. Printed by Thomas Pearson and sold by J. Johnson St. Paul's Courtyard.
Letter to the Inhabitants of the Town of Birmingham. London. 19th July 1791.
Letter to the Morning Chronicle. London. 7th March 1793.

A Sermon preached at . . . Hackney, April 1793. . . . for a General Fast. London, Printed for J. Johnson St. Paul's Courtyard.

A Sermon preached at the Gravel Pit Meeting in Hackney (28th February 1794), With a Preface containing the Reasons for the Author's leaving England. London, printed for J. Johnson St. Paul's Courtyard, 3rd edition 1794.

Autobiography (1806) Reprint 1970, with introduction by Jack Lindsay. Adams & Dart, Bath, Somerset.

An Address by the United Irishmen to Dr. Joseph Priestley. (1794) Dublin.

Burke. Edmund, BA, LL.D, MP.

An Appeal from the New to the Old Whigs, in consequence of some late Discussions in Parliament relative to the Reflections on the French Revolution. (1791) Originally anon. but definitely Burke. 3rd Edition. London, printed for J Dodsley, Pall Mall.

An Answer to Dr. Priestley's Letter to the Rt. Hon. Edmund Burke, by a Layman of the Established Church (anon. ?Burke) London, printed for J F & C Rivington.

Berington. Rev. Joseph

The Rights of Dissenters from the Established Church, in relation principally to English Catholics (1789) Birmingham, Printed and sold by M. Swinney

Rigby. Edward, MD

Dr. Rigby's Letters from France etc. in 1789. Edited by his daughter, Lady Eastlake. First published in 1880. London, Longmans, Green & Co.

Wollstonecraft. Mary

Vindication of the Rights of Men. (1790) 1st edition – anon. 2nd edition in her own name (1790). London, published by J Johnson, St. Paul's Courtyard.

Originals Reprinted

Burke, Edmund

Thoughts on the Present Discontents. (1770). London (1886). Cassell's National Library

Burke's Writings and Speeches – volume 4. The World Classics, Oxford University Press (1907)

Reflections on the Revolution in France. (1790) pp.1–275.

A Letter to a Member of the National Assembly. (1791) pp.277–322.

Thoughts on French Affairs. (1791) pp.325–375.

Heads of Consideration on the Present State of Affairs. (Nov. 1792) in Writings and Speeches, vol.4 Bickers & Son Ltd., Leicester Square. Printed by The Colonial Press, C H Simmons & Co., Boston, USA.

Locke. John

An Essay concerning the True Original Extent and End of Civil Government. (1690) London and Oxford. Basil Blackwell (1946)

Paine. Thomas, MA

The Case of the Officers of the Excise. (1772) Lewes, Suffolk, William Lee.

Common Sense. (1776) Reprint 1984. Introduction by Issac Kramnick. Penguin Books

Dissertations on Government, the Affairs of the Bank and Paper Money. (1786) Philadelphia.

Prospects on the Rubicon. (1787) London.

Rights of Man, Part I (1791) pp.55–169. *Part II* (1792) pp.173–300. Pelican Classics
– reprint (1982)
The Age of Reason. (1794 and 1796) New York. Card Publishing Group Edition,
1995.
Agrarian Justice, opposed to Agrarian Law and Agrarian Monopoly. (1796) Paris,
London.

Secondary Sources

Dictionary of National Biography for Burke, Paine, Price, Priestley, et al.

Ayer. A J
Thomas Paine. (1988) London. Secker & Warburg.

on **Barbauld.** Anna Laetitia
Aikin. Lucy
The Works of A L Barbauld. (1825) 2 volumes. London. Produced by Longman,
Hurst, Rees, Orme, Brown & Green.
Includes: *The Curé of the Banks of the Rhone.* (1791) vol. 2. p.260.
*Sins of Government, Sins of the Nation, a Discourse for the Fast appointed
on April 19, 1793.* vol. 2, p.381.
McCarthy. William P and Kraft. Elizabeth
The Poems of A L Barbauld. (1994) University of Georgia Press, Athens and London.
Rodgers. Betsy
Georgian Chronicle, Mrs Barbauld and her Family. (1958) London, Methuen & Co.
Ltd

Belloc. Hilarie
The French Revolution. London, OUP. 2nd edition 1911. 1945 reprint.
James the Second. (1928) London, Faber & Gwyer.

Marie Antoinette
London. Methuen & Co. (1909.)

Bronowski, Jacob
The Ascent of Man. (1973) London, BBC.

Brooke. John
King George III London, Book Club Associates (1972)

Bush. M L
The English Arisiocracy. (1984) Manchester University Press.

Chesterton. G K
A Short History of England. (1917) London, Chatto & Windus.

Churchill. Winston S
A History of the English Speaking Peoples. 3rd edition 1967.
Vol.3. Age of Revolution. London, Cassell & Co. Ltd.

Cobbett. William
A Short History of the Protestant Reformation in England and Ireland. Dublin, J
Duffy & Co. Ltd. Late 19th Century edition printed by Edmund Burke & Co.

Collinson. P
The Mythology of a Protestant Nation. London. the Tablet. 25.3.1995. pp.384–6

Cronin. Vincent
Louis and Antoinette. (1974) London, Purnell Book Services Ltd. Book Club edition.

Davie. Donald
The Clarke Lectures. (1976) London, Routledge & Keegan Paul (1978)

Dickens, Charles
Barnaby Rudge. (1841) (Gordon Riots)
Tale of Two Cities. (1859) (French Revolution)

Dumas. Alexandre
Taking the Bastille.

Gottschalk. Louis R
The Criminality of Jean Paul Marat. South Atlantic Quarterly. 25 (1926) pp.154–167

Harris. Nathaniel
Spotlight on the American Revolution. (1988) Hove, Sussex, Wayland Ltd.

Hibbert. Christopher
The French Revolution. (1982) London, Penguin Books.

Hobsbawn. E J
The Age of Revolution in Europe (1789–1848). London, Sphere Books Ltd. Cardinal Reprint (1988).

Holt. Victoria
The Queen's Confession – Marie Antoinette. (1970) London, Collins, Fontana Books

Howard. John
The state of the Prisons in England and Wales. (1777) Warrington, printed by William Eyres for T Cadell in the Strand and N Conant in Fleet Street.

Keane. John
Tom Paine (1995) London, Bloomsbury Publishing plc.

King James VI and I
Political writings. Cambridge Texts in the History of Political Thought, 1994. C.U.P.

Lewis. C S
The Four Loves. (1960) London, Fontana Books. (1963)

McCracken. J L
in *A New History of Ireland.* Edited by Moody. T W, and Vaughan. W E. Volume IV. (1986) OUP.

McLachlan. Herbert
Warrington Academy. (1943) Manchester, Chetham Society, volume 107.

Martin F X and Moody.T W
The Course of Irish History 1967. Cork, The Mercier Press.

Newman. John Henry
The Idea of a University. New impression (1912) London, Longmans, Green & Co.

Nuttall. G F
Phillip Doddridge 1702–51, His Contribution to English Religion. (1951) London, Independent Press Ltd.

O'Brien Conor Cruise
The Great Melody. A Thematic Biography and Commented Anthology of Edmund Burke (1992) London, Sinclair Stevenson, Minerva.

O'Brien. P
Warrington Academy (1757–86) its Predecessors and Successors. (1989) Wigan, Owl Books.

On Priestley and his associates

Baugh. A C and **Cable.** Thomas
A History of the English Language. (1983) 3rd edition. Chapter 9 has many references to Priestley as a linguist. London, Routledge & Kegan Paul.

Bird. V
The Priestley Riots, 1791, and The Lunar Society. (1991) Birmingham and Midlands Institute.

Gibbs. F W
Joseph Priestley, Adventurer in Science and Champion of Truth. (1965) London, Thomas Nelson Ltd.

Gillam. John G
The Crucible. The Story of Joseph Priestley. (1954) London, Robert Hale Ltd.

Martineau. A D
Playing Detectives, Fresh Thinking on the Priestley Riots 14th–17th July 1791. (1991) Birmingham and Midlands Institute.

Orange. A D
Joseph Priestley – Lifelines 31. Aylesbury, Bucks., Shire Publications Ltd.

Schofield. Robert E
The Lunar Society of Birmingham. (1963) Oxford University Press.

Schwartz. A T and McEvoy. J G
Motion Towards Perfection. The Achievement of J Priestley. Boston, Mass., Skinner House Books, Unitarian Universalist Association.

Reynolds. E E
The Dawn of Emancipation (Catholic Relief Act. 1778). London, The Tablet (weekly) 3 November 1978. pp.530–1.

Selby. John
The Road to Yorktown. (1976) London, Book Club Associates.

Smith. Adam
The Wealth of Nations. (1776) London, Grant Richards, World Classics (1904)

Thackeray, William M
The Book of Snobs, by one of Themselves. (1848) Gloucester, Alan Sutton (1989)

Tomalin. Claire
The Life and Death of Mary Wollstonecraft. (1974) London, Wiedenfeld & Nicholson, Penguin (1985)

Trevelyan. G M
History of England. London, Longmans Green & Co. Ltd. 3rd edition 1952 reissue. Illustrated English Social History. Book Club Edition (1963).

Wardropper. John
Kings, Lords and Wicked Libellers. Satire and Protest 1760–1837. London, John Murray Publishers (1973).

Webster. Nesta H
The French Revolution. A Study in Democracy. (1919) London, Constable & Co. Ltd.

Wells. Roger
Insurrection. The British Experience 1795–1803. Gloucester, Alan Sutton (1983)

Wilkes, John
The North Briton. No. 45 23 April 1763. London.

Wollstonecroft, Mary
Vindication of the Rights of Men and Vindication of the Rights of Woman. Cambridge Texts in the History of Political Thought. (1995). C.U.P.

Yeats. W B
The Winding Stairs and Other Poems. (1933)

Index

For the views of individuals on particular subjects, see those subjects.